Public and Private Justice

A. Uzelac
C.H. van Rhee

Public and Private Justice

Dispute Resolution in Modern Societies

intersentia

IUS COMMUNE

Inter University Centre Dubrovnik IUC

A. Uzelac
C.H. van Rhee

Public and Private Justice
Dispute Resolution in Modern Societies

ISBN-13: 978-90-5095-683-3
D/2007/7849/51
NUR 828

http://www.intersentia.com

This book was published with the financial support of the MATRA programme of the Ministry of Foreign Affairs of the Kingdom of the Netherlands.

Acknowledgements

This book would not have been possible without the support of many. Financial support was given by the Dutch embassy in Zagreb (Croatia) and the Research School Ius Commune. In revising the English of those who contributed to this book, invaluable assistance was given by: Prof. Erica Beecher-Monas (Detroit), Prof. Tony Diloff (Detroit), Giuseppe Biondo (Detroit), Dr. Morag Goodwin (Maastricht), Michael Krucker (Detroit), Lauren Trible (Detroit) and Dr. Ng Gar Yein (Maastricht). Editorial assistance was obtained from Marjo Mullers of the Ius Commune Research School. Many organisational and related issues were successfully solved due to the assistance of Ognjenka Manojlović (Zagreb). The book is the result of a course organised by the editors at the Inter University Centre Dubrovnik (Croatia). The editors and the authors benefited tremendously from the discussions following the oral presentation of their papers in Dubrovnik as well as from the moral support of the Croatian Minister of Justice and the Major of Dubrovnik, who opened the course sessions at Dubrovnik in May 2006.

Table of Contents

LIST OF AUTHORS

Nina Betetto, Judge at the Supreme Court of the Republic of Slovenia, Member of the CEPEJ Working Group on Mediation (CEPEJ-GT-MED), Mediator in Court-Annexed Proceedings in Slovenian Courts.

Dalibor Čepulo, Associate Professor of Legal History at the University of Zagreb (Croatia), Faculty of Law.

Marie-Hélène Enderlin, Justice and Home Affairs sector manager, European Commission Delegation to Croatia.

Nanny Granfelt, President of the District Court Raasepori (Finland), Advisor and Expert in the CARDS 2002 Twinning project Reform of the Judiciary in Croatia.

Aida Grgić, Référendaire at the European Court of Human Rights.

Dirk Heirbaut, Professor of Legal History at the University of Ghent (Belgium), Faculty of Law.

Jon T. Johnsen, Dean of the Law Faculty of the University of Oslo (Norway), Professor at the department of Public and International Law, Former Member of the CEPEJ's Task Force for Timeframes of the Judicial Proceedings (TF-DEL) and Member of the SATURN Centre for judicial time management of the CEPEJ.

Marko Petrak, Associate Professor of Roman Law at the University of Zagreb (Croatia), Faculty of Law.

C.H. (Remco) van Rhee, Professor of European Legal History at the University of Maastricht (Netherlands), Faculty of Law.

Satu Seppanen, Judge and Head of the Justice Team EUPT Kosovo, Advisor and Expert in the CARDS 2002 Twinning project Reform of the Judiciary in Croatia.

Alan Uzelac, Professor at the University of Zagreb (Croatia), Faculty of Law, Croatian delegate in the CEPEJ and Former President of the TF-DEL, Member of the SATURN Centre for judicial time management of the CEPEJ.

Richard Verkijk, Researcher at the University of Maastricht (Netherlands), Faculty of Law, Attorney at Law and mediator, mainly in the field of labour law and family law.

Mario Vukelić, Judge and Head of the IT Department of the High Commercial Court of the Republic of Croatia, National Correspondent of the CEPEJ, Mediator and Member of the International Insolvency Institute.

INTRODUCTION

The present volume addresses the delivery of justice by the state courts (public justice) and alternative means of dispute resolution (private justice). It brings together views and ideas regarding dispute resolution from old, new and future Member States of the European Union. The underlying assumption of the book is that both types of dispute resolution collaborate and contribute to the same goal, i.e. the establishment of a fair and effective justice system.

The main focus of this book is the comparison and evaluation of current developments in the national justice systems of various European countries. Particular emphasis is placed on legal, political and economic processes in the transition and post-transition countries. Its aim is to analyze not only norms, laws and regulations, but also the role and the actual functioning of the law and its institutions.

The texts in this book approach dispute resolution in an interdisciplinary manner. They analyze the role and functioning of the law and its institutions as mechanisms for the regulation of social conflicts in present-day Europe. In understanding the contemporary problems, this book also offers a historic perspective on the development of dispute resolution, as well as a legal and sociological analysis of contemporary issues in the administration of justice.

The book is divided into four sections. The first section discusses the relationship between public and private justice and the assessment of their performance. In this section, Alan Uzelac discusses the methodological issues connected to research devoted to the functioning of justice systems (public justice *and* private justice). The author poses the question whether objective, well-founded and rational assessment of a particular justice system is possible and, if so, what criteria should be applied. In addition, Uzelac addresses the issue to what extent the current European justice systems can be compared on the basis of their assessment according to particular methodologies, more specifically the methodologies and indicators developed by the European Commission for the Efficiency of Justice of the Council of Europe (CEPEJ) and the Doing Business indicators of business regulations and their enforcement developed by the World Bank.

The second section of the book discusses the history and the development of public and private justice systems. Remco van Rhee discusses the origins of public justice systems in Europe, systems that on the European Continent find their origin in Roman Law, more specifically in the extraordinaria cognitio of the later Roman empire and the Romano-canonical procedure of the medieval period. Although the differences between the various public justice systems in Europe are still very pronounced, the author is of the opinion that some kind of approximation is taking place, even between Continental systems and the systems of the Common Law. This development was clearly visible in the 20th century.

One century earlier, i.e. in the 19th century, far-reaching changes took place in the public justice systems of various countries due to the French Revolution and its aftermath. In his contribution to this volume, Dirk Heirbaut states that the ideals of the French Revolution in this particular area can best be described as 'deprofessionalization' and simplification. Deprofessionalization refers to the fact that the Revolutionaries wanted to take the judicial system out of the hands of the legal professionals as much as possible by removing them altogether from the courts, or, if this was not possible, by at least putting them under stringent controls. Simplification meant that a rational court structure was aimed for without the large numbers of special and specialized courts that existed before the Revolution. The author shows how deprofessionalisation was not a success in France, Belgium and the Netherlands. However, simplification of the court structure was successful in at least one of these countries, namely the Netherlands, even though this country rejected many principles of the French Revolution. The Netherlands is a state with very few specialized courts, and a court structure that may serve as an example for many other European countries due to its simplicity and efficiency.

The third paper in the historical section tries to uncover the origins in Antiquity of what one would now call the protection of private rights. Its author, Marko Petrak, discusses theories about the historical origins of civil procedure in ancient Roman law that are often invoked in textbooks on civil procedure. Some of these theories argue - on the basis of a Darwinist type of approach - that civil procedure was originally conceived as private justice. The author focuses on the criticism that was launched against these theories in the 1940s and later, and comes to the conclusion that it was not a system of private justice, but rather a system of public justice, based on religious rituals, that lies at the basis of the Roman system of the protection of 'private rights'.

The second section closes with a paper by Dalibor Čepulo, who studies the formation of the public justice system in Croatia in the period 1848-1918. Due to the complicated political situation in Croatia, as well as the fact that Croatia was part of the Kingdom of Hungary - albeit being a relatively autonomous part of it - the judicial system of the country consisted of a combination of indigenous and European influences. The paper studies the various stages of the development of the Croatian judicial system until the breakdown of the Austrian-Hungarian Double Monarchy at the end of WW I.

The third section of the volume is devoted to the creation of accessible and efficient systems of dispute resolution. It studies the functioning of the public justice system from the perspective of the European Court of Human Rights (length of the proceedings and legal aid), as well as the functioning of the Croatian judicial system from the perspective of the country's future accession to the European Union.

The paper by Jon T. Johnsen concentrates on Article 6 (and Article 13) of the European Convention of Human Rights and legal aid. The author observes that this is an important topic since it directly concerns access to justice. Few cases on the entitlement to legal aid have, however, been brought before the European Court of Human Rights. The paper discusses methods of increasing the accessibility of the courts as well as the data that have been collected on legal aid and their interpretation by the European Commission for the Efficiency of Justice (CEPEJ). The author concludes by discussing ways in which national governments can be induced to implement legal-aid reforms.

The paper by Aida Grgić also concentrates on Articles 6 and 13 of the European Convention of Human Rights, but this time from the perspective of the administration of justice within a reasonable time. After having discussed the criteria which the European Court of Human Rights takes into consideration in determining whether or not this requirement of the Convention has been met, she continues with an analysis of the Court's findings in cases brought against Croatia. The substantial number of cases brought before the European Court of Human Rights against Croatia in which violations of the right to a trial within reasonable time are at stake, define a series of problem areas. The author comes to the conclusion that extensive research is needed with the aim of identifying all the structural problems which unnecessarily protract the proceedings in Croatia.

That research is already being undertaken is apparent from the last paper of the third section of this book. It is written by three experts (Enderlin, Granfelt and Seppanen) who participated in various capacities in judicial assistance projects aimed at Croatia. These projects took place in the context of Croatia's possible accession to the European Union. They monitored the functioning of Croatia's public justice system and made recommendations for its improvement. The authors note that 2007 will be a decisive year for Croatian justice reform, as the key implementation tools are then expected to be adopted and in place. The list of reforms that are needed is long: rationalisation of the court system, a new judicial map, the introduction of integrated case management in a large number of courts, transparency as regards access to the legal profession, a reform of criminal procedure, etc.

The fourth and final section of the book concentrates on private justice. In his paper, Richard Verkijk discusses the problems that arise when instituting compulsory court-annexed mediation. The author asks whether mandatory mediation should be regarded as informal *injustice*. More specifically, he discusses three questions: (1) what does it mean that mediation is mandatory?; (2) in which European countries can mandatory mediation be found?; and (3) why mandatory mediation is a problematic issue. Verkijk observes that although mediation is by its nature a voluntary process, nevertheless there seems to be a tendency to make it mandatory, a tendency he dislikes due to the many questions that remain unanswered regarding mandatory mediation.

Even though many questions remain to be answered, many countries have adopted court-annexed mediation programmes. This type of mediation is also popular in the new Member States of the European Union, often due to the fact that it is extensively advertised in these countries by representatives of the old Member States. In her paper, Nina Betetto explains that court-annexed mediation may be the only option in these countries. Mediation outside the courts is often not possible due to a lack of experience with mediation. An infrastructure outside the courts does not exist. The author describes a mediation project at the District Court of Ljubljana in Slovenia. She emphasizes the need of a commitment of key players in the judicial field such as the Ministry of Justice in order to make programmes such as these a success.

The fourth section of the book is concluded by a paper in which the legal basis as well as the institutions dealing with Alternative Dispute Resolution and mediation in Croatia are being discussed. The author, Mario Vukelić, explains in which types of cases mediation may be used as a means for solving disputes, and lists the various Acts in which a type of Alternative Dispute Resolution is referred to. Furthermore, he discusses issues such as educating mediators, advertising the possibility of mediation to the public and the activities that are undertaken in Croatia for strengthening mediation as an alternative type of dispute resolution.

Zagreb/Maastricht, April 2007
Alan Uzelac
Remco van Rhee

I. Public and Private Justice: Working together for Common Goals

A. Uzelac

PUBLIC AND PRIVATE JUSTICE: THE CHALLENGES OF RATIONAL ASSESSMENT OF PERFORMANCE IN THE CONTEMPORARY JUSTICE SYSTEMS

1. Challenges of Assessment: How to make Hard Statements on a Soft Ground?

On November 8, 2006 the Commission of the European Communities issued the Croatia 2006 Progress Report.[1] The purpose of the report was to review Croatia's capacity to assume the obligations connected to future EU membership. Among the areas which deserve more attention in the process of accession to the EU, a prominent place was given to the reform of the judicial system. The Report noted that the judicial reform strategy 'has begun', with 'some progress' in reducing the case backlog, but that 'reform is at an early stage and the judicial system continues to suffer from severe shortcomings'.[2]

The report indicated some areas for improvement. The actions that need to be taken were summarized as follows:

- to reduce significant case backlog;
- to reduce the length of court proceedings;
- to improve case management;
- to rationalize the court network;
- to ensure proper enforcement of judgements;
- to reform legal aid;
- to ensure impartiality in the procedures for the appointment, training and disciplining of judicial officials.

In conclusion, the Report stated that 'Croatia is still some way from enjoying an independent, impartial, transparent and efficient judicial system'. This statement was a serious warning, all too clear for the otherwise very diplomatic language of

1 COM(2006) 649 final.
2 Commission 2006, p. 8.

this document. The Report further warned that the establishment of such a judicial system 'will be an important indicator of Croatia's readiness for eventual [EU] membership ...'.[3]

In this paper, we will neither deal with the rather interesting findings of the Croatia 2006 Progress Report, nor with the particular Croatian problems with the administration of justice.[4] Instead, the intention is to use the EU Commission statements on Croatia to raise some general methodological issues connected with every public debate devoted to the functioning of a concrete justice system.

These general methodological issues are best comprised by the following questions:

- To what extent can an assessment of a national justice system be legitimized as objective, well-founded and rational?
- What are the criteria for the rational assessment of a particular justice system?
- Are contemporary European justice systems comparable, and, if so, what should be the basis for comparison?

We would submit that the answers to these questions are neither trivial nor self-evident. While in so many other areas convergence has led to standardization and harmonization, contemporary justice systems in Europe and elsewhere may still be viewed as fortresses of parochialism. Every outside observer who ventures to undertake comparative research of judicial systems and their functioning may become perplexed by immense differences and colourful variations in institutional settings, approaches and terminology.

Indeed, in such a situation it is easy to disregard unpleasant assessments as biased and unfounded. In fact, the assessments from the cited 2006 Progress Report were mostly described by Croatian opinion-makers as political statements, and it appears that the reactions to them were largely political. While the political factor is not to be underestimated, the question remains whether political actions taken to produce the *impression* of reform are sufficient to cause any real change, and, indeed, whether – without objective means of evaluation and assessment – one can even be sure whether *any* change has in fact taken place.

To clarify, let us use the following hypothetical example.[5] We start with the initial political assessment that the court network should be rationalized. On our agenda we have a proposal that two or more specialized courts should merge with other courts. Without clear criteria of assessment, any action taken to meet this objective may be presented either as an important improvement (i.e. as a positive

3 Commission 2006, p. 8.

4 More on these issues can be found in the paper by Enderlin *et al.* in this volume.

5 Although hypothetical, this example bears some similarities with the findings of the EU CARDS 2002 Twinning programme for Croatia. See 'Support to a more efficient, effective and modern operation and functioning of the Croatian court system', Activity B 1.1., Distribution and size of the courts, <http://www.pravosudje.hr> and <https://quickplace2.tietoenator.com/QuickPlace/cards2002/Main.nsf> (last consulted 20 March 2007). See also Enderlin *et al.* in this volume.

change), as no improvement at all (i.e. as a neutral action or the maintenance of *status quo*) or even as a negative change. So, for instance, a change in territorial jurisdiction that reduces the number of courts may be presented as the effective use of resources that enhances access to justice, or as reshuffling that effectively changes nothing, or even as a waste of effort, time and money that impairs access to justice for the citizens. As all of these arguments might be encountered in the public debate, the neutral/objective/rational assessment of the justice systems inevitably raises the question of which criteria we might use to achieve a well-informed consensus for our choice.[6]

Of course, the result of the discussion on criteria might ultimately lead to relativism - to the conclusion that all of the possible methods of assessment are, in fact, subjective, and that no firm, universal criteria can exist in this area. Lawyers always have been prone to relativism, so this result would be no surprise. Statements like 'delays have always existed, and will exist in courts', 'two lawyers, three opinions' demonstrate this affection for 'soft' grounds - an affection that may be deeply rooted in the very nature of the legal profession. Therefore, especially if one encourages the debate among legal professionals, there is a high likelihood the debate will end in an agreement to disagree.

The attraction of relativism does not end here. This polite consensus of relativists is not only a kind of professional deformation of a legal *Fachidiot* who likes to be in the position to advocate, with equal conviction and vigor, two diametrically opposite theses. There may be another, deeper existential reason - the one rooted in self-interest. As many jokes about lawyers demonstrate, the interests of justice cannot unequivocally be equalized with the interests of justice professionals. Thus, while legal certainty might be among the ideals of justice, legal uncertainty produces more work and therefore more profit to attorneys around the globe. It may explain why there are, on average, among legal professionals so few sincere proponents of more comprehensive reforms. On the other hand, legal professionals are among the most influential opinion-makers and, ultimately, they are invited to be the driving force and implement the very reforms that they meet with scepticism. Their position, regularly, is that they are the only real experts who are acquainted with the functioning of the justice system, while everyone else is, at best, benevolent but uninformed, i.e. an *amateur*.[7]

6 The issue of territorial jurisdiction was found to be important for access to justice in the report produced for CEPEJ by B. Hess, D. Chemla and A. Lindgren. Some criteria for the allocation of courts and cases were noted, but the conclusion was 'that in most countries issues relating to territorial jurisdiction followed traditions, cultures and historical reasons and that, as a consequence, in most countries, both the number of courts and their location remained the same throughout several decades'. Hess, Chemla & Lindgren 2003, p. 36, at 17.

7 The commitment to reforms also depends on the methods of selection and recruitment of judges and other judicial professionals. Paradoxically, this commitment may be higher in places where the justice system functions better. If the selection and the role of legal professionals suffers from far-reaching flaws, the likelihood that those who have profited from it will be against the change is higher. For an evaluation of this statement in respect to Croatia, see Uzelac 2000, p. 23-66; Uzelac 2003, p. 303-329.

The purpose of this text is to come to a rather different conclusion. First, we hope to demonstrate that objective criteria of evaluation and assessment in the justice area are, in fact, imaginable and - in spite of the fact that current methodologies and approaches are far from perfect - have good chances to evolve in the next few years. Second, we contend that, for establishing, monitoring and adjusting these criteria, a special task force is needed, which should come from the outside, and not from inside the closed circles of judicial institutions. Justice is too precious to be left to justice professionals only. As the saying *nemo iudex in causa sua* indicates, an outside view of the dispute is the only guarantee for a proper assessment. In the same sense, an outside view of the functioning of justice is the only guarantee for its proper evaluation. Which outside view? This text will be devoted in part to the issue of 'insiders' and 'outsiders' in the justice system, and there we will suggest the need for establishing a new discipline of *justice system administration* as a special professional, scientific and academic field of research (the science of justice system assessment) which is clearly distinguishable, both in personal and systemic respect, from the day-to-day administration of justice.

2. Assessment and Reform

The notion of 'judicial reform' mentioned in the Croatia 2006 Progress Report, is now familiar to a number of jurisdictions across Europe and the globe.[8] Most countries, in fact, undertake some reforms of their national justice systems, for diverse reasons, either internal or external. Internal, national reasons include some generally accepted observations, statements and goals within a particular system, such as the need to accelerate proceedings and/or improve their quality; the wish to cut the costs of the system for the state or for the citizens; or the desire to enhance communication among the actors of the justice system; or to adjust to on-going social changes. Among the external factors, there are those resulting from the process of international integration (such as the EU), involving the need to adjust to a new layer of normative acts (e.g., EU directives) and/or to the intervention of the supra-national courts (such as the European Court of Human Rights in Strasbourg, Court of Justice in Luxembourg or international tribunals in the Hague or Rome). Finally, as the process of globalization advances, some of the reasons are mixed, as cross-border relations and transactions with an international element become increasingly apparent in every jurisdiction, and all national jurisdictions face the same global threats of pollution, war and terrorism.

The ever-increasing need for reforms in justice brings along the need for a universally acceptable methodology and makes greater the need to establish universal assessment criteria. Without objective and rational criteria of assessment, it is hard to imagine rational reform plans for the justice system.

8 For a comprehensive bibliography on the topics of legal and judicial reform see Decker & Messick 2005.

There are several elements that, taken together, make the assessment rational. Here is a brief summary of some key features for evaluating whether the assessment is objective:

- transparent starting points;
- defined goals;
- clear criteria and performance indicators;
- impartiality and integrity of assessors;
- continuing analysis, dialogue and discussion;
- institutional structures for assessment;
- long-term planning and monitoring;
- commitment to the goals of the process.

Each of these elements would deserve a more elaborate presentation. However, this is not something that we attempt in this paper. For the time being it suffices to say that not all of these elements of rational justice reform are present in the justice systems that undergo the most intensive changes. We may comfortably make such a statement at least in respect to the more limited geographic area of Central and South-Eastern Europe – the area that is sometimes connected to the notion of 'countries in transition'. Croatia may be a representative example, especially in the light of the fact that, irrespective of the statements in the Progress Report, it is still among the more advanced and more active countries in the region (and the only one with the EU Candidate status). The Progress Report may have been too kind when speaking of the beginning of the 'judicial reform strategy', as the existing strategy, belated for at least a decade, was announced and accepted by the government only at the end of 2005[9] and approved by the parliament in February 2006.[10] Although this document attempts to declare goals and define an action plan for its implementation, it is still very far from the idea of transparent starting points; defined methodology; broad discussion and dialogue of all stakeholders; and reliable ways of steering the process and monitoring its achievements.[11]

3. Dual Approaches: 'Insiders' and 'Outsiders'

The elements of a rational approach are not the only relevant aspects that influence the process of assessment. All key features enumerated *supra* are decisively determined by unspoken starting premises – by the perspective of those who shape and undertake the evaluation process. In a slightly simplified, model-type manner,

9 The government submitted the text of the Strategy to the Sabor (parliament) on 6 October 2005. This was not the first text of this kind – already during the late 1990s the then Minister of Justice issued a similar document, without much impact.

10 Proceedings of the 18. session of February 3, 2006 (Croatian *Sabor*). For the text of the strategy and the discussion about it, see Barbić 2006, p. 73-162.

11 On several problematic aspects of justice reform in Croatia *cf.* Uzelac 2004, p. 105-130; Uzelac 2004a, p. 283-313; Uzelac 2002, p. 37-80.

we would like to distinguish two main types of approaches to the evaluation of justice systems.

One approach is to focus on the judicial institutions and their personnel. This approach predominantly takes into account the interests of judicial bodies that conduct legal proceedings - the courts, other tribunals, and their collateral parts and services - as well as the interests of those who are in charge of these bodies and work in them - the judges, the administrative staff of the courts and, to a certain extent, others who visit courts on a more or less regular basis (e.g. lawyers or experts). Therefore, we will call this approach the *'insiders'' approach,* or a traditional, *institution-oriented approach.* As indicated in the name, this is the approach that prevailed in the past, and for most countries still is the dominant (if not only) approach to the evaluation of justice systems.

The other approach is to concentrate on the social role and function of judicial institutions. If we regard the purpose of the justice system as the resolution of legal disputes (at least limited to the more numerous, although publicly less visible civil cases), then the methods of evaluation should investigate the extent to which the courts have managed to fulfil the needs of those for which they ultimately work: the parties. The reference to 'parties' here should not be, as often in the institution-oriented approach, identified with the party representatives (professional lawyers), but with the citizens and legal persons who ultimately are (or should be) the *domini litis,* the masters (or owners) of the litigation. Therefore, this approach - the *'outsiders'' approach,* or the *user-oriented approach,* evaluates the interests of the public as a whole, and assesses the performance of the justice system as a public service shaped to fulfil an important need of the citizens: the need for justice. Although in matters of justice one may easily gain the impression that nothing has changed much over the centuries, this approach is, in fact, relatively novel, and has its roots only in the second half of the 20th century.[12] In most European countries, this approach is still unknown or suppressed, but it is slowly evolving, often mixed with the other, institution-oriented approach.[13]

Let us discern several typical differences between the two approaches.

The *institution-oriented approach* mainly monitors the difficulties that are burdening the institutional players and the institution as such. So, e.g., the principal way of monitoring court performance is to monitor its *caseload* (and, more generally, *workload*), with a view to ensure the smooth *case flow* and avoid *backlogs* of cases.[14] The performance indicator stemming from this way of monitoring is the ability to assimilate the incoming cases, measured by the ability to have the output rate of

12 See Uzelac forthcoming.

13 On European national systems of administration of justice as systems that 'should operate, and should be seen to operate, as a public service to all EU citizens', see Zuckerman 2006, p. 61.

14 For definitions of the terms *caseload* and *workload* see Compendium of 'best practices' on time management of judicial proceedings, CEPEJ document CEPEJ(2006)13 of 8 December 2006, p. 23. The term *backlog,* defined in the same document as 'quite ambiguous', is used here in a more narrow sense - as the difference between the number of cases received and the cases disposed of in a certain period of time.

closed cases as close as possible to the input rate of new cases. A very similar methodology may be applied for the evaluation of the work of particular units within the court, or the performance of individual judges. The success of the process is evaluated by the product, and, ultimately, the product delivered is the decision by which the case is closed for the particular court.

Of course, just as in any factory, there may be instances of 'failed products'. In the courts, this corresponds to the decisions that are struck down or changed on appeal. In order to avoid such failures, special attention is paid to the uniform application of law and the consistency of judicial decisions, which has precedence over the substantive result of the adjudication and its impact on the parties.

Also, in general, the way the case is disposed of is not decisive in this method of evaluation - a decision declining jurisdiction on technical grounds is regarded as equally effective (if not more!) as a complex judgement on the merits after thorough examination of all legal and factual issues. As cases are monitored only from the perspective of an individual institution, there is no need to have an insight into those parts of the proceedings that have preceded, or that will follow. Both for the first-instance court and for the appellate court, what matters is *their* part of the proceedings, and thus, e.g. a case that is followed by an appeal is in principle viewed as *two* cases (one case of the first-instance court, and the other of the appellate court). In short, the logic of this approach is to evaluate and measure the *resolved cases,* and not the *resolved disputes.*

On the other side, the *user-oriented* approach would assume the perspective of those who are under the jurisdiction of the judicial institutions - of those whose disputes these institutions are supposed to resolve. The concerns of this approach are *time, costs* and *final result and effect* of the judicial proceedings. The performance indicators that would correspond to this approach should, therefore, take into account *what is at stake* for the parties in the proceedings; *what are the costs* of dispute resolution for the parties; *the length* of the process of dispute resolution; and, finally, the *effectiveness* of the whole process and the time needed to *finally implement* the judicial decision. This approach thus attempts to evaluate and measure the efficiency of *dispute resolution* and its ability to realize the purpose of the process in the eyes of its principal stakeholders - the *users* of the justice system.

The main features of the two approaches are contained in the following table:

	Institution-oriented approach (insiders' approach)	*User-oriented approach (outsiders' approach)*
Perspective	*Institutions*: courts, tribunals, other judicial bodies *Stakeholders:* Judges, administrative personnel	*Users*: parties to proceedings (citizens, businesses), other interested parties *General public*
Indicators	Court caseload Court workload Backlogs of cases Success of appeals Consistency of judgements	Transparency and foreseeability Time needed to obtain legal protection of claims Costs of proceedings Efforts engaged Reasonableness and justifiability of end result
Purpose	To measure the ability to *resolve cases*	To measure the ability to effectively *resolve disputes*

4. Public Justice Assessment Examples: *CEPEJ* v *World Bank*

We will provide two illustrative examples of these two model approaches. Our intention is not to prove that the concrete evaluation mechanisms that exist in particular countries and particular courts can be clearly attributed to only one approach. On the contrary, due to the fact that the collection of data and statistical evaluation of the justice systems is regularly done by the Ministries of Justice, which should, in theory, as political bodies represent both the insiders (legal professionals) and the outsiders (public), it should be expected that the available performance monitoring has both components. Yet, the following two examples indicate that official performance monitoring in Europe still suffers from an apparent imbalance in favour of the insiders' approach, with important *lacunae* in regard to data that would reflect the user's perspective. In such a situation, the compilation of data and monitoring from the outsiders' perspective is left to external bodies, which are often not close enough to the sources of information and therefore cannot systematically fill in the vacant space.

The first example deals with the ability of the European justice systems to monitor one of the most essential indicators from the perspective of the users of the justice system - the *length of judicial proceedings.* Notorious statements, like 'justice delayed, justice denied' and the well-publicized right to trial within a reasonable time, would imply that one of the first tasks of the bodies responsible for the organization, conduct and oversight of judicial proceedings is the monitoring of their timeframes. Yet, even the first pilot evaluation of European judicial systems, developed by the European Commission for the Efficiency of Justice (CEPEJ), demonstrated that this is not the case.[15] During the evaluation process, complete and accurate data was collected on institutional issues, e.g., numbers of courts and legal professionals. However, when it came to length of proceedings, the results were completely different. The report on the results of the evaluation scheme stated

15 More on the first round of CEPEJ Evaluation in Uzelac 2006, p. 41-72.

that '... the processing time of cases brought to court has become one of the key issues regarding the efficiency of justice' and emphasized that 'it has been a main point of attention for the CEPEJ, which has adopted a Framework Programme on this issue'.[16]

However, when analyzing the collected data on the processing time of three common types of court cases - robbery cases, employment dismissal cases and divorce cases, the Report had to conclude that 'only a few countries were able to report on the length of all three types of cases', in particular noting the lack of the ability to report on the total length of the proceedings.[17] The same thing happened in the next evaluation round in 2006 - as noted during the collection of data, 'especially with length of proceedings, most of the Member States could not present (reliable) data'.[18] This failure to collect or dispose of the information that is essential for the length of and delays in the relevant types of proceedings led the Task Force on the Timeframes of Proceedings (TF-DEL) to adopt the *Time management checklist* as the first document produced by this working group of the CEPEJ.[19] The purpose of this checklist was to give practical help to all those justice systems that still need to collect appropriate information and analyze relevant aspects of the duration of judicial proceedings. In fact, this problem was seen in a large majority of Council of Europe countries.

On the other hand, an example of evaluating justice systems from the perspective of users may be found in the World Bank studies of doing business in various countries.[20] The World Bank attempted to develop indicators of the business environment and applied them to all countries of the world, from Albania to Zimbabwe, presenting them in one, publicly accessible, database. The World Bank's focus is on the assessment of business regulations and laws, but also on the assessment of their implementation - as explained on the home page of the database, it should 'provide objective measures of business regulations and their enforcement'.[21] Under the topic 'Enforcing Contracts', the World Bank expert team is rating countries according to three criteria:

- number of procedures from the moment the plaintiff files a lawsuit in court until the moment of payment;
- time in calendar days to resolve the dispute, and

16 CEPEJ 2005, p. 52.

17 CEPEJ 2005, p. 54.

18 Meeting report of the Working party on the evaluation of judicial systems (CEPEJ-GT-EVAL), 4th meeting, 1-3 March 2006, document CEPEJ-GT-EVAL(2006)1E / 10 March 2006, at 26. See <http://www.coe.int/cepej> (last consulted 20 March 2007).

19 See *Time management checklist. Checklist of indicators for the analysis of length of proceedings in the justice system,* adopted by the CEPEJ at its 6th plenary meeting (7-9 December 2005), Strasbourg, Council of Europe Publishing, 2006, p. 4.

20 *Doing business in 2004. Understanding Regulation; Doing business in 2005. Removing Obstacles to Growth; Doing business in 2006. Creating Jobs. Doing Business in 2007. How to Reform* (all publications by the World Bank, the International Finance Corporation and Oxford University Press).

21 <http://www.doingbusiness.org> (last consulted 20 March 2007).

- cost in court fees and attorney fees, where the use of attorneys is mandatory or common, expressed as a percentage of the debt value.[22]

Some of the collected data are summarized in the World Bank reports. Thus, the report for 2004, *inter alia* notes 'the striking differences in the efficiency of contract enforcement across countries', and provides the example of Slovenia, where 'the creditor must complete 22 procedures and spend 1.003 days to get paid'. This is contrasted to Tunisia, where 'it takes only 14 procedures and 7 days to take a debt recovery case from filing to enforcement of judgement. The costs of the debt recovery were compared as well - assessed with $ 360 or 7.2% of the claim amount for Slovenia.[23]

The approach of the World Bank obviously starts from the user's perspective, and strikingly resembles the intent of the CEPEJ Time management checklist, insofar as it inquires into the total time, cost and effectiveness of the legal proceedings. Yet, the results of the evaluation appear to be somewhat puzzling, both on the negative and on the positive side. So, among the good news for 2006, the World Bank report announced that 'Serbia and Montenegro, the country with the third longest delay in 2003, went from 1.028 days to 635 days',[24] and concluded that this country successfully 'cut nearly 400 days off the time it takes to go through the court'.[25] The explanation for this revolutionary change was found in the legislation: 'Two new laws - on civil procedure and enforcement of judgements - were passed. These contain strict time limits. For example, a debtor has only 3 days to file an appeal after the judge rules. The judge then has 3 days to decide its merit. Previously this back-and-forth could take 10 months'.[26] It was also noted that Slovenia reduced delays. But, browsing the same database in 2007, the statistics demonstrate that the number of required procedures for Slovenia rose to 25, and the total time for enforcement of the claim to 1.350 days. All in all, comparing the data for former Yugoslav republics, the result would be the following:

Country	Bosnia & H	Croatia	Macedonia	Serbia	Slovenia
Procedures	36	22	27	33	25
Total time	595	561	385	635	1.350
Costs (% of debt)	19.6	10	32.8	12.7	15.2

In itself, nothing is wrong with the data presented. Yet, the result contradicts sharply the intuitions of every person knowledgeable in the field of dispute resolution in Central and Eastern Europe. The usual perceptions about the level of development which corresponds to the effectiveness of court practices might be deceptive, although it is still very improbable that court proceedings in Macedonia

22 <http://www.doingbusiness.org/ExploreTopics/EnforcingContracts/> (last consulted 20 March 2007).

23 *Doing business in 2004, supra* note 20, p. 42.

24 *Doing business in 2004, supra* note 20, p. 62.

25 *Doing business in 2004, supra* note 20, p. 61.

26 *Doing business in 2004, supra* note 20, p. 62.

last 3.5 times less (and are twice as expensive) as court proceedings in Slovenia. However, the level of volatility of the collected data raises serious doubts. Knowing that real changes in the functioning of the judiciary happen rarely and slowly, the data about cutting the average judicial timeframes from 1000 to 600 days is hard to believe. The distrust in the presented facts is only strengthened by the references to the basis for the conclusion - the introduction of 'strict time limits'. As demonstrated by the situation in some post-Yugoslav countries, the normative changes and strict regulation of the timing of court actions in the legislation has hardly ever produced tangible effects.[27] Without realistic measurement and reporting, the pure legislative time limits are, to use the language of the CEPEJ Framework Programme, the *bogus solutions* that one should beware of.[28]

Therefore, the approach of the World Bank, though in principle acceptable and well-directed, suffers from far-reaching deficiencies.[29] The primary source of these problems may be the distance from the real facts of the adjudication, as the concrete, reliable data on duration of judicial proceedings and other aspects should be collected directly at the source - in the courts and other judicial institutions. Thus, the approach of the CEPEJ Time management checklist does not have any alternative. Six indicators for the analysis of the length of proceedings in the justice system[30] are aimed principally at all those who shape, oversee and execute the administration of justice: legislators, policy-makers, Ministries of Justice, court administrators and judges - precisely because no full insight and reliable information are possible without their co-operation. All other institutions and agencies, especially those who have such resources and will as the World Bank, may contribute by their particular findings, but cannot replace the lack of activity by the

27 E.g. all family laws passed in Croatia from the mid 1990s to today contained the 'strict time limit' that the first hearing *must* be held within 15 days from filing. See Article 269/2 ObZ (1998), NN 162/98; Article 265/2 ObZ (2003), NN 116/03. In spite of this rule, the available data shows that the average (median) time from filing to the first hearing was in total 108 days - data for the Municipal Court in Zagreb. See *National Center for State Courts, International Programs Division, Functional Specifications Report for Computerization in Zagreb Municipal Court of the Republic of Croatia, Municipal Courts Improvement Project - Croatia,* Sponsored by the U.S. Agency for International Development Delivery Order # 801, AEP-I-00-00-00011-00, September 2001 - unpublished, p. 12 (hereinafter referred to as: NCSC Report). See also Uzelac forthcoming, p. 4.

28 See CEPEJ Framework Programme: *A new objective for judicial systems: the processing of each case within an optimum and foreseeable timeframe*, 11 June 2004, CEPEJ (2004) 19 REV 1 at 23.

29 Somewhat more reliable information, that provides 'a strong complement to Doing Business (DB) indicators', are to be found in the Business Environment and Enterprise Performance Survey (BEEPS), developed jointly by the World Bank and the European Bank for Reconstruction and Development (EBRD). The BEEPS, unlike the DB indicators, does not assess the contents of various government policies, rules and procedures, but only how concrete businesses (firms) assess such policies and their impact on their everyday business. See Anderson & Gray 2006, p. 30; Anderson, Bernstein & Gray 2005.

30 The indicators are: 1. ability to assess the overall length of proceedings; 2. established standards for duration of proceedings; 3. sufficiently elaborate typology of cases; 4. ability to monitor course of proceedings; 5. means to promptly diagnose delays and mitigate their consequences; 6. the use of modern technology as a tool for time management in the justice system. See *Time management checklist, supra* note 19.

responsible bodies - they can supplement, but not substitute internal assessment and monitoring mechanisms.[31]

5. Assessing Private Justice - Alternative Dispute Resolution as a *Litmus Test* for Public Justice

Nowadays, alternative dispute resolution is often mentioned in the context of justice reforms. However, we may legitimately ask whether the use of alternative dispute resolution is at all relevant for the assessment of the functioning of the justice system. Admittedly, the use of the alternative dispute resolution mechanisms - arbitration and mediation[32] - has today a significant political support, both at national and international level. This is best demonstrated by a number of positive statements in various documents of international bodies, starting with the recommendations of the Council of Europe,[33] by the programmatic documents of the European Union in the field of mediation,[34] and by many recently enacted mediation laws in various countries.[35]

But, what is behind the encouraging declarations at the high political level? When advocating mediation, arbitration and other private methods of dispute resolution, the emphasis is often on the positive impact that such alternative dispute resolution (ADR) mechanisms may have on clearing backlogs of public *fora,* discharging judges from their burdens and, consequently, reducing the length of court proceedings.[36] For these assertions, however, there is so far no conclusive proof.

The first example of the weakness of the habitual approach to assessing alternative dispute resolution as a way of discharging the courts relates to

31 Another argument to the same effect can be derived from the fact that every particular initiative inevitably only raises issues in the interest of a single group of users. In the case of the World Bank, the users of the justice systems that it dominantly represents are businesses, in particular those active in international trade. Others - private persons, citizens and non-commercial organizations - and their viewpoints are necessarily left aside, and it is questionable whether there is any representative organization that would take into account their interests.

32 In this paper we will intentionally include arbitration under the term of ADR, in the sense of *private justice* that is complementary to state mechanisms of dispute resolution. This inclusion is strictly functional, and made without prejudice.

33 See Recommendation R (98) 1 on family mediation; Recommendation R (99) 19 concerning mediation in penal matters; Recommendation R (2002) 10 on mediation in civil matters.

34 See Green Paper on alternative dispute resolution in civil and commercial law, COM(2002) 196 final; Draft Directive on certain aspects of mediation in civil and commercial matters, SEC (2004) 1314; European Code of Conduct for Mediators. See more on the internet pages of the EJN - European Judicial Network in Civil and Commercial Matters, <http://ec.europa.eu/civiljustice/adr/adr_ec_en.htm> (last consulted 20 March 2007).

35 New legislation on mediation is numerous and comes both from the 'old' EU members, like Austria - see *Mediationsgesetz,* BgBl. No. 29 of 6 June 2003; 'new' members like Poland - *see* The Law of July 28, 2005 (Polish Mediation Law); or candidate countries like Croatia, see Zakon o mirenju, NN 163/2003.

36 Similarly in the CEPEJ Framework Programme, *supra* note 28, at 31.

arbitration. As civil dispute resolution depends on the private initiative of the parties, a very simple, market-oriented logic (or, in the more sophisticated language of the law and economics movement, the theory of the rational choice of forum) may imply that the overburdening of courts and their inability to deliver satisfactory results within a reasonable time would stimulate parties to seek an alternative that could bypass the clogged courts and result in a decision of equal force. So, in the standard Croatian civil procedure textbook, one could read the following submission:

> 'The rise in the use of arbitration may be interpreted as a symptom of the critical conditions in the public justice system. *Srećko Zuglia,* our teacher and Nestor of the science of civil procedural law, advocated the statement according to which the intensity of the activity of arbitral tribunals is functionally dependent on the quality of performance of the public judicial fora; the more the public courts work reliably, efficiently, and cost-effectively, the less the parties have reasons to *run from these courts* and use instead private venues, the arbitral tribunals that enjoy their trust'.[37]

Immediately, however, the authors note that this rule 'was not verified in Croatia for a series of specific reasons'.[38] These reasons were, in another text, explained by the practice of evading responsibility (which had originated in socialism and was continuing in the transition period):

> 'Those compatriots of ours who have been appointed as managers of companies continue to believe strongly that adroitness in outsmarting and overcharging one's business partners is the key to success. This conviction is reinforced by the continuous experience that they are not held responsible for their misbehaviour...'.[39]

This explanation for the lack of expected arbitration practice was later called in one law and economics study the *Triva-conjecture.*[40] This conjecture was stretched to cover all or most transition countries, and some other institutional factors were added as possible explanations for 'the puzzling underuse of arbitration', such as lack of knowledge about arbitration, legal illiteracy, shortage of lawyers and adequate legal advice, and lack of proper enforcement of arbitral awards.[41] However, no concrete empirical evidence was found to conclusively explain the puzzle – 'as it turns out the successes yielded by the rational choice of forum approach are very limited'.[42]

The underlying methodology that often leads to similar findings about the 'puzzling underuse of arbitration' is based on the comparison between the numbers of cases and decisions in the systems of public and private justice. When applied to arbitration, this comparison will indeed lead to devastating results. So, in several

37 Triva & Dika 2004, § 178/3, p. 854.
38 Triva & Dika 2004, § 178/3, p. 854.
39 Triva 1991, p. 24. See *infra* note 40).
40 Schönfelder 2005, p. 3. See <http://www.tu-freiberg.de> (last consulted 20 March 2007).
41 Schönfelder 2005, p. 3-22.
42 Schönfelder 2005, Abstract, p. II.

arbitration meetings and conferences in Croatia in the end of the 1990s and the beginning of the 2000s it was popular to contrast the figure on the annual influx of about 1.500.000 new cases in the public court system, and some 20-30 cases initiated before private arbitration tribunals in the same period.[43] Massive information campaigns and intensification of promotional activities were announced as a reply to this situation, and some new initiatives did in fact take place. Yet, the overall figures on the use of arbitration did not dramatically change at all until today.

Very similar is the situation in the field of mediation. Mediation, as already noted, became popular in public discourse as a promising method to settle civil and commercial disputes later than arbitration. Propagation of arbitration happened on a larger scale in particular in the last five to six years (symbolically starting in 2002, when three international organizations issued their key documents on dispute settlement by mediation).[44]

In spite of the considerable institutional support, the real figures about mediation still turn out to be much more modest and much less reliable.

Within the first two rounds of the evaluation of the European justice systems, the CEPEJ *inter alia* collected data about the use of mediation. In the first questionnaire, questions 97 to 101 asked about the numbers of registered mediators, public budget devoted to mediation, numbers of incoming and resolved mediation cases and the areas in which mediation is most practiced and successful.[45] However, after processing the data, the reporters learned that the collected information regarding mediation is 'limited' in value, and that 'the information collected can not be used for cross country comparison'.[46] Therefore, only some figures on public budgets for mediation and the number of accredited mediators were included.[47] The report, however, stated that 'the report shows that many countries are in the process of developing mediation practices'.[48] But, two years later, in the next report, the situation was not significantly different. Based on the problems diagnosed in the first evaluation round, the questions were rephrased, supplemented and formulated in a deliberately open way.[49] Nevertheless, the report once again contained only some individual information, concluding that 'it is difficult to gather coherent statistical data taking into account the number and type of mediation

43 For official statistics on public justice see <http://www.pravosudje.hr> (last consulted 20 March 2007); for some data on arbitration cases in the second part of the 1990s see Uzelac 1998, p. 115-119.

44 Three organizations are: the United Nations (cf. 2002 UNCITRAL Model Law on International Commercial Conciliation); the European Union (cf. 2002 Green Paper of the Commission); and the Council of Europe (2002 Recommendation on Mediation in Civil and Commercial Matters). We hereby refer only to the last wave of interest for ADR. The history of mediation is, of course, much longer - on some historic examples see the reports on the history of ADR by Wijffels 2005; Verkijk 2005; Verkijk 2005a; Van Orshoven 2005 and Oberhammer & Domej 2005.

45 CEPEJ 2005, p 104.

46 CEPEJ 2005, p. 76.

47 CEPEJ 2005, p. 135.

48 CEPEJ 2005, p. 76.

49 CEPEJ 2006. See questions 101 to 104, p. 193-194 and explanatory notes on p. 213-214.

proceedings'.[50] Only 16 countries were able to provide some 'more precise information', and according to these, in 2004 there were 181 mediation procedures in Bosnia and Herzegovina, 4 in Bulgaria, 130 in Croatia, 433 in Hungary, 569 in Liechtenstein, 6 in Luxembourg, 4414 in Netherlands and 694 in Portugal.[51] At the same time, the figures on the total numbers of civil cases in the public courts of those countries was measured in the hundreds of thousands (e.g. 417 000 in Croatia, 635 000 in Hungary, 680 000 in Bulgaria and 628 000 in Portugal).[52]

Under the habitual approach, exemplified *supra* by the statements of Zuglia, based on the collected data, in assessing the current use of both arbitration and mediation in Europe, one must arrive at catastrophic conclusions. Even though alternative dispute resolution need not necessarily have the same figures and results as the mainstream dispute resolution, from the perspective of relieving the public court system from its burden of backlogs, the existing ADR mechanisms appear to be no alternative at all. Of course, one might always argue that mediation is a relatively novel trend in dispute resolution and therefore deserves some grace period before assessment. Still, we are sceptical about this argument and the prospects of a dramatic change in future figures. Arbitration, at least, is not an entirely new method of dispute resolution - it has been dynamically evolving on an international scale at least since the 1950s, when the New York Convention was adopted by the UN.[53] Although arbitration services and arbitration laws have been developing over the last 50 years, this has not been accompanied by any exponential rise in the figures relating to arbitration cases. Still today the most prominent arbitral institutions in the world have an annual caseload of only a few hundred cases.[54]

We would, therefore, suggest a change in approach. The very method of evaluation of the private justice mechanisms may be a *litmus test* for the dominant view on all types of dispute resolution mechanisms (including the public justice system). The assessment of alternative dispute resolution based on numbers of cases, and the goal of advancing private justice primarily as a method of steering cases from the public courts, is again a symptom of the *institution-oriented, insiders' approach* described *supra* in this paper. This approach is even less appropriate when applied to private justice, and therefore the outcome of the evaluation can be even weirder than the conclusions of the World Bank about contract enforcement in some countries. Among other things, here are three reasons for this conclusion.

50 CEPEJ 2006, p. 151.

51 CEPEJ 2006.

52 CEPEJ 2006, p. 89.

53 See Convention on the Recognition and Enforcement of Foreign Arbitral Awards (New York Convention) of 10 June 1958. This Convention, as one of the most universally accepted instruments of the UN, is ratified today by some 142 countries (data for February 2007).

54 One of the most prominent institutions for international arbitration, the International Court of Arbitration of the International Chamber of Commerce, has announced in February 2007 under the heading 'ICC arbitration tops records in 2006' that it had received in 2006 'a total of 593 new cases… equaling the record set in 2002'. See <http://www.iccwbo.org/court/arbitration/> (last consulted 20 March 2007).

First, this approach disregards the interests of the users: it disregards the specific weight and importance of the matters handled in the process as well as the social importance of the particular cases and the values that are at stake for the parties. This is visible already on a very superficial level, e.g., when comparing the amounts in disputes regarding monetary claims. As arbitration is most developed in resolving international commercial disputes, the amounts adjudicated there can be voluminous.[55] Even in the national arbitral *fora,* the relatively minor number of cases can still involve socially relevant issues, and matters that can determine the fate of social processes and even the means of existence for hundreds or thousands of persons.[56]

Second, the numerical comparison of cases solved through public and private dispute resolution mechanisms may be problematic. Irrespective of its social importance and value, one successfully resolved case in the public court is not necessarily equally valuable to one dispute resolved by mediation. The cases resolved in adjudication have a tendency of multiplying. As the result of an adjudicatory process is imposed from above, the likelihood of not accepting it is greater, and new processes will often follow (e.g., launching of legal remedies, initiation of new suits, etc.). On the other hand, a successful ADR process has a much higher level of acceptance and can bring an end to current litigations, as well as prevent future ones. Also, on the side of expenses, litigations regularly last significantly longer and bring with them considerably higher costs, which should not be disregarded. Finally, the effect of the successful implementation of ADR mechanisms may have a general impact on avoiding disputes in formalistic *fora* of public justice. Parties with the experience of ADR might wish to adhere to autonomous methods of dispute resolution as often as possible in their future dealings with their partners.

Third, when assessing the success of private justice mechanisms according to the numbers of cases that were steered from the public courts to them, it is often forgotten that private justice does not exist in order to 'receive' or 'steal' cases from the public courts, but to offer services that are freely available to their potential users. Regularly, the cases are neither administratively distributed nor mandatorily referred to mediation and arbitration.[57] Therefore, from the side of the users, the private dispute resolution services should be evaluated on the basis of their

55 E.g. according to the 2005 Statistical Report of the ICC Arbitration Court, in 54.3% new cases the amount in dispute exceeded one million US dollars. See <http://iccwbo.org/court/arbitration> (last consulted 20 March 2007), as well as the full report in the *ICC International Court of Arbitration Bulletin,* 17/1, 2006.

56 The statistics show that in 2001 the leading Croatian national arbitral institution, the Permanent Arbitration Court at the Croatian Chamber of Commerce in Zagreb 'had only 0.6% of the caseload of the largest commercial court in the country (the Commercial Court in Zagreb), but at the same time the aggregate value of its cases was about 25% (i.e., one quarter) of the annual aggregate value of the same court', i.e. about 300 million euros. The dominant part in this amount was related to domestic disputes relating to privatization of state companies. See Uzelac 2003a, p. 7.

57 For some arguments in favour of the voluntary nature of mediation, see the paper of Verkijk in this volume.

availability and their effectiveness. Under the assumption that such services exist, that they are accessible, and that their functioning and effects are known, *any* figures will be exactly appropriate, as the goal in itself is not to impose any system on the users, but to fulfil the needs that they themselves experience.

Therefore, the only failing that may be indicated by the lack of alternatives to public justice can, in fact, be attributed to public justice itself. The shaping of the landscape of dispute resolution services is, ultimately, the duty of those who shall see to it that the citizens' needs are fulfilled - the public authorities. The architecture of the dispute resolution services should take into account that each dispute resolution service has its place, purpose, and limitations, and act accordingly, enabling the development and free initiative both on the side of service providers and their users.

6. Conclusions - Towards a True Public-Private Partnership?

As demonstrated, the assessment of how well the contemporary justice systems function is still a considerable challenge. On one side, we have more or less benevolent impressions, backed by everyday experience, but dependent on subjective, personal points of view. The assessments based on this methodology, although possibly accurate, derive their force from the institutional position of the assessor. Yet, they are an easy target for those who dislike their results or their recommendations. Just as in the case of the Croatia 2006 Progress Report, the findings may be perceived as 'political' and, therefore, the reactions on them can be political, too. Without the firm ground of solid and generally accepted indicators for assessment, it is also easy to distort the real nature of ongoing processes in the justice system, and create an impression of change while nothing is changing (or where changes go in the negative direction).

On the other side, current attempts to develop objective indicators to assess the justice systems of Europe still need to be thoroughly evaluated and discussed.[58] Important steps forward were made under the auspices of some international organizations, such as the World Bank and the CEPEJ. These organizations are also pioneers in attempts to promote the *user-oriented approach* - the approach that centers on the users of the justice system. However, so far they were more successful in collecting information that originates from the *institution-based approach* - the comparative data on existent structures (e.g. numbers of courts, legal professionals etc.), simply because the current national justice systems, still deeply impregnated by the insiders' approach, mostly do not monitor processes and collect information that provide an objective picture which would be relevant from the users' perspective (e.g., data about the length of legal processes, including their enforcement). Just as the data originating from the *institution-based approach* is not sufficient to assess and compare the functioning of the justice systems, the fragmentary and unreliable data on legal processes may cause the *user-oriented*

[58] Regarding evaluation of ADR more was achieved in the Anglo-American circle, where the limitations of old, traditional evaluation criteria are recognized. See e.g. Tyler 1989, p. 20.

approach to arrive at false conclusions which may ultimately compromise the goals and projects of those who use them. Therefore, a lot of ground-laying work still has to be done, assisted by the community of independent researchers and academic institutions which may help in the process of formulating adequate methodologies and performance indicators for the future, and in the testing of the soundness of the current ones and their use. Strategic planning and thinking about the justice systems has to be done with the support of impartial and professional experts in the analysis of the administration of justice, who study justice systems and judicial procedures as one important social service, just as the botanist scientifically studies plants, or myrmecologist studies ants.

The private justice mechanisms are an especially good example of the weaknesses of the current assessment exercises. The use of institutional indicators applied on private dispute resolution methods produces particularly weak results, and usually also indicates misunderstanding of the proper function and use of these methods. The appropriate evaluation of ADR (arbitration and mediation) at the level of national justice systems would need elaboration of a complex system of indicators which would take into account general features of the justice system, the culture of dispute resolution and the institutional and extra-institutional space for mechanisms of private justice. Public justice and private justice are not adversaries, competitors or alternatives to one another. For both public and private justice there is no alternative. They should both be taken as partners in the same venture - the fulfilment of the fundamental needs of the users of the justice system.

Bibliography

Anderson, Bernstein & Gray 2005
Anderson, J.H., Bernstein, D.S. & Gray, C.W., *Judicial Systems in Transition Economies. Assessing the Past, Looking into Future*, Washington: World Bank Publications, 2005.

Anderson & Gray 2006
Anderson, J.H. & Gray, C.W., *Transforming Judicial Systems in Europe and Central Asia*, paper for ABCDE Conference, St. Petersburg, January 2006.

Barbić 2006
Barbić, J. (ed.), *Strategija reforme pravosudnog sustava*, Zagreb: HAZU, 2006, p. 73-162.

CEPEJ 2005
CEPEJ, *European Judicial Systems 2002 – Facts and figures on the basis of a survey conducted in 40 Council of Europe Member States*, Strasbourg: Council of Europe Publishing, 2005.

CEPEJ 2006
CEPEJ, *European judicial systems. Edition 2006 (2004 data)*, CEPEJ and Council of Europe Publishing, No. 1, 2006.

Commission 2006
Commission of the European Communities, *Croatia 2006 Progress Report*, Brussels, 2006.

Decker & Messick 2005
Decker, K. & Messick, R., *World Bank Annotated Bibliography, Legal Institutions of the Market Economy*, <http://www.worldbank.org/publicsector/legal/> (last consulted 20 March 2007).

Hess & Chemla 2003
Hess, B., Chemla, D. & Lindgren, A., *Territorial Jurisdiction*, Strasbourg: CEPEJ, 2003.

Oberhammer & Domej 2005
Oberhammer, P. & Domej, T., 'Germany, Switzerland and Austria', in: Van Rhee, C.H. (ed.), *European Traditions in Civil Procedure* (Ius Commune Europaeum, 54), Antwerpen: Intersentia, 2005, p. 215-221.

Van Orshoven 2005
Van Orshoven, P., 'Belgium', in: Van Rhee, C.H. (ed.), *European Traditions in Civil Procedure* (Ius Commune Europaeum, 54), Antwerpen: Intersentia, 2005, p. 213.

Schönfelder 2005
Schönfelder, B., *The Puzzling Underuse of Arbitration in Post-Communism – A Law and Economics Analysis*, Freiberger Arbeitspapiere - The Freiberg Working Paper, 07/2005, <http://www.tu-freiberg.de> (last consulted 20 March 2007).

Triva 1991
Triva, S., *Arbitražno rješavanje domaćih i međunarodnih trgovačkih sporova', Arbitraža i poduzetništvo*, Zagreb: Progres, 1991.

Triva & Dika 2004
Triva, S. & Dika, M., *Građansko parnično procesno pravo*, Zagreb: Narodne novine, 2004.

Tyler 1989
Tyler, T.R., 'The Quality of Dispute Resolution Procedures and Outcomes: Measurement Problems and Possibilities', *Denver University Law Review*, 1989, p. 419-436.

Uzelac 1998
Uzelac, A., 'A Log of the Activities of the Permanent Arbitration Court at the Croatian Chamber of Commerce', in: Uzelac, A. *et al.* (eds.), *Croatian Arbitration Yearbook*, vol. 5, Zagreb: HGK, 1998, p. 111-119.

Uzelac 2000
Uzelac, A., 'Role and Status of Judges in Croatia', in: Oberhammer, P. (ed.), *Richterbild und Rechtsreform in Mitteleuropa*, Wien: Manz, 2000, p. 23-66.

Uzelac 2002
Uzelac, A., 'Amendments to the Law on Courts and Law on State Judicial Council – Elements of the Reform of the Organizational Judicial Legislation', in: Lalić, G. (ed.), *Croatian Judiciary: Lessons and Perspectives*, Zagreb: HHO, 2002, p. 37-80.

Uzelac 2003
Uzelac, A., 'Reform of the Judiciary in Croatia and Its Limitations (Appointing Presidents of the Courts in the Republic of Croatia and the Outcomes)', in: Vujadinović, D. *et al.* (eds.), *Between Authoritarianism and Democracy: Serbia, Montenegro, Croatia: Vol. I – Institutional Framework*, Belgrade: CEDET, 2003, p. 303-329.

Uzelac 2003a
Uzelac, A., Croatian national report, in: Paulsson, J. (ed.), *International Handbook on Commercial Arbitration*, Suppl. 39, Deventer: Kluwer, 2003, p. 1-59.

Uzelac 2004
Uzelac, A., 'The Rule of Law and the Judicial System: Court delays as a barrier to accession', in: Ott, K. (ed.), *Croatian Accession to the European Union*, Zagreb: IJF, 2004, p. 105-130.

Uzelac 2004a
Uzelac, A., 'Accellerating Civil Proceedings in Croatia - A History of Attempts to Improve the Efficiency of Civil Litigation', in: Van Rhee, C.H. (ed.), *The Law's Delay, Essays on Undue Delay in Civil Litigation* (Ius Commune Europaeum, 47), Antwerpen: Intersentia, 2004, p. 283-313.

Uzelac 2006
Uzelac, A., 'Kann die Effizienz der Justiz gemessen werden? Versuch eines Vergleichs der europäischen Justizsysteme', in: Gottwald, P. (ed.), *Effektivität des Rechtsschutzes vor staatlichen und privaten Gerichten*, Bielefeld: Gieseking, 2006, p. 41-72.

Uzelac forthcoming
Uzelac, A., *Turning Civil Procedure Upside Down*, contribution at the Ghent Symposium on the Bicentennial of the Code de procédure civile, University of Ghent, 27 October 2006, forthcoming.

Verkijk 2005
Verkijk, R., 'The Netherlands', in: Van Rhee, C.H. (ed.), *European Traditions in Civil Procedure* (Ius Commune Europaeum, 54), Antwerpen: Intersentia, 2005, p. 207-212.

Verkijk 2005a
Verkijk, R., 'England and Wales', in: Van Rhee, C.H. (ed.), *European Traditions in Civil Procedure* (Ius Commune Europaeum, 54), Antwerpen: Intersentia, 2005, p. 223-231.

Wijffels 2005
Wijffels, A., 'France', in: Van Rhee, C.H. (ed.), *European Traditions in Civil Procedure* (Ius Commune Europaeum, 54), Antwerpen: Intersentia, 2005, p. 197-205.

Zuckerman 2006
Zuckerman, A.A.S., 'How to work together to make practical solutions', *Justice for All: Practical approaches to solving cross-border civil and family disputes*, Civil and family law conference, 24-26 October 2005, Edinburgh: DCA, 2006.

II. Public and Private Justice: History and Development

C.H. van Rhee

PUBLIC JUSTICE: SOME HISTORICAL REMARKS

1. Introduction

This paper addresses the history of the public justice systems in Europe, and especially the procedure of the courts in civil matters. It focuses more specifically on the fact that the differences between the European systems of civil procedure seem to have become less pronounced than they were in the past.

However, before turning to this issue, something needs to be said about a phenomenon that becomes quickly apparent to any student of the history of civil litigation in Europe, i.e. the tension between the adjudication of civil disputes by the organs of the state (public justice) on the one hand, and the adjudication or settlement of civil disputes by private individuals or bodies or by the litigants themselves (private justice) on the other.

If one looks at classical Roman law this tension is not so apparent. In fact a mixture between the two extremes may be found. In the formula process - and even in the earlier procedure by way of *legis actiones* - litigation was started before a state official, the *praetor*, but after the *praetor* had decided whether or not an action should be granted and, if so, what action should be granted, one finds that the adjudication of the lawsuit was left to a private citizen chosen by the parties, i.e. the *iudex privatus*.[1] This approach guaranteed that the legal part of the case rested firmly in the hands of the state, but at the same time it made sure that those aspects of litigation which were of lesser importance to the state, i.e. confronting the applicable legal rules with the facts of the case, were left to the private domain. This was an attractive approach, since it required a minimum amount of state investment in the distribution of justice and, at the same time, guaranteed the necessary state influence.

This situation changed in the post-classical period as a result of the introduction of a manner of litigation which became known as the *extra-ordinaria cognitio*.[2] This type of litigation, which is an ancestor of the procedural model of the

1 Kaser & Hackl 1996, p. 192 *et seq*. See also Petrak in this volume.
2 Kaser & Hackl 1996, p. 435 *et seq*.

European continent, brought the whole action under the control of state-appointed judges. It reflected the wish to control all aspects of the functioning of the state in a detailed manner. Although its name suggests that this procedure was exceptional, it was the leading type of procedure at the time of the emperor Justinian, even though we also find remnants of the other types in Justinian' code of law, the *Corpus Iuris Civilis*. From classical times until Justinian, therefore, the history of litigation may be characterised as a movement from semi-private to public.

In large parts of Europe, Roman civilization and its culture had disappeared or was in the process of disappearing at the start of the medieval period (from ca. 500 AD) and the same was true for the Roman state organisation. In the absence of an organised state, the adjudication of disputes was carried out by those who were effectively in a position of power, i.e. those who controlled a certain area. More than once, this resulted in a spectacular growth of private 'justice': either this meant that one was only able to effect one's right by force of arms, or that one was dependant on the assistance of others who often only acted out of self-interest. In the best possible situation, this would mean that one had to resort to a local court organised by a local ruler where justice was being done not according to the rules of procedure developed in Roman law, but according to a procedure which, from a modern perspective, would be classified as non-rational. It was a mode of procedure in which the supernatural played a role in that, particularly at the evidential stage, considerable faith was placed in the direct intervention of God (ordeals, trial by battle, etc.).[3]

Due to the feudal system, the administration of justice at the local court came to be seen as a prerogative of the local lord, also because justice was not free of charge; it often represented a considerable source of income. The administration of justice became, as it were, private property. This manner of administering justice can, in my opinion, be classified as private justice, not so much in the sense that it was the parties themselves who arranged the adjudication of their case (as was the case in Roman law where they played a role in the nomination of the *iudex privatus*), but more in the sense that they brought their case before a court that was not organised by a state or a comparable institution.

From around the 12th century, when Europe entered a more developed phase in its history (a purely agricultural society gave way to a society in which trade and manufacture played a considerable role), the local 'private' justice system was confronted with justice systems organised on a supra-local and even supra-regional level. It is at this moment that the history of modern litigation begins, first only within the confines of ecclesiastical courts known as officialities, and later also in courts organised by the various kings, princes, dukes and counts that reigned medieval Europe. The latter were interested in the administration of justice in their own courts because this would result in the highly desirable centralisation of the administration of their various territories.

Private justice in the sense of locally organised courts 'owned' by local rulers was detrimental to the ambitions of these kings and princes. Public justice in the

3 Van Caenegem, p. 8 *et seq.*

sense of a court system organised on a central level, on the other hand, favoured their ambitions since it would result in the administration of the law becoming independent of the private interests of local rulers.

Although one might not consider this development so much as a movement from private to public justice, since the interests of local rulers were only replaced by the interests of other, more powerful rulers, i.e. kings and princes, I would nevertheless maintain that this is a development towards a public justice system, as the interests of a society and its kings and princes - at least according to contemporary learning - coincided. The interests of these kings and princes went beyond what I have categorized as private interests at the local level. These kings and princes were building the foundations - albeit in a rudimentary form - of modern statehood, something that was absent at the local level where the administration of justice was first and for all seen as a useful source of income.

The organisation of a public justice system at a central level (later to become the 'national level') has been very successful. On the Continent, this is due to the French Revolution and the consequent abolition of the last remnants of the feudal system. As a result, the last traces of a private justice system (in the sense of the local administration of justice as a kind of private property of the local ruler) have disappeared. Consequently, the competition between this type of private justice and public justice has disappeared with them.

Unfortunately for the state courts, this did not mean that the battle was won, since competition between private and public justice is still with us today. Nowadays, however, private justice should not be understood as the adjudication of claims by private local courts, but rather as justice organised by the parties themselves; a type of dispute settlement we already encountered when discussing the formula process and the *iudex privatus* of Roman law.

But let us now turn to the main theme of this paper: the history of civil procedure in the state courts (public justice). I would like to discuss a common European trend in this area of the law, i.e. the fact that the differences between the systems of civil procedure in Europe are slowly becoming less pronounced. In my opinion, one may even speak of a 'convergence' of civil justice systems in Europe.

2. Convergence of Civil Justice Systems?

During the last decade or so, the question whether or not European legal systems are converging has been debated fiercely.[4] According to the main proponent of the anti-convergence argument, Pierre Legrand, no convergence is taking place. This author holds that differences in legal culture prevent the various national systems from growing together despite the introduction of similar rules of law in the different Member States of the European Union.[5] Other authors, on the contrary, are

4 The sections that follow are based on Van Rhee 2003, p. 217-232 and Van Rhee 2003a, p. 201-216.

5 E.g. Legrand 1996, p. 52 *et seq.*; Legrand 2002, p. 61 *et seq.*

convinced that approximation of the national systems of law is taking place.[6] Some of these authors also believe that the creation of a harmonised set of legal rules for the European Union is a feasible option. This conviction is shown strikingly in the second edition of *Towards a European Civil Code* edited by A.S. Hartkamp and others.[7] Unlike the first edition of this book, the considerably revised second edition takes the feasibility of a European *ius commune* for granted; it directly addresses the possible content of harmonised European rules.[8]

On an earlier occasion,[9] I have expressed the opinion that I tend to agree with the authors who favour the convergence argument. Although one might concur with Legrand that common rules of law do not necessarily guarantee their uniform interpretation and application, it cannot be denied that the introduction of similar rules nevertheless brings legal systems somehow closer together than they were before. Additionally, the existence of similar rules may trigger their uniform interpretation, at least to some extent, in situations where information on their interpretation and application in one or more jurisdictions is readily available to courts and practitioners. An example of such a situation may be found in the Netherlands at the time of the introduction of the 1838 Code of Civil Procedure: not only was this Code to a large extent modelled on the French *Code de procédure civile*, so, too were French treatises on civil procedure, which were apparently widely available and cited frequently in the first decades of the Code's existence.[10]

The above example is a special case in the sense that it deals with an area of the law which for a long time has been considered to be immune from foreign influences and, therefore, from anything but the most incidental and haphazard converging tendency (mistakenly so, as the example shows). In support of the thesis that civil procedure is a purely national branch of the law, it has been claimed that procedure is very much linked to court organisation, an area of the law which is traditionally considered to be the exclusive domain of the national legislature. Additionally, it is held that the way in which litigation is conducted is closely linked to national convictions and traditions. It seems, however, that these ideas are subject to erosion. After all, Article 65 of the *Treaty Establishing the European Community* lays down that

> 'Measures in the field of judicial cooperation in civil matters having cross border implications, to be taken in accordance with Article 67 and insofar as necessary for the proper functioning of the internal market, shall include: [...] c) eliminating obstacles to the good functioning of civil proceedings, if necessary by promoting the compatibility of the rules on civil procedure applicable in the Member States'.

Even before the introduction of this Article, however, international attempts to harmonise procedural legislation had already been made. Of course, the report of

6 E.g. Glenn 1993, p. 567; Markesinis 1994, p. 30; Watson 2000.
7 First edition Nijmegen 1994; second edition Nijmegen 1998.
8 Cf. the prefaces to the first and the second editions.
9 Van Rhee 2000a, 589 *et seq.*
10 French textbooks are, for example, frequently cited by Oudeman 1842; De Pinto 1845.

the Storme Working Group immediately comes to mind as regards harmonisation of procedural law within the European Union.[11] Further attempts have been made on an even wider international level under the aegis of the *American Law Institute* and *Unidroit*.[12]

The present paper seeks to question the anti-convergence argument from the perspective of legal history. It gives a brief overview of the shared legal past of most modern systems of civil procedure in Europe and tries to identify areas of procedural law which have been susceptible to convergence, areas of the law which in my opinion merit further investigation. The main focus of attention will be on the influence of continental civil procedure on its English counterpart. Before addressing this theme, however, something needs to be said about the terminology *ius commune* which I use in this article as well as about the reception of the Romano-canonical procedure in secular courts.

3. *Ius Commune*

Today, *ius commune* is often used to denote a common law of Europe, i.e. a set of rules shared by the various Member States of the European Union. In that sense, *ius commune* is to a large extent something of the future, a goal to be achieved. In the past, however, this was not the case. At that time *ius commune* was in many instances *not* used to refer to a common set of legal rules. As P. Nève has shown,[13] the historical term *ius commune* had many different meanings. Usually, it could best be defined as a common legal science (doctrine),[14] mainly based on Roman Law (*Corpus Iuris Civilis*) and Canon Law (*Corpus Iuris Canonici*). In the field of procedure, however, the situation might have been different. In order to make this clear, we need to have a look at the early history of the modern systems of procedural law.

As we all know, the 'mother' of most modern systems of civil procedure on the European Continent is the so-called Romano-canonical procedure, which came into existence in the 12th century. It was developed on the basis of materials derived from the *Corpus Iuris Civilis* as well as from some other sources, for example those belonging to Canon Law.[15] According to Nève,[16] unlike substantive private law, procedure consisted from the outset of a blend of Roman and Canon Laws. It could therefore rightly be considered to be a *ius commune*, not in the traditional sense, but in the sense of a single system of procedural law built from elements of the two learned laws.

Quickly, the new procedure became a separate field of study, something which appears from the considerable body of contemporary literature solely dealing

11 Storme 1994.
12 American Law Institute & UNIDROIT 2006.
13 Nève 1995, p. 3-58. See also Nève 1997, p. 871 *et seq*.
14 Schulze 1993, p. 442.
15 Van Caenegem, p. 16.
16 Nève 1995, p. 20-21.

with procedural topics.[17] This was a new development, since procedure was not treated as a separate subject in the *Corpus Iuris Civilis*. There, rules concerning procedure (often rules of the procedure *extra ordinem* from the time of Justinian) were not grouped together and, consequently, it was the task of the early students of Roman Law to bring the scattered procedural rules from the *Corpus Iuris* together.

The new procedure was applied by a new type of ecclesiastical courts known as officialities. These officialities were spread all over Europe and dealt with a wide range of issues. As a result, the Romano-canonical procedure became known in the greater part of the medieval Christian world.

As regards the particular way in which the Romano-canonical procedure was applied at the ecclesiastical courts, final conclusions cannot be drawn at the present stage of research. The available evidence suggests, however, that it was not applied in an identical manner (something that would, indeed, have been surprising in the light of the local differences that exist even today in a single codified legal system); variations can be observed.[18] As regards the ecclesiastical courts in England, for example, R.H. Helmholz states: 'It would be fair to say that the procedure used in the English spiritual courts always followed the outlines of that found in contemporary *ordines* and other procedural manuals, but that it often did so in simplified fashion'. These variations may prevent us from referring to the Romano-canonical procedure as a *ius commune* in the sense of a common procedural law for the ecclesiastical courts in Europe. However, after listing the differences between the law on the books and the rules of procedure actually applied in the spiritual courts, professor Helmholz also remarks that '[t]hese, and other such features, seem to have been permissible variants of Romano-canonical procedure. Not all were features one could read about directly in the medieval handbooks. But neither were they contrary to the canon law'.[19] Whether one can refer to the Romano-canonical procedure as *ius commune* in the sense of a common European law of procedure is, therefore, to a large extent a matter of personal preference. In the present article I opt for using the terminology *ius commune* in referring to the learned Romano-canonical procedure. One should, however, be aware of the limitations of this terminology.

4. The Reception of the Procedural *Ius Commune* in Secular Courts

4.1. *Reception on the Continent*

The introduction of a learned procedure in the domain of the secular courts of the European Continent[20] was the result of different factors (which can only be

17 On the early procedural literature, see Fowler-Magerl 1999.

18 Also Van Caenegem 2002, p. 20.

19 Helmholz 1997, p. 653.

20 When mentioning continental Europe, one should not forget that Scotland, at least from the 16th century, also belonged to the continental tradition. The supreme civil court in Scotland, →

discussed here in part). One of them was that clerics regularly acted as judges in superior lay courts. Apart from a thorough knowledge of substantive Roman and Canon Law, they were usually acquainted with the Romano-canonical procedure. These lawyers often had recourse to the *ius commune* when it was possible and necessary to supplement and modify the rules of procedure of the secular courts to which they were attached. Additionally, European rulers introduced Romano-canonical rules when they made attempts to modernise and centralise the administration of justice in their realm, i.e. when they deliberately introduced new rules of process. This was to some extent the result of the apparent superiority of the new procedure as compared with indigenous legal practice. Trial by battle and ordeals, for example, was a common feature of the old procedure. These methods lost their appeal in the quickly changing late medieval society. This society needed a new, rational procedure for which the Romano-canonical procedure was able to provide the model.

The reception of Romano-canonical rules of procedure did not result in a uniform procedure on the European Continent. As stated above, even at the level of the ecclesiastical courts, procedure showed local differences. Such differences were even more likely within the atmosphere of the secular courts since these courts were not subject to a single Pope and a single Canon Law, but to different princes and different regional customs. The differences that may be observed in the various procedures of the secular courts in Europe are so numerous, that it is wrong in my opinion to use the terminology *ius commune* in order to refer to these procedures. Nevertheless, marked similarities did exist. I will mention just a few examples.

First, the Romano-canonical model gave rise to procedures that were mainly written. These procedures relied heavily on documents; all steps in a lawsuit had to be recorded. This was in sharp contrast to indigenous legal practice, where the oral element was preponderant. As a result of the reception of the Romano-canonical forms of process, the oral element in the procedures of continental Europe became less important and nearly disappeared in some places.[21] Secondly, the Romano-canonical procedure furnished European lawyers with a procedural terminology and concepts that were, at least to a certain extent, standardised. All European lawyers were (and are) familiar with terms such as *citatio, exceptio* or *litis contestatio*.[22] This, of course, facilitated the international legal debate. Finally, the influence of the Romano-canonical model resulted in particular procedural rules to be the same in some or all continental European states. A notable example of a shared rule on the European Continent was that a single witness did not suffice for full proof. The availability of counterclaims is another.[23]

established as a 'college of justice' in May 1532, for example, used a procedure that had a distinct Romano-canonical outlook. See Finlay 2000, esp. Chapter 5.

21 Van Caenegem, p. 12.

22 For the Romano-canonical variant of procedure applied at one of the supreme courts of the Low Countries, the Great Council of Malines, see Van Rhee 1997.

23 It should be noted, however, that, although counterclaims were (and are) allowed in most continental jurisdictions, a difference of opinion existed (and still exists) regarding whether →

4.2. *Reception in England*

The reception of the Romano-canonical procedure in English lay courts was less successful than on the European Continent. This was due to the fact that at the time of the initial reception of the learned laws on the Continent, i.e. in the 12th century, in England the 'common law emerged [...] from the efficient and rapid expansion of institutions which existed in an undeveloped form before 1066'.[24] This common law may rightly be called a *ius commune* for England in the sense of a system of rules common to the whole realm. While other European 'nations' turned to Roman Law for modernisation of the law, England developed its own legal system.[25] This system was sufficiently modern to meet the demands of the time. Therefore, Roman Law did not gain as much ground there as on the Continent. The same was true for the Romano-canonical procedure. The exclusion of this procedure was reinforced by the fact that under the common law, procedure and substantive law were interrelated subjects. Forms of action dominated the scene and the particular procedural rules to be followed were determined by the available writ.[26]

However, even though the common law furnished England with its own substantive and procedural law, this did not mean that English and continental systems of procedure lacked common features. On the contrary, similarities did exist. Some of these similarities might have been remnants of older forms of process which were incorporated in the Romano-canonical procedures of the Continent and the common law forms of action. An example are the so-called 'essoins'.[27] Both according to the medieval common law[28] and according to procedure on the Continent,[29] a litigant who failed to appear in court was allowed to send excuses by messengers, so-called 'essoiners', which in French procedural language and in English Law French were called 'essoins'. The messengers could excuse the defaulter from being absent by explaining that he was sick, abroad, on the king's service, cut off by a flood, a broken bridge, and so forth. 'Essoins' secured delays of varying length.

The observance of (aspects of) the rule *audite et alteram partem*, i.e. the rule that both parties should be given equal opportunities to be heard by the court, may also be an example of continuity in European civil procedure finding its origin in the period from before the introduction of the new systems of procedural law in England and on the Continent.[30] This rule dominated (and still dominates) procedure both in common law and civil law jurisdictions. Observance of the rule

or not a counterclaim needs to be related to the original claim. This subject is discussed in Van Rhee 2000, p. 227 *et seq*.

24 Baker 2002, p. 12.

25 Van Caenegem, p. 15.

26 Maitland 1968, p. 2: 'The choice [between forms of action] is not merely a choice between a number of queer technical terms, it is a choice between methods of procedure adapted to cases of different kinds'.

27 Van Caenegem, p. 9.

28 Plucknett 1956, p. 384.

29 For France, see Tardif 1885, p. 55-56. For the Low Countries, see Wielant 1573, p. 89-91.

30 On the history of this rule from Roman times, see Coenraad 2000.

appears where courts go to particular lengths to make the parties appear before them.[31] Defendants need to be summoned. If they do not make their appearance in court, proceedings are postponed. After appearance, the litigants have the opportunity to respond to the allegations of their opponents. Although differences may be observed in this area of the law,[32] the basic rule is the same everywhere.

Apart from the above similarities, further similarities came into being as a result of the fact that the *ius commune* influenced English procedure in various ways. A channel through which English law was influenced by Roman and Canon Law at an early stage was equity. Equity aimed at mending defects of the common law. J.H. Baker mentions the example of the debtor who gave his creditor a sealed bond, but did not ensure that it was cancelled when he paid up. The common law regarded the bond as incontrovertible evidence of the debt, and so payment was no defence. In such situations, petitions for relief were presented to the English King. The King had these petitions decided by his Chancellor, not according to the rules of common law but on the basis of equity and justice. Slowly, this gave rise to a new jurisdiction which became known as equity.[33]

At an early stage most Chancellors were clerics and, therefore, acquainted with Roman and Canon Law as well as with the Romano-canonical procedure. It is not surprising that they, just as their colleagues at the secular courts on the European Continent, made use of this knowledge and, as a result, the body of law which became known as equity shows marked influences of the the learned law.[34] Even professor J.H. Baker, who in his *Introduction to English Legal History* is generally rather sceptical as regards the influences of the learned law on English law, states: 'The procedure [of the Court of Chancery] clearly owed something to the inquisitorial[35] procedure of the canonists'.[36] This is, however, not to say that only

31 For common law jurisdictions, see Plucknett 1956, p. 385.

32 In common law jurisdictions, for example, it is usually the plaintiff who has the last word, whereas on the Continent the last word is traditionally reserved for the defendant.

33 See e.g. Reppy 1949, p. 21 *et seq.*

34 Van Caenegem, p. 45: 'The special nature of the chancellor's intervention and the fact that he was a cleric and surrounded by a staff of clerics led to the adoption of a procedure that was very different from that of the Common Law and very close to the Romano-canonical procedure, especially in the summary form of the decretal *Saepe*, which had been issued in the early fourteenth century'. See also Millar 1928, p. 19-20, who calls chancery procedure 'the joint product of canon and common law'; Clark 1993, p. 69 ('the common Romano-canonical influences on ... chancery ... procedure'); Clark 1993, p. 75-76 ('Equity courts ... were viewed as Romano-canonical').

35 Even though it must be admitted that the Romano-canonical procedure can be described as inquisitorial in certain respects, describing this procedure as 'inquisitorial' *tout court* is in my opinion overstating the case. The same is true for modern systems of civil procedure on the European Continent, which, however, incidentally are also described as inquisitorial by some Anglo-American lawyers. Indeed, before the introduction of the recent reforms in English civil procedure, the powers of the English judge were rather limited (they still are for today's American judge). A comparison of his position with that of his continental counterpart inevitably leads to the conclusion that continental systems are less adversarial. Nevertheless, some kind of party autonomy has always been a feature of both modern continental systems of civil procedure and of the Romano-canonical procedure. Therefore, calling these →

equity was influenced by the *ius commune* and that the common law remained immune from these influences. An example of civilian influences on the common law in the early-modern period can be found in the area of proof (a subject which, at least from a continental perspective, clearly belongs to the domain of procedural law).

In his excellent book on *The Law of Proof in Early Modern Equity*,[37] Michael Macnair explains that, in the period discussed by him, the common law should be viewed as local positive law, within the general hierarchy of laws accepted in later medieval and early modern thought (the hierarchy being divine law, natural law, the law of nations and positive law). Within this framework, he claims, the basic ideas of the law of proof were considered to be of divine law, since they could be supported from the Bible. As such they were binding on all tribunals. Divine law as a source was later replaced by more general natural law concepts drawn from the universal usages of nations. A substantial part of these concepts was to be found in the civilian and theological literature and did directly influence the common law of proof. According to the learned author, this may have been due partly to the fact that courts of equity sought to offer relief from the defects of the common law. Some of these defects were to be found in the existing rules of proof at common law (for example those concerning common law estoppels and the absence of compulsion of witnesses). By reforming their proof rules, common law lawyers could prevent the intervention of equity courts and consequently increase their business.

The question whether or not, in adapting the common law, English common law lawyers consulted civilian and theological sources themselves has often been answered negatively. It has been suggested that these lawyers copied 'civilian' concepts of proof from equity. Equity might indeed have been the origin of these concepts at common law since, according to Michael Macnair, there are at least three reasons to suppose that equity proof was a system which applied the general principles of the Roman-Canon Law of proof (although the author also claims that the rules of proof in equity were certainly not equivalent to those of the Roman-Canon Law). The author states: 'The first [of these reasons] is parallelism of content; the second linguistic echoes; and the third instances of direct citation'.[38] There are various situations in which rules indeed might have been copied by common law lawyers from equity (for example rules concerning 'discovery' and *subpoenas ad testificandum*). However, in other areas the sources for equity proof doctrine largely

procedures 'inquisitorial' in the sense of completely judge-driven gives, I respectfully submit, the wrong impression. J.M.J. Chorus agrees with this point of view, at least as regards modern continental systems of civil procedure. See Chorus 1992, p. 32 *et seq.* See also Chorus 1997, p. 299: 'At the outset we must forget this inquisitorial label. It is an unfortunate label because to lawyers of today it no longer refers to the great traditions of continental Romano-canonical procedure and, indeed, those of the old Court of Chancery and the Court of Session of the 17th and 18th centuries, which might, with greater justification, be styled inquisitorial (with a positive connotation)'.

36 Baker 2002, p. 103. On the history of the Court of Chancery, see the introduction to Yale 1961, p. 7-207.

37 Macnair 1999.

38 See Macnair 1999, p. 289.

begin at the same period as the first steps in common law evidence doctrine (e.g. documentary originals, exceptions to witnesses) and, as a result, equity could not have been a source. According to Michael Macnair, in the latter areas there is direct or near-direct evidence of common law lawyers referring directly to civilian sources on proof matters.[39]

Consequently, it can be stated that the law of proof was in its own time a *convergence* (albeit not a complete one) between the common and the civil laws. True, later developments (mainly the abolition of the old law of proof in continental Europe at the end of the 18th century) resulted in continental law and English law, after a period of convergence, growing apart again in this particular area of the law. But, the point I would like to stress here is that even the common law of proof did not flourish in 'noble isolation' from the learned law. As will be shown hereafter, more examples in the area of procedure can be mentioned, examples that sometimes have resulted in lasting similarities between England and the Continent. These date mainly from the 19th century, and it is on this period that I would like to focus attention now.

5. Codification of Procedure

The 19th century was the age of codification. It witnessed the birth of various codes, including Codes of Civil Procedure. Although the codification movement was very successful on the European Continent, it did not gain ground in England, the country of Jeremy Bentham who seems to have coined the term 'codification'. However, even in 19th century England, the legislature was active in the field of procedure. England gave birth to some very important statutes regarding judicial organisation and procedure. The most important Acts date from 1873 and 1875 and are known as the Judicature Acts. These Acts resulted in a streamlined court system. Courts of common law and equity were fused and the forms of action were abolished. The Judicature Acts provided a uniform 'code' of civil procedure and pleading.[40]

On the Continent, the law, including procedure, lost some of its European appearance as a result of the activities of the national legislatures. However, similarities continued to exist in the juridical landscape. Most codifications did not break with tradition. The codification of judiciary law was based on Romano-canonical models. In France, for example, the ordinance on procedure of 1667,[41] which combined Romano-canonical and indigenous elements, formed the basis of the Code of Civil Procedure (1806). In Germany the *Zivilprozessordnung* (1877) had a distinctly Romano-canonical flavour even though it contained important innovations.[42]

39 See Macnair 1999, p. 38.

40 Holdsworth 1994, p. 128.

41 *Ordonnance civile pour la réformation de la justice* of Louis XIV (also known as Code Louis).

42 I do not agree with P.H. Lindblom, who states: 'In Germany, there seems to be no reason to characterise the national procedural law as a version of the procedural law of *ius commune*' (Lindblom 1997, p. 18).

Similarities on the European scene were caused not just by the Romano-canonical background of many codified rules. Additionally, the influence of some of the procedural codes and ideas in other countries resulted in a similarity of different national procedures. The French *Code de Procédure Civile* of 1806 was very influential. The Netherlands, Belgium, Germany, Italy, Spain and Switzerland were all influenced by this code.[43] In Holland and Belgium the French Code of Civil Procedure continued to apply after the defeat of the French emperor. In Belgium it remained in force for more than 150 years until the introduction of the new 1967 Code (in 1970). Although the Netherlands only left the French code in force until 1838, the new Dutch code nevertheless leaned heavily on the French example; many of the rules it originally contained were a direct translation from the provisions of the French code. In the more recent past, Austrian-German procedure has been very influential, for example in France and Italy.[44]

Although the activities of the national legislatures might have caused continental procedure to lose some of its European appearance, the opposite is true for the English Judicature Acts. In England, the new legislation brought procedure closer to continental models. J. Chorus states:

> 'In England ... the new forms of process, as laid down in the Judicature Acts of 1873 and 1875 and in the Rules of Court which came to supplement these Acts, must be regarded as the triumph of chancery, and thus the triumph of civilian ideas'.[45]

How did this change come about? Unfortunately, not all details concerning the drafting of the Judicature Acts have been explored. We do not know completely, for example, to what extent foreign examples (including those from Scotland) were used as a source of inspiration. Nevertheless, it seems likely that developments across the Atlantic played a role, since some of the more important innovations introduced by the Judicature Acts in English procedural law had several decades before been incorporated in the Code of Procedure for the State of New York. Surprisingly enough, until now references to this so-called Field Code (after its main drafter) have only been found very sparingly in sources related to the drafting of the Judicature Acts.[46]

The Code of Procedure of New York was one of several codes drafted by David Dudley Field (1805-1894), who dominated the American codification scene for a considerable part of the 19th century.[47] The Code of Procedure was one of the few codes which were actually enacted. This happened in 1848. The new procedure for New York combined elements of the forms of action at common law and the procedure in equity,[48] the emphasis being, at least according to some authors, on the

43 Van Caenegem, p. 91.

44 Stürner 1992, p. 23.

45 Chorus 1997, p. 296.

46 Jacob 1982, p. 315-316.

47 On Field, see Field 1949.

48 Cf. Reppy 1988, p. 337: 'They [i.e. Field and the other Code commissioners] used the merger of law and equity as much as an occasion for conforming equity to common-law procedure as the reverse'; Reppy 1988, p. 338: 'It was more obvious to those closer to David Dudley Field's →

latter procedure. The Field Code shows a marked influence of the Romano-canonical procedure. This might have been the result of two factors: (1) the fact that Field used equity as a source for his new procedure; and (2) the fact that some New York rules of procedure were related to procedural rules enacted in the State of Louisiana, a civil law jurisdiction (additionally, the drafters of the Field Code occasionally refer to Scotland). The 1825 Louisiana Code of Procedure was, according to D. Clark, probably the most important vehicle for Field's ideas about the codification and content of civil procedure. This Code was based on French, Spanish, and Roman civil law sources as well as the common law tradition. The *Corpus Iuris*, the *Siete Partidas*, and the writings of Jean Domat (1625-1696) and Robert Pothier (1699-1772) were, for example, consulted when drafting this piece of legislation.[49] If it can be shown that the procedural rules of the Judicature Acts have been influenced by the Field Code and, consequently, by the Romano-canonical procedure - either directly or through some intermediate stage (possibly the procedural legislation for British India, dating form the 1850's)[50] - this would be an extra argument for the thesis that the gap between continental Europe and England is not as wide as is usually thought. Further research into this topic is very much needed.

6. Common Elements of Civil Procedure in Europe

The developments described above justify the conclusion that procedural law is not as national a subject as has long been held. Similarities between the national procedures can often be explained on the basis of contacts with foreign legal systems. I will discuss some of these similarities below. In doing so, I will focus on similarities between the Continent and England. First I will discuss the 19th century and afterwards I will deal with an important example of convergence in the 20th century.

6.1. *Shared Elements of Civil Procedure in 19th Century Europe*

According to T. Plucknett, one of the most significant themes in the study of legal history is the growth of the power to think of law apart from its procedure.[51] This development is already apparent from Roman Law, although even at a late stage in its development procedure was discussed as an integral part of substantive law: the *Corpus Iuris Civilis* does not separate procedural issues from substantive law. The definition of procedure as a separate field of study is due to the medieval students of the Roman and Canon Laws (even though it must be admitted that elements of substantive law continued to play a significant role in procedural treatises).[52] In

times that this Code was confining and formalistic and that Field was deeply tied to common-law procedural thought'.

49 Clark 1993, p. 74.

50 I consulted *The New Procedure of the Civil Courts of British India*, 4th edition, London 1860.

51 Plucknett 1956, p. 381.

52 See e.g. Wielant 1573.

England, however, the separation of substantive and procedural law occurred much later in history. Although first traces of attempts to describe substantive law apart from procedure may be found in the medieval treatises of Glanvill and Bracton, the first serious attempts to separate substantive law from procedure seem to date from the 18th century. Inspiration for doing so came, according to Plucknett, from abroad. In the 18th century English lawyers took an interest in French and Dutch works, and 'under this stimulus they attempted to think in terms of substantive law rather than merely of procedure'. Blackstone's *Commentaries* are a good example of this attempt. However, only the reforms of the 19th century made it possible to effectively separate substantive law from procedure[53] (these reforms seem to have followed the example of the American Field Code in this respect). Currently we find both in England and on the Continent separate textbooks dealing with procedure. Additionally, courses solely concentrating on the law of procedure are a feature of many European law faculties.

A similar tendency of convergence can be witnessed in the area of forms of action available for bringing a lawsuit. At a certain point in time, the Roman Law possessed a more or less closed system of actions. Only where the complaint could be brought under one of the available *formulae* granted by the Roman *praetor* could a lawsuit be started. The writ system of the English common law resulted in a similar situation.[54] However, things changed. As a result, the Romano-canonical procedure, as well as the continental European systems derived from it, only know a single, general action for bringing a lawsuit. The same development occurred in England as a result of the Judicature Acts. The forms of action were abolished. In their place a single, general action was created. It is not unlikely that this development was the result of civil law influences through the example of the 1848 Code of Procedure for the State of New York (Field Code): the Field Code was the first piece of legislation to mandate a single form of action in a common law jurisdiction. As in Louisiana, this action was called the 'civil action'.[55]

The concept 'cause of action' is possibly another element in the Judicature Acts that has been influenced by continental legal thinking, possibly through the Field Code. According to Stephen Subrin, 'Field and the others [i.e. the other members of the codification commission] used the term 'cause of action' to try to describe those groupings of facts to which legal consequences attach'. He further mentions: '"Cause of action" was their way of describing a right of citizens that could be enforced in court'.[56] Section 142 of the Field Code specifically mentions the 'cause of action' where it states that

> '[t]he complaint shall contain ... [a] statement of the facts constituting the *cause of action*, in ordinary and concise language, without repetition, and in such manner as to enable a person of common understanding to know what is intended ...'.

53 Plucknett 1956, p. 381-382.
54 On this issue, see Pringsheim 1935, p. 347.
55 Field Code §§ 1 & 4. Cf. Clark 1993, p. 79 & p. 82.
56 Subrin 1988, p. 329.

According to Clark, the concept of 'cause of action' can be traced back through the Louisiana Code of Practice (Article 172; there it is rendered in French as 'les motifs de l'action' and 'la cause de l'action') to the French Code of Civil Procedure.[57] However, further investigation into this matter is needed since other authors claim that 'cause of action' is a concept which can already be found in English 15th century legal sources, and it is not clear whether its definition in English legal practice (as opposed to its definition in the Field Code) is related to the civil law.[58]

Pleading is also an interesting subject for those interested in a possible convergence of civil procedural law, even though at first glance pleading is, of course, a very technical area which sets the common law apart from continental jurisdictions. According to Holdsworth, however, pleading in the Judicature Acts owed something to the system in use in the Court of Admiralty.[59] This court had a procedure based on the Romano-canonical model.[60] Additionally, the Romano-canonical model might have influenced the new rules of pleading through the American Field Code which, in its turn, might have influenced the Judicature Acts. It seems that for his rules on pleading (which put an emphasis on pleading facts, i.e. 'fact-pleading' or 'code-pleading')[61] Field drew primarily on the Romano-canonical system as illustrated by French and Spanish law.[62] He permitted only four types of pleadings: the complaint, answer, reply, and demurrer (§ 156). A reply was only allowed when an answer contained new matter (§ 153). As a result, in most suits in which the defendant raised no affirmative defence, the pleading stage could be completed in two or maybe three (with a demurrer to make dilatory objections) steps.[63]

Particularly interesting from the 'convergence perspective' are counterclaims. Counterclaims were not allowed at common law. Only the relief for which the suit had been instituted could be granted. Since counterclaims are brought in pending lawsuits, they can by their very definition never be the relief for which the suit is instituted. On the Continent the Romano-canonical procedure and the systems based on it allowed counterclaims (under the 1806 Code of civil procedure in France such claims were also allowed, even though they were not mentioned as such; see currently the new *Code de Procédure Civile*, Article 64).[64] The Judicature Acts made counterclaims generally available in England. Holdsworth claims that this change was based on a rule of practice prevailing in the ecclesiastical courts (the 1848 Field Code did not contain provisions on counterclaims; in 1852, however, a provision was included).[65] This rule allowed the court to give the relief to which the parties

57 Clark 1993, p. 82-83.
58 Clark 1923, p. 820 *et seq.*
59 Holdsworth 1994, p. 134. See also Holdsworth 1991, p. 684.
60 Chorus 1997, p. 296.
61 Fact-pleading also became a feature of English civil procedure. See Glenn 1993, p. 573: 'Certaines institutions de la procédure civile s'alignent aussi sur le modèle civiliste. On ne plaide plus, en principe, le droit ...'.
62 Clark 1993, p. 76.
63 Clark 1993, p. 83.
64 On counterclaims in continental jurisdictions, see Van Rhee 2000, p. 227 *et seq.*
65 Clark 1923, p. 823; Subrin 1988, p. 332.

were entitled though the suit had been instituted for a different kind of relief.[66] Since the procedure of the ecclesiastical courts is of Romano-canonical origin, the rise of counterclaims in English procedure is possibly another illustration of civil law influence on the British Isles.

A last example of convergence in the 19th century is the appeal. Originally, the common law did not know a system of appeal, i.e. a means of recourse by way of rehearing a case in a higher court. Without a hierarchy of courts, which originally did not exist in England, such a system of recourse is not feasible.[67] English lawyers got acquainted with the appeal system through the Romano-canonical procedure of the ecclesiastical courts. This system was copied in England, at least in externals.[68] Later, the Judicature Acts introduced a system of appeals which might have been derived from the Field Code, which in its turn might have been based on the Louisiana Code. At the same time, these Acts, like the Field Code (§ 323), abolished the writ of error of the common law, a means of recourse which aimed at reviewing questions of law (error in the proceedings) which appeared on the record of the court below.[69] Under the new procedure, an appeal could also be lodged in cases where formerly the writ of error had been available.[70]

6.2. *Convergence of Civil Procedure in the 20th Century*

Reforms of civil procedure in the 20th century have been the cause of convergence of the rules of procedural law in many European countries. In the present paper I would like to discuss only one example of convergence, albeit a very important one: the importance of the judge in the conduct of civil litigation in England and the Continent.

Traditionally, both the systems inspired by the Romano-canonical procedure and the forms of action at common law are aimed at avoiding arbitrary decisions. They seek to guarantee that judicial decisions are based on the truth (be it the formal or the substantive truth). In order to reach this goal, they assign to the judge and the parties a fixed role in the proceedings. Both systems have, to a certain extent, an adversarial character,[71] even though some present-day common law lawyers are inclined to describe continental civil procedures as inquisitorial.[72] The adversarial character of the procedures both on the Continent and in England appears from the fact that in England as well as on the Continent the principle of

66 Holdsworth 1994, p. 135. See also Holdsworth 1991, p. 684-685.

67 Van Caenegem, p. 30: 'The Common Law knew nothing of an appeal, i.e., a rehearing of a case [...] (the term 'appeal' was used for a criminal accusation), consequently there were no real appeal courts either. Appeal was linked with Roman Law, which was alien to the Common Law, and it presupposed a hierarchy of courts unknown in England [...]'; Van Caenegem 1998, p. 4-6.

68 Plucknett 1956, p. 387-388.

69 Van Caenegem, p. 30-31; Plucknett 1956, p. 388.

70 Holdsworth 1994, p. 131. Cf. Field Code § 325.

71 Cf. Van Caenegem 2002, p. 51-53.

72 Jacob 1987, p. 7.

party presentation (*Verhandlungsmaxime*) applies.[73] The principle prescribes that the scope and the content of the judicial controversy are to be defined by the parties or, conversely, that the court is restricted to a consideration of what the parties have put before it.[74] In addition, the principle of 'party control over the subject matter' (*Dispositionsmaxime*) is a feature of both continental and English civil procedure. This means that the aggrieved party decides whether or not a lawsuit will be started, that the defendant decides whether or not he will introduce his defence, and that each party takes the sundry procedural steps.[75] As a result, the judge is relatively passive, even though it cannot be denied that judges do have some power to take initiatives in the conduct of the proceedings without requiring any demand by the parties or counsel to do so.[76] Nevertheless, in the end, it is the parties who dominate the litigation, not the judge.

Undue delays in the proceedings and high costs have, however, resulted in measures increasing the directive powers of the judge. Of course, these measures are not as extreme as those introduced in 18th century Prussia under Frederick the Great, which resulted in a procedure that could rightly be called inquisitorial.[77] Nevertheless, there has been a slow movement in the direction of a more active role for the judge. This is especially true for England. Although the Judicature Acts did not seriously affect the principle of 'party presentation,' they gave the court slightly larger powers to regulate the course of the procedure.[78] Unfortunately, they did not solve the existing problems, since English procedure remained expensive and cumbersome. However, the recent reforms of civil procedure in England will most likely be more successful. The basis of these reforms was two reports by Lord Woolf entitled *Access to Justice*,[79] in which the negative aspects of the English adversarial system were pointed out.[80] The main characteristics of the reforms are an increase in the directive powers of the judge and the emphasis on a cultural move towards court control of litigation practices. It should be the courts, and not the parties, who determine the pace of the litigation process and its intensity.[81] The adversarial

73 Holdsworth 1994, p. 116: '[...] common law procedure has, like the systems of procedure in Roman and early German law, adopted the principle of 'party presentation', and not the principle of 'judicial investigation'. Pollock has made it clear that this has been true of the procedure of the common law throughout its history and is still true today'; Millar 1928, p. 19-20: 'Whatever of investigative character manifested itself in the chancery procedure was borrowed from the canon procedure, and that the civil procedure of the canon law at all times yielded first place to the principle of party presentation can admit of no doubt'.

74 Millar 1928, p. 19-20.

75 Van Caenegem, p. 14.

76 Cf. Chorus 1987.

77 Van Caenegem, p. 92. See also Chorus 1992, p. 34 *et seq.*

78 Holdsworth 1994, p. 132.

79 *Access to Justice: Interim Report to the Lord Chancellor on the civil justice system in England and Wales*, London 1995; *Access to Justice: Final Report to the Lord Chancellor on the civil justice system in England and Wales*, London 1996.

80 See Zuckerman 1995, p. 75.

81 Zuckerman 1995, p. 62. See also Zander 1995, p. 80: 'The mood of the times, both here and in other common law countries, is to follow the lead of the United States and embark on a period of reform under a banner called 'Judicial Case Management'.

principle, which was so dominant a feature of English civil procedure, is therefore under attack.[82] Consequently, we may conclude that also in this area of procedure convergence between England and the Continent is taking place.

7. Summary

I would like to sum up. I started this paper with the tension between public justice and private justice. I focused on the different balances that have been struck throughout the ages between the adjudication of civil disputes by the organs of the state (public justice), and the adjudication or settlement of civil disputes by private individuals or bodies or by the litigants themselves (private justice). A mixture of the two systems could be found in the Roman formulary procedure, whereas the ancestor of most modern systems of civil procedure, the *extra-ordinaria cognitio*, may be brought under the heading of public justice.

After having discussed the fate of private and public justice in medieval times and later, I continued with a discussion of the relationship between the various systems of public justice in Europe. I have shown that interaction between the various systems has been taking place for at least 800 years. In this respect, the reception of the Romano-canonical procedure in secular courts and the changes brought about by the English Judicature Acts and by Lord Woolf are crucial. The convergence of procedure resulting from this interaction makes it likely that the approximation of public justice systems in the European Union is a feasible option. In my opinion initiatives aimed at harmonisation may benefit from having regard to the rich history of the procedure of the state courts. I am convinced that knowledge of the history of procedure will smooth the path for those who feel that a fragmented Europe in the field of procedural law distorts the proper functioning of the internal market and is undesirable.[83]

82 See already in 1993 Glenn 1993, p. 573-574: 'Même cette procédure [i.e. the adversarial procedure] est de plus en plus contestée; elle est souvent absent dans les phases préparatoires du procès. Le fardeau de l'acte de jugement s'impose partout'.

83 On differences in procedure and distortions in the proper functioning of the internal market, see Wolf 1992, p. 35 *et seq.*; Kerameus 1990, p. 47 *et seq.*; Kerameus 1998, 121 *et seq.*

Bibliography

American Law Institute & UNIDROIT 2006
American Law Institute and UNIDROIT, *Principles of Transnational Civil Procedure*, Cambridge: Cambridge University Press, 2006.

Baker 2002
Baker, J.H., *An Introduction to English Legal History*, 4th edition, London etc.: Butterworths, 2002.

Van Caenegem
Van Caenegem, R.C., 'History of European Civil Procedure', in: *International Encyclopedia of Comparative Law XVI*, Tübingen/Paris/New York: J.C.B. Mohr etc., n.d.

Van Caenegem 1998
Van Caenegem, R.C., *Judges, Legislators and Professors. Chapters in European Legal History*, Cambridge: Cambridge University Press, 1998.

Van Caenegem 2002
Van Caenegem, R.C., *European Law in the Past and the Future. Unity and Diversity over Two Millennia*, Cambridge: Cambridge University Press, 2002.

Chorus 1987
Chorus, J.M.J., *De lijdelijkheid van de rechter: historie van een begrip*, Deventer: Kluwer, 1987.

Chorus 1992
Chorus, J.M.J., 'The Judge's Role in the Conduct of Civil Proceedings', in: Carey Miller, D.L. & Meyers, D.W. (eds.), *Comparative and Historical Essays in Scots Law*, Edinburgh: Butterworths, 1992, p. 32-46.

Chorus 1997
Chorus, J.M.J., 'Civilian Elements in European Civil Procedure', in: Carey Miller, D.L. & Zimmermann, R. (eds.), *The Civilian Tradition and Scots Law. Aberdeen Quincentenary Essays*, Berlin: Duncker & Humblot, 1997, p. 295-305.

Clark 1923
Clark, C.E., 'The Code Cause of Action', *Yale Law Review*, 1923-1924, p. 817-837.

Clark 1993
Clark, D.S., 'The Civil Law Influence on David Dudley Field's Code of Civil Procedure', in: Reimann. M. (ed.), The *Reception of Continental Ideas in the Common Law World (1820-1920)*, Berlin: Duncker & Humblot, 1993, p. 63-87.

Coenraad 2000
Coenraad, L., Het *beginsel van hoor en wederhoor in het Romeinse procesrecht,* Rotterdam: Gouda Quint, 2000.

Field 1898
Field, H.M., *The Life of David Dudley Field,* New York: Charles Scribner's Sons, 1898.

Finlay 2000
Finlay, J., *Men of Law in pre-reformation Scotland* (Scottish historical review monograph, 9), East Lothian: Tuckwell Press, 2000.

Fowler-Magerl 1984
Fowler-Magerl, L., *Ordo iudiciorum vel ordo iudiciarius,* Frankfurt a. M.: Klostermann, 1984.

Glenn 1993
Glenn, H.P., 'La civilisation de la "common law"', *Revue Internationale de Droit Comparé,* 1993, p. 559-575.

Helmholz 1997
Helmholz, R.H., 'The Universal and the Particular in Medieval Canon Law', in: Landau, P. & Mueller, J. (eds.), *Proceedings of the Ninth International Congress of Medieval Canon Law* (Monumenta Iuris Canonici, Series C: Subsidia, vol. 10), Vatican City: Biblioteca Apostolica Vaticana, 1997, p. 641-659.

Holdsworth 1991
Holdsworth, W.S., *A History of English Law XII,* London: Sweet and Maxwell/ Methuen, 1991.

Holdsworth 1994
Holdsworth, W.S., *A History of English Law XV,* 4th edition, London: Sweet and Maxwell/Methuen, 1994.

Jacob 1982
Jacob, J., 'The Judicature Acts 1873-1875, Vision and Reality', in: *The Reform of Civil Procedural Law and Other Essays in Civil Procedure,* London: Sweet and Maxwell, 1982, p. 301-321.

Jacob 1987
Jacob, J., *The Fabric of English Civil Justice,* London: Stevens, 1987.

Kaser & Hackl 1996
Kaser, M. & Hackl, K., *Das Römische Zivilprozessrecht,* Munich: C.H. Beck, 1996.

Kerameus 1990
Kerameus, K.D., 'Procedural Unification: The Need and the Limitations', in: Scott, I.R. (ed.), *International Perspectives on Civil Justice*, London: Sweet and Maxwell, 1990, p. 47-66.

Kerameus 1998
Kerameus, K.D., 'Procedural Implications of Civil Law Unification', in: Hartkamp, A. *et al.* (eds.), *Towards a European Civil Code*, Nijmegen: Ars Aequi, 1998, p. 121-132.

Legrand 1996
Legrand, P., 'European Legal Systems are not Converging', *International and Comparative Law Quarterly*, 1996, p. 52-81.

Legrand 2002
Legrand, P., 'On the Unbearable Localness of the Law: Academic Fallacies and Unseasonable Observations', *European Review of Private Law*, 2002, p. 61-76.

Lindblom 1997
Lindblom, P.H., 'Harmony of the Legal Spheres: A Swedish view on the construction of a unified European procedural law', *European Review of Private Law*, 1997, p. 11-46.

Litewski 1999
Litewski, W., *Der römisch-kanonische Zivilprozess nach den älteren ordines iudiciarii*, 2 vols., Kraków: Wydawnictwo Uniwersytetu Jagiellonskiego, 1999.

Macnair 1999
Macnair, M., *The Law of Proof in Early Modern Equity*, Berlin: Duncker & Humblot, 1999.

Maitland 1968
Maitland, F.W., *The Forms of Action at Common Law: A Course of Lectures*, Cambridge: Cambridge University Press, 1929.

Markesinis 1994
Markesinis, B.S., 'Learning from Europe and Learning in Europe', in: Markesinis, B.S. (ed.), *The Gradual Convergence: Foreign Ideas, Foreign Influences, and English Law on the Eve of the 21st Century*, Oxford: Clarendon Press, 1994, p. 1-32.

Millar 1928
Millar, R.W. (ed.), *A History of Continental Civil Procedure*, Boston: Little, Brown and Company, 1927.

Nève 1995
Nève, P.L., 'Ius Commune oftewel "gemeen recht": traduttore traditore?', in: Tellegen-Couperus. O.E. *et al.* (eds.), *Tertium datur: Drie opstellen aangeboden aan Prof. mr. J.A. Ankum*, Tilburg: Tilburg University Press, 1995, p. 3-58.

Nève 1997
Nève, P.L., '(Europäisches) Ius Commune und (nationales) gemeines Recht: Verwechslung von Begriffen?', in: Köbler, G. & Nehlzen, H. (eds.), *Wirkungen europäischer Rechtskultur, Festschrift für Karl Kroeschell zum 70. Geburtstag*, Munich: C.H. Beck, 1997, p. 871-884.

Oudeman 1842
Oudeman, A., *Het Nederlandsch Wetboek van burgerlijke regtsvordering, naar deszelfs beginselen ontwikkeld en door formulieren in praktijk gebragt*, 4 vols., Groningen: Wolters, 1842-1845.

De Pinto 1845
De Pinto, A., *Handleiding tot het Wetboek van burgerlijke regtsvordering*, 2 vols., 's-Gravenhage: Gebroeders Belinfante, 1845.

Plucknett 1956
Plucknett, T.F.T., *A Concise History of the Common Law*, 5th edition, Boston: Little, Brown and Company, 1956.

Pringsheim 1935
Pringsheim, F., 'The Inner Relationship between English and Roman Law', *Cambridge Law Journal*, 1935, p. 347-365.

Reppy 1949
Reppy, A., 'The Field Codification Concept', in: Reppy, A. (ed.), *David Dudley Field Centenary Essays. Celebrating One Hundred Years of Legal Reform*, New York: New York University School of Law, 1949, p. 17-54.

Van Rhee 1997
Van Rhee, C.H., *Litigation and Legislation. Civil Procedure at First Instance in the Great Council for the Netherlands in Malines (1522-1559)*, Brussels: Algemeen Rijksarchief, 1997.

Van Rhee 2000
Van Rhee, C.H., 'De vordering in reconventie in Nederland en Europa', in: Hondius, E.H. *et al.* (eds.), *Liber Amicorum Paul Meijknecht. Van Nederlands naar Europees Procesrecht?!*, Deventer: Kluwer, 2000, p. 227-242.

Van Rhee 2000a
Van Rhee, C.H., 'Civil Procedure: a European Ius Commune?', *European Review of Private Law*, 2000, p. 589-611.

Van Rhee 2003
Van Rhee, C.H., 'Towards a Procedural Ius Commune?', in: Smits, J. & Lubbe, G. (eds.), *Remedies in Zuid-Afrika en Europa* (Ius Commune Europaeum, 43), Antwerp: Intersentia, 2003, p. 217-232.

Van Rhee 2003a
Van Rhee, C.H., 'English and Continental Civil Procedure: Similarities Today and in the Past', in: Sondel, J. *et. al.* (eds.), *Roman Law as Formative of Modern Legal Systems. Studies in Honour of Wieslaw Litewski*, Krakow: Wydawnictwo Uniwersytetu Jagiellonskiego, 2003, p. 201-216.

Schulze 1993
Schulze, R., 'Allgemeine Rechtsgrundsätze und europäisches Privatrecht', *Zeitschrift für Europäisches Privatrecht*, 1993, p. 442-474.

Storme 1994
Storme, M. (ed.), *Approximation of Judiciary Law in the European Union*, Dordrecht etc.: Martinus Nijhoff, 1994.

Stürner 1992
Stürner, R., 'Das Europäischen Zivilprozessrecht - Einheit oder Vielfalt?', in: Grunsky, W. *et al.* (eds.), *Wege zu einem europäischen Zivilprozessrecht. Tübinger Symposium zum 80. Geburtstag von Fritz Baur*, Tübingen: Mohr, 1992, p. 1-23.

Subrin 1988
Subrin, S.N., 'David Dudley Field and the Field Code: A Historical Analysis of an Earlier Procedural Vision', *Law and History Review*, 1988, p. 311-373.

Tardif 1885
Tardif, A., *La procédure civile et criminelle aux XIIIe et XIVe siècles ou procédure de transition*, Paris: Alphonse Picard *et al.*, 1885 (reprint Aalen: Scientia Verlag, 1974).

Watson 2000
Watson, A., *Legal Transplants and European Private Law* (Ius Commune Lectures on European Private Law, 2), Maastricht: METRO, 2000.

Wielant 1573
Wielant, Ph., *Practijke Civile*, Antwerp: Henrick vander Loe, 1573 (reprint Amsterdam: Graphic, 1968).

Wolf 1992
Wolf, M., 'Abbau prozessualer Schranken im europäischen Binnenmarkt', in: Grunsky, W. *et. al.* (eds)., *Wege zu einem europäischen Zivilprozessrecht. Tübinger Symposium zum 80. Geburtstag von Fritz Baur*, Tübingen: Mohr, 1992, p. 35-67.

Yale 1961
Yale, D.C.C. (ed.), *Lord Nottingham's Chancery Cases* (Selden Soc. Publ. 79), London: Selden Society, 1961.

Zander 1995
Zander, M., 'Why Lord Woolf's Proposed Reforms of Civil Litigation should be Rejected', in: Zuckerman, A.A.S. & Cranston, R. (eds.), *Reform of Civil Procedure. Essays on 'Access to Justice'*, Oxford: Clarendon Press, 1995, p. 79-95.

Zuckerman 1995
Zuckerman, A.A.S., 'Reform in the Shadow of Lawyers' Interests', in: Zuckerman, A.A.S. & Cranston, R. (eds.), *Reform of Civil Procedure. Essays on 'Access to Justice'*, Oxford: Clarendon Press, 1995, p. 61-77.

D. Heirbaut

THE REVOLUTION BETRAYED: THE EVOLUTION OF THE JUDICIAL SYSTEM IN FRANCE, BELGIUM AND THE NETHERLANDS SINCE THE FRENCH REVOLUTION*

This article makes a comparative study of the history of the judicial system in France, Belgium and the Netherlands since the French Revolution. Needless to say, this is such a huge subject, that only a few topics can be dealt with. Therefore, this article will focus on the civil courts, leaving the criminal and administrative courts out of the picture, and even then many interesting themes, like the internal organisation of the courts, cannot be studied here.

1. The French Revolution was not really Necessary

The traditional points of reference for today's judicial system in France, Belgium and the Netherlands are the French Revolution and Napoleon. An example of that is the constant reference by today's justices of the peace in Belgium to a French 1790 statute. However, this has been criticised because, even though today's peace courts can indeed be traced back to that statute, they no longer resemble their colleagues from 1790.[1] In fact, they have changed so much as to become their opposite. Moreover, even disregarding later changes it is to be doubted whether the French Revolution was really as important as is claimed.

The Revolution[2] had two great ideals, as far as the judicial system was concerned: deprofessionalisation and simplification,[3] the latter being a general theme of Revolutionary reforms, whether in the judicial system or in law in general and it was sorely needed. After all, the Old Regime's judicial organisation can best be described as chaotic, because apart from the many royal courts, there were also

* I would like to thank Prof. em. dr. R. van Caenegem, P. Carson and G. Sinnaeve, who have read the draft of this text, for their comments. Needless to say any remaining errors are entirely my own.

1 Vuye 1998, p. 413-414; Nandrin 1992, p. 19-38.

2 For an overview of the court system in France during the Revolution, see e.g. Jugnot 1998, p. 63-79. Very good surveys are the graphics in Rousseaux 1999, p. 37-58.

3 Cf. Halperin 1996, p. 233-256.

church and most of all seignorial courts, of which there may have been about 80.000 at the end of the 18th century. This was due to 'feudalism', which gave the many lords judicial power over other persons and their lands. Hence, the abolition of feudalism by the Revolution on 24 August 1789, which also led to the disappearance of the seignorial courts, was more important for the history of the judicial system in France than any other piece of legislation.

The abolition of feudalism was to the benefit of the state courts because they were henceforward without competitors. However, they were themselves also in need of a better organisation, as they had not been established in a planned way, but had gradually and almost organically come into existence. Far from being a uniform structure, France's judicial 'system' before the Revolution was a patchwork of overlapping jurisdictions and this does not even take into account special courts for privileged persons or for special matters. The situation was most complicated on appeal: against the decisions of some courts no appeal was possible, whereas after those of other courts there might be up to six possibilities for appeal. Given these circumstances, conflicts of jurisdiction were numerous and one can easily understand why the French people in 1789 called for a reform of the judicial system.[4]

However, this had been on the agenda of French politics long before the Revolution and Napoleon. In fact, to a certain extent, what the French Revolution did was just to abolish some exceptional situations and to streamline the judicial system,[5] as one can already see before the Revolution the shape of the typical four-layer hierarchy of courts and a procedure in three instances (small claims courts at the lowest level, ordinary courts, appellate courts and above them all a predecessor of the Court of Cassation). True, this system was marred by its many exceptions, but even in abolishing those the Revolution was less revolutionary than one may think, as there had been reformers, like Maupeou in 1771 and Lamoignon in 1788, who had already planned to do the same.[6] In the Southern Netherlands (now called Belgium) this is also evident, as a few years before the annexation by the French its then prince, the Habsburg emperor Joseph II, had tried to replace the old tribunals and courts with a new system, which is very similar to one later introduced by the French.[7] Likewise, in the Batavian Republic, as the Netherlands were called from 1795 till 1806, reformers made plans for a new judicial system without much recourse to the French example.[8]

However, there is a difference between the Revolution and these other reformers: they failed, whereas the Revolution succeeded and the French 'pyramidal' system of courts as sketched above was also imposed upon Belgium and the Netherlands by the Revolution and by Napoleon, even though at first there

4 See about the French judicial system before 1789 in general, Dahlmanns 1982a, p. 2491-2505; and, for a regional example: Crubaugh 2001.

5 For a detailed study of this, see Lafon 2001.

6 Dahlmanns 1982a, p. 2505-2509.

7 Van Hille 1972; Warlomont 1959, p. 269-289 and the monumental Dhondt 2002.

8 Van Boven 1990.

was still some resistance to it.[9] It is a tribute to the flexibility of the French model that in Belgium this resistance disappeared after one generation. In fact, when the country became independent in 1830 and a Judiciary Act reorganised the Judicial system two years later, not much changed. A third court of appeal was established in Ghent and also a Belgian Court of Cassation. Apart from that, the situation remained unchanged.[10]

However, by now, the judiciary system in France, Belgium and the Netherlands has undergone so many changes that the old model of the French Revolution and Napoleon does no longer exist as such. Either it has been amended so much that it has turned into the opposite of what the French Revolutionaries wanted (France and Belgium), or it has been rejected altogether (the Netherlands). Yet, strange as it may sound, the latter country may have remained more faithful to the spirit of the French Revolution than the former.

2. Amending the Revolutionary and Napoleonic Model in France and Belgium

Next to simplifying the judicial system, the French Revolution wanted to take it out of the hands of the legal professionals as much as possible by removing them altogether from the courts or, if this was not possible, by at least putting them under stringent controls. In the light of the situation under the Old Regime this was understandable, as the law had then been the preserve of a group of university trained lawyers, guardians of an arcane and esoteric knowledge, who in many cases had bought their office and intermarried, so that it would not be too exaggerated to talk of a 'caste' of lawyers before the Revolution.[11] An instrument for enfranchising the law from them were the codifications, texts which made the law accessible to the people and which judges had to apply faithfully.[12] Even more important than these was the reform of the judicial system, but unlike the idea of codifications, the deprofessionalisation has not survived.

2.1. *From Subservient Judges to a Regained Independence*

If not for the courts, or rather the most important of them, the Parlement of Paris, the French Revolution would never have been. The Revolution started when this highest court forbade the king to introduce a new tax without first convocating the Estates General, the assembly representing the French nation, or at least its nobility, clergy and bourgeoisie. However, the Estates General and the various parliaments which succeeded them did everything they could to subordinate the judiciary. The principle of separation of powers, as formulated by the Act of 16 and 24 April 1790,

9 Van Goethem 1997, p. 289-300.

10 Gilissen 1983, p. 565-574 & p. 585-596; Dahlmanns 1982, 2585. See also Nandrin 1998 and Nandrin 1995.

11 Royer 1979; Royer 2001, p. 107-139.

12 Van Caenegem 1992, p. 128-134.

meant most of all that no interference by judges in politics would be tolerated. To express this subordinate position of the judiciary towards the nation and its assembly, parliament, judges were to be elected.[13] However, this backfired, most of all in annexed territories like Belgium, because the population could by the process of election ensure it had judges who were likely not to cooperate with the Revolutionary authorities and who could claim a democratic legitimacy.[14] This was not what the Revolution, or thereafter Napoleon, wanted and it contributed to the replacement of elected by nominated judges under Napoleon. Needless to say, whereas the elected judges could have been amateurs, the nominated judges were professionals.[15] Still, even under Napoleon the judiciary remained subservient, but now towards the executive, the justice minister and ultimately the emperor, and not the legislature. For obvious reasons, any interference of judges in administrative affairs was out of the question in this situation. Subjects could only hope that an administrative institution would be willing to listen to their complaints. This has led to the establishment of a separate administrative court system, which, by now, is flourishing in France and Belgium, as there is a plethora of administrative courts in these countries today.[16]

Even though the dual court system is still in existence, the stranglehold of the executive over the judiciary has been very much weakened, most of all because constitutions have ensured that judges cannot be removed from office, though this principle has been less absolute in history than one might assume. After all, a constitution does not guarantee that those who came to their office before the constitution can remain in it. Thus, those nominated by a previous regime can lose their position, as happened in Belgium after independence with two 'cleansing' operations in 1830 and 1832.[17] Their effect was that the new judges were very interested in the stability of the new state, to which they contributed by supporting the current government in parliament until 1848, when being a member of parliament was no longer compatible with being a judge.[18] In France constitutions and regimes changed so many times before the country found some stability in 1958, that the history of the French judiciary in the nineteenth and the first half of the 20th century seems to have as its main theme the struggle of judges to hold on to their positions under yet another new regime.[19] Control of political authorities over the judiciary was less by removal from office, than by the nomination of new judges. In Belgium one Minister of Justice, shortly after independence, even managed to have more than four hundred judges nominated in one royal decree,

13 Chauvaud 1995, p. 29-41.

14 Van Goethem 1997, p. 291-296; see also Humberts 1997, p. 351-369.

15 See e.g. Bourdon 1942.

16 A major step was the establishment of the *Conseil d'état* (see about the Napoleonic *Conseil d'état* e.g. the publications by Charles Durand and Tony Sauvel). For the other courts, one can consult for France: Perrit 2004, p. 201-243.

17 Nandrin 1995, p. 257-259; Nandrin 1998a, p. 153-202; Nandrin 1997, p. 405-429. See also Rousseaux & Nandrin 1993, p. 13-69.

18 Witte 1981, p. 828-882.

19 Royer 2001; Royer, Martinage & Lecocq 1982; Lecocq & Martinage 1983, p. 215-248; Bancaud 2002; Association française pour l'histoire de la justice 1993.

which a historian has called 'the foundation charter of political nominations of judges in Belgium'.[20] By now, by competitive exams, schools for magistrates, high councils of justice and so on, political interference in the nomination and promotion of judges has been largely eliminated, with in this case Belgium lagging behind France (and also the Netherlands).[21] However, the new mechanisms for ensuring the independence of magistrates are dominated by judges and other lawyers, which means that the judiciary is once again firmly in the hands of professionals.[22] As far as this is concerned, a historian can only conclude that the French Revolution was only an intermezzo and that after some time the continuity with the Old Regime, in which law was also dominated by the professionals, has resurfaced. Thus, although today's judicial system may have its origin in the French Revolution, its spirit is more akin to that of the Old Regime.

2.2. *The Court of Cassation: from Parliamentary Watchdog to Supreme Court*

That the revolutionary ideals have changed into their opposite is also visible for the Court of Cassation. It started out not as a Court, but as a mere Tribunal, because the Revolutionaries wanted it to be anything but a supreme court.[23] It had to be only an agent of parliament, ensuring that the courts and most of all the appellate ones would not follow the road their predecessors had taken by promulgating *arrêts de règlement*, decisions which were binding for all courts in their province.[24] If any such judgement was taken, it had to be nullified. Thus, originally the Tribunal of Cassation was parliament's bullyboy to whip the courts into submission and yet another token of the distrust of the professionals, which permeated the judiciary system of the French Revolution. However, very soon another task of the Tribunal took on more importance. France (and likewise Belgium and the Netherlands) did not have one national legal system before the Revolution, but hundreds of local customary laws. These were abolished by Revolutionary and Napoleonic law and replaced by national statutes and codifications. Yet, there was a danger that the courts would have their own local interpretations of the new unitary law and that this, in time, would lead to a resurrection of local customs, the more so if the new law were to be interpreted locally in the light of the hitherto prevailing local custom. To ensure that this would not happen, there was a possibility to bring a case before the Tribunal of Cassation, when there was doubt about the interpretation of a statute or a code.

The Tribunal of Cassation was established not to safeguard the interests of the citizens, but those of the nation, or rather its main body, parliament, and this becomes clear in the procedure which was followed in case of an appeal to the Tribunal. First of all, the Tribunal would not deal with the facts, but only with

20 Nandrin 1998a, p. 53-202.

21 For Belgium, see Storme 2005.

22 Cf. Bancaud & Robert 2001, p. 184-185.

23 About the *Tribunal de Cassation*, see Halpérin 1990, p. 25-51; Halpérin 1987.

24 Payen 1997; Payen 1999; Lemonnier-Lesage 1999.

questions of law and, if the judgement of the lower court was nullified because the law had been misapplied, the Tribunal would send the case to another court of the same instance for a new trial. If the second court once again misapplied the law, the Tribunal would remit the case to a third court, but, if that one followed its peers, the Tribunal had to pass on the problem to parliament, so that an Act of parliament could settle the issue.[25] Under Napoleon power shifted from the legislative to the executive and the ultimate decision would no longer be taken by parliament, but by the government, but, as far as the judiciary was concerned not much changed. Cassation was still meant to control the judges and to make them subservient. For the Tribunal itself, however, there was one important, albeit rather symbolic change: it was no longer to be called a Tribunal, but a Court and, thus, its name finally expressed its superior position.[26]

The next step was for the Court of Cassation to become the head of the judiciary. In France this happened, more or less, by neglect. In 1828 the Napoleonic system in which government had the final say had been modified somewhat, government henceforth no longer taking the final decision, but only drafting an interpretation, which would be enacted by parliament. However, subsequent governments neglected to do so in many cases and in 1837 the system was changed and took on its current form. After a second appeal to Cassation its interpretation is binding for the third court to which the case is remitted.[27] As a practical solution this was not bad, but it effectively gave the Court of Cassation control over the judicial interpretation of statutes and thus made it the undisputed head of the judiciary.[28] From a watchdog of the judges the Court of Cassation had become their champion.

Evolution in Belgium and the Netherlands at first was different from the one in France. In the United Kingdom of the Netherlands (in which, from 1815 until 1830, the Southern (i.e. Belgium) and the Northern (i.e. today's Netherlands) Netherlands were united) there was a possibility of cassation, but not a specialised court to take care of it. There was a circular, instead of hierarchical, system of cassation, in which the courts of appeal functioned as courts of cassation towards their fellow courts.[29] In the context of this kingdom uniting Belgium and the Netherlands this was an elegant solution, as it eliminated the need to choose in which part of the kingdom the Court of Cassation would be situated. In fact, the Dutch Court of Cassation, called the *Hoge Raad* (High Council) would only start to function in 1838, some years after Belgium had become independent. It was a Court of Cassation of the newer type, without a referral to parliament.[30]

25 About this, see Miersch 2000; Alvazzi del Frate 2005.
26 Lemosse 1990, p. 53-70.
27 Beauthier 1999, p. 67-70.
28 Cf. Montazel 1998, p. 87-89; Gouron 1996, p. 53-82.
29 Beauthier, p. 70-73.
30 Holthöfer 1993, p. 19-20 & p. 22-23. See more in general about the history of the Hoge Raad, Van Soest 1988.

In Belgium the new style of cassation appeared somewhat later, in 1865.[31] Nevertheless, Belgium's Court of Cassation may have even more prestige and importance than its Dutch and French counterparts thanks to the Court's attitude during the two World Wars. During World War I Belgium was almost completely occupied by the Germans and the Court of Cassation tried to obstruct German occupation as much as possible, serving as a guiding beacon for the country's other courts. In 1918 the confrontation between the Court of Cassation and the occupying forces even escalated so far that the Court went on strike and was promptly followed by the rest of the Belgian judiciary.[32] After the war, the Court of Cassation, and most of all its General Prosecutor, de facto Minister of Justice during the war, could, with justification, claim that they had been as patriotic as the soldiers who had been fighting the Germans in the trenches.[33] The Belgian king, during the war the leader of Belgium's armed forces, acknowledged this and made an official visit to the Court in honour of its patriotism.[34] The First World War provided the scenario for the Second. Once again, the Court of Cassation tried to work against German occupation as much as it could, thus ensuring that Nazi control over Belgian courts was less than in neighbouring countries[35] and, once again, the Court gained in prestige. By now, Belgium's Court of Cassation has also become crucial in keeping Belgium united, although there is an ever growing rift in public opinion and amongst lawyers about legal issues, while calls for a regionalisation of justice are growing stronger. In this climate, in which even a justice minister may take sides with one part of the country against the other, the Court is one of the few institutions which still tries to bridge the gap between Dutch and French speaking Belgium[36] and it is a bit of a shame that the Court of Cassation is never mentioned in the traditional (and very short) list of what still keeps Belgians together: the king, the national soccer team and social security.

2.3. *The Justice of the Peace: from Anti-Judge to Member of the Legal Establishment*

Originally, the highest 'judge' was not really a judge and neither was the 'lowest' one, the justice of the peace. That there had to be judges close to ordinary people was evident for the French Revolution. After all, tens of thousands of seignorial courts had been abolished by the Revolution and, whatever their defaults had been, they had stood in close contact with the population.[37] The Revolution replaced them

31 Beauthier 1999, p. 74-92.

32 Janssens 1977, p. 102-104.

33 Cf. the following speech by the General Prosecutor: Terlinden 1918, p. 1169-1182 & p. 1201-1225.

34 Rousseaux & Weber 2004, p. 82.

35 Michielsen 2004.

36 Heirbaut 2005, p. 80. It may happen that Dutch and French speaking chambers of the court have a diverging view about a certain point of law, but then they can resolve this in a plenary session (Du Jardin 2001-2002, p. 649-676).

37 See about the predecessors of the *juge de paix*, e.g. Métairie 2004; Humbert 1995, p. 5-30.

with the justices of the peace, who, and not only in the geographical sense, were close to the people. The justice of the peace was not only local, he also had to judge according to dictates of equity, not those of law. Hence, in the peace court trained professional lawyers were not needed: the judge did not have to be a lawyer and advocates were anything but welcome (the Revolution had abolished them too), as the judge's main goal was to try to reconcile the parties, thus eliminating the judgement. The preliminary stage in which the judge tried to mediate between the parties originally was a general element of the civil procedure of Revolutionary courts, but in 1806 the Napoleonic Code of Civil Procedure abolished it for all other courts (except for some special procedures) and only in the peace courts did it survive and thrive.[38] Another Revolutionary element which was stronger in these courts was the election of judges, though here it did not last much longer than in other courts, as it disappeared already under Napoleon who was in favour of nominated judges over whom he had much more control. In fairness, one has to add that the nomination of judges also ensured a better quality than elections. Elected judges may have been popular, but they were not very professional and to ensure some quality of the proceedings, the justice of the peace always had two associate judges. When Napoleon replaced elected with nominated judges, this was no longer needed and the peace court became a single-judge court.[39] Even though no longer elected, because of the more easygoing procedure and mentality and because of the geographical proximity, the justice of the peace remained a 'popular' judge in all senses of the word.

After Napoleon, there is a marked contrast between France and Belgium. France abolished the peace courts in 1958,[40] whereas in Belgium the justice of the peace is, by far, the most successful judge. Paradoxically, today's Belgian justices of the peace have become the victims of their own success because the legislator is heaping ever more powers and thus work on them.[41] With some exaggeration, the articles in Belgium's Judiciary Code about the justice of the peace's jurisdiction are called 'kilometric'.[42] Today's favour with parliament has obscured the original hostility of Belgian politics towards the justice of the peace. At the time of independence, the plan was to greatly curtail their number and to come to larger jurisdictions. Despite that, there are even a few more peace courts today than during the French era.[43] What saved them was their popularity - no decision about the court system is as likely to lead to as much grass roots protest as the one to 'rob' a place of its peace court - and statistics. Strange as it may sound, in the mid-19th century, when Belgium was a pioneer in this field, its judicial statistics were sooner available and more accurate than the ones published today, because then both government and parliament were very much aware that good statistical data

38 Nandrin 1992, p. 23-29.
39 Nandrin 1992, p. 27.
40 Benat-Berger 2003, p. 225-247.
41 Cf. Velle 1999, p. 8-21.
42 Storme 1995, p. 24.
43 See Van Royen 1989.

enabled them to keep track of what the judiciary was doing.[44] Sometimes this could be to the advantage of the latter and it certainly was in the case of the justices of the peace, as the early statistics showed that they were functioning to the satisfaction of people. Long before 'access to justice' became a slogan, they embodied this principle and there were few appeals against their decisions, and even fewer of those were successful. The then governments and parliaments deserve some credit for what they did when these facts became known. They shelved the plans to cut back on the peace courts and, instead, decided to invest in them. The Ministers of Justice started by only nominating trained lawyers as justices of the peace and an 1848 Act of parliament made a law degree obligatory.[45] From then on the justice of the peace no longer differed from his colleagues because they were professionals, whereas he was not always one, but by his accessibility, because the professional justices of the peace in this continued the policies and mentalities of their predecessors. Consequently, they managed to keep the trust of the people, which is the major factor in their ongoing success.[46] However, the continuity in easy access does not mean that today's justices of the peace are justified in referring proudly to their Revolutionary origins, as they are professionals and thus the complete opposite of what the Revolution wanted.

Whereas the history of the Belgian justice of the peace is a success story, in France it was not.[47] Professionalisation took place much later than in Belgium and the rural depopulation complicated matters. The upshot was that in 1958 the peace courts were displaced by the *tribunaux d'instance*, which were responsible for a much larger area, as more than 2000 peace courts were succeeded by less than 500 *tribunaux d'instance*.[48] In these conditions, it was hard to achieve the Revolutionary ideal of the lowest judge as a very accessible judge. Moreover, since 1970 the judges of the *tribunaux d'instance* are judges of the *tribunaux de grande instance* (the courts which had replaced the courts of first instance), who are on detached duty for a renewable term of three years.[49] This ensures that the new judges are even less embedded in local life. By the end of the 20th century a growing chorus of critics was expressing its disappointment with this system. True, the 1958 reform was not that bad from a managerial or a budgetary point of view, but it had distanced the court system from the people. Hence, many legal scholars called for a 'proximity justice'. In one of these strange twists of events, which make history either so endearing or so maddening, some of them even referred to the 'Belgian' justice of the peace, who had started life as a French immigrant.[50] Turning back the clock by bringing back the old peace courts was not possible, but in 2002 a new type of courts saw the light, the *juridictions de proximité*, whose judges are to be less

44 Tixhon 1999, p. 976-981; Rousseaux & Tixhon 2004, p. 163-183.
45 Nandrin 1995a, p. 155-166; Nandrin 1992, p. 29-37; Nandrin 1998.
46 See about this also Franssen, Van Loon & Delrue 1997-1998, p. 1241-1246.
47 For a comparison between Belgium and France, see the following excellent article: Nandrin 1997a, p. 85-102.
48 Nandrin 1997a, p. 85.
49 Nandrin 1997a, p. 98-99.
50 Cf. Gridel 1994.

professional and more accessible.[51] Future historians will have to judge whether they will be a success or not,[52] but the French experience has shown that, even though the Revolution was wrong in its dislike of law professionals, it hit the mark in its preference for judges who are accessible. (And it did not even need Mauro Cappelletti to point that out.)

2.4. *The Triumph of the Specialised Courts*

As has been repeatedly stated in this article, the two goals of the French Revolution for the judicial system were deprofessionalisation and simplification. The latter combined with the general abolition of privileges meant that any special court for a privileged group had to disappear,[53] but in the case of the commercial courts this came into conflict with the principle of deprofessionalisation. On the one hand they should have been abolished, on the other the merchants pointed out that the judges of their courts were democratically elected and this saved them, so that the tribunals of commerce are the only courts which can proudly say that they antedate the Revolution.[54] Unfortunately, this meant that a precedent was set and that thereafter it became easier to establish new specialised courts, because the principle of simplification had already been broken. The first newcomer was the *Conseil des prud'hommes* (labour tribunal; the literal meaning is: Council of wise men), competent to judge disputes about labour contracts. The oldest employment tribunal appeared in 1806 in Lyon and thereafter many others would follow.[55] In Belgium the growth of special courts has been limited to the commercial courts and employment tribunals. In France some other courts joined them in the 20th century for dealing with agricultural tenancy and social security. All these specialised courts share some characteristics: in many cases their judges are elected, they are laymen and, if possible, it is a 'joint tribunal', i.e. they sit with equal representation for both sides.[56] For example, in a *Conseil des prud'hommes*, two of the judges will be employers and two will be employees.

The more recent French courts are less interesting than the commercial and labour tribunals. They were only established where the state thought they were needed. Hence, their distribution over France and Belgium was very uneven. In general, rural areas did not have a commercial or labour tribunal, but it would be wrong to assume that a lot of economic activity would automatically lead to the establishment of a new tribunal. For example, in Belgium the very important

51 Perrot 2004, p. 106-110.

52 Cf. Cadiet & Jeuland 2004, p. 109.

53 This article will not deal with the short-lived family courts during the Revolution (Commaille 1989, p. 205-223; Demars-Sion 2005, p. 385-420).

54 Hilaire 1989, p. 243-266. However, this remark is only true for France. (See for Belgium, Logie 1998a, p. 67-68.) For more details about the history of the commercial courts, see Ithurbide 1970; Szramkiewicz 1995, p. 7-14; Baudoin 1997; Pene Vidari 1998, p. 403-423.

55 Perrot 2004, p. 121. See also Scholl 1956, p. 1047-1080; Dubois 2000; Cottereau 1987; David 1974, p. 3-21.

56 Perrot 2004, p. 110-136.

industrial city of Charleroi did not have a commerce tribunal, whereas the Bruges district, which had sharply declined since its medieval days of glory, had two of them.[57] This shows that new commercial and labour tribunals were the product of circumstances and not of planning. Moreover, the fact that important cities could do without them proved that they were not needed. After all, if there was no specialised court, the ordinary court, the court of first instance, took care of commercial and labour disputes and it seems to have done so without trouble. Therefore, logic would have dictated the abolition of these specialised tribunals. Instead, the opposite happened. Local lobbying for a specialised court and other factors have made their numbers grow and they are stronger than ever.

In Belgium this evolution has somewhat of a Greek tragedy, because in the 1960's the authors of the new Judicial Code, Van Reepinghen and Krings, had originally planned a court system in which there would no longer be specialised courts. The resistance from special interest groups finally made Van Reepinghen and Krings sacrifice this idea to save the rest of their Code (which would indeed become law in 1967). The most important opposition had come from the Unions, which did not trust the judges of ordinary courts, as these were seen as too employer-friendly. Not only did they manage to abort the plan for the abolition of the specialised courts, they could strengthen their position. The old *Conseils des prud'hommes* were replaced by new labour tribunals of which there would be one in every judicial district. Likewise there would be a commercial court in every judicial district. The new labour tribunals also became competent for social security cases and next to the courts of appeal special labour courts of appeal would be established. The specialised courts had not only beaten off the attack, they had become even more firmly entrenched. Their crowning achievement came in 1970, when the constitution was changed to mention the labour tribunals (the commercial courts had been in the constitution from the start).[58] France is, in this, lagging behind Belgium. Since 1979 there are one or more *Conseils de prud'hommes* in the jurisdiction of a *Tribunal de grande instance*, but tribunals of commerce are still absent from some places.[59]

Another difference between France and Belgium is professionalisation. As for the justices of the peace, Belgium has chosen for professionals. The 1967 Judicial Code organises both the commercial and the labour courts in the same way: each chamber has a professional judge as its president and two laymen as his associates. France is more faithful to the original model with only lay judges and, at the most, a professional lawyer to help them. Because of that, the specialised courts are more criticised in France than in Belgium. However, commercial tribunals in Alsace-Lorraine, which was German between 1870 and 1918, have an organisation more like the Belgian one. Moreover, since 1982 there have been several efforts at reforming the system, referring to the Alsatian or the Belgian example, but up to

57 Fettweis 1961, p. 80 & p. 85.

58 Krings 2003, p. 169; Verwoerd 1982, p. 331-332; Cambier 1968, p. 262-276.

59 Perrot 2004, p. 111 & p. 127.

now these have not led to concrete results.[60] Strange enough, there are no like proposals for the *Conseils de prud'hommes*.[61] Nevertheless, the parallels with the justices of the peace cannot be overlooked. Like in that case, Belgium has chosen to take the road of professionalisation earlier and further than France and consequently the court concerned has strengthened its position.

The Belgian professionalisation is also due to the elimination of elected judges. Whereas their French counterparts are still elected, in Belgium the professional who presides over the commercial and labour courts is nominated, as are his lay associates, though in their case the nomination generally takes place at the recommendation of representative organisations. The choice in favour of nomination was at first a stopgap measure, at least as far as the commercial courts are concerned. In 1933 their judges were elected for eight years, but thereafter the war and its aftermath made new elections impossible.[62] Thus, the switch from election to nomination was the product of chance and not of policy.

2.5. *History's Stepchildren: the Courts of First Instance and the Appeal Courts*

The highest and lowest judges, Cassation and the justice of the peace, have been well studied, like the special courts. However, historians have paid less attention to the courts of first instance and the appeal courts[63] and this is a shame, as the courts of first instance are the ordinary courts and the courts of appeal are the courts which really shaped law in the 19th century and which can be seen as the successors of the pre-revolutionary highest courts, the *parlements*. It is remarkable that they could dominate the law in their jurisdiction, as the French Revolution had tried as much as it could to avoid this. Originally, the Revolution had a very simple mechanism for eliminating the courts of appeal. There was a possibility for appeal, but no specialised court to take care of it. Instead of a hierarchical appeal a circular appeal was set up, i.e. the court in appeal was to be another court of the same type in another city. Even when Napoleon finally established specialised courts for appeals, these were not called courts, but tribunals, to better express the idea that they should not be thought of as 'superior'.[64] Nevertheless, it took only a few years for the name 'appeal courts' to be used. Terminology thus reflected reality, as the appeal courts were indeed the most important higher courts in the 19th century,

60 Elliot & Vernon 2000, p. 64-65; Perrot 2004, p. 119-121.

61 Even though they are also criticised (Vincent *et al.* 2003, p. 393).

62 Fettweis 1961, p. 82.

63 One can easily see this, if one consults the *Bibliographie. Histoire justice en France (1789-2004)* (<http://www.criminocorpus.cnrs.fr/rubrique.php3?id_rubrique=2>, last consulted 20 March 2007), which contains separate directories about the history of the Court of Cassation, the commercial courts, the labour courts and the justices of the peace, whereas these are lacking for the courts of appeal and the courts of first instance. There are exceptions to this rule. For example, there are several studies about these courts and their judges for the French and the Dutch era in Belgium (e.g. Logie 1998) and there are also some archival guides (Gadeyne 1997-2001; Depoortere 1999).

64 Perrot 2004, p. 9.

even eclipsing the Court of Cassation.[65] Many courts of appeal were helped in asserting their superiority by their links to their predecessors, the *parlements*,[66] and to old regional identities. For example, in Belgium the Liege court of appeal remained during the 19th century a focal point of Liégois particularism, a last remnant of the fact that before the French Revolution the principality of Liege had not been a part of the Southern Netherlands.[67] The continuity with the past was helped by the absence of major changes in the courts of appeal, the one exception being that in France from 1958 the courts of appeal deal with all appeals, whatever the court in first instance was, whereas before 1958 the court of first instance could sit in appeal, e.g. when decisions of justices of the peace were attacked.[68] In Belgium the court of first instance can still sit in appeal, but for that country another change has to be mentioned: the creation of new courts of appeal, the country now having five courts of appeal instead of the original two. The new courts were necessary because of the industrial development of certain regions and also to preserve equilibrium between the Dutch and the French speaking part of the country.[69]

In contrast to this, Belgium has been more stable than France as far as the courts of first instance are concerned. In Belgium they still exist, but in France they were replaced by the *tribunaux de grande instance* in 1958 in a reform which completely overhauled the jurisdictional landscape. Instead of one court of first instance in each district, there is now one *tribunal de grande instance* in each 'department' (the districts are subdivisions of the departments), though in departments with a high population there may be several *tribunaux de grande instance*, but their distribution is determined by other factors than the division of the department into districts.[70] Budgetary considerations had caused the 1958 reorganisation, as on the one hand in some districts the workload of the courts of first instance was becoming unbearable, whereas the depopulation of the rural districts had resulted in some courts sitting in idleness. In those circumstances, it was not justified to keep up a minimum staff of three judges, one public prosecutor and one court clerk in every district. Of course, instead of redistributing the courts, the French might also have chosen in 1958 for single judge courts, but the distrust of

65 Van Dievoet 1943, p. 307.

66 Jugnot 1998, p. 115.

67 There were many Liégois reviews and some of their names expressly refer to the Court of Appeal: *Chronique Liégeoise, Gazette des tribunaux du ressort de la Cour d'appel de Liège, L'audience, Journal des tribunaux, Gazette des tribunaux de la province de Liège, L'Echo judiciaire, La chronique des tribunaux de la province de Liège, Recueil des arrêts notables de la Cour d'appel de Liège, Jurisprudence de la Cour d'appel de Liège et de son ressort.*

68 Perrot 2004, p. 141-142.

69 The Ghent court of appeal was established after independence because of the industrial importance of Ghent, then Belgium's biggest city; the Antwerp court of appeal in 1970 both because of the economic importance of the Antwerp port and because of the need to have a Dutch speaking court of appeal for the Dutch speaking province of Limburg, which for historical reasons had belonged to the territory of the French speaking court of Liège. There was no real reason for a fifth court of appeal in Mons, except for the need to have as many Dutch as French speaking courts of appeal, the Brussels court being bilingual.

70 Perrot 2004, p. 93; Vincent *et al.* 2003, p. 358.

a judge working on his own – a heritage from the Revolution – was too great for that.[71] Even nowadays, the *tribunal de grande instance* is only very exceptionally a single judge court.

Belgium has diverged from France, as most chambers of the court of instance are staffed by a single judge, collegiate administration of justice being the exception. Even in courts of appeal, certain cases may be taken care of by a single judge. Like in France, budgetary constraints have led to this. When the backlog has become too great, the authorities can either nominate more judges or they can make the judges take more cases. The latter, being cheaper, had the preference. By taking a chamber of three judges and turning it into three single judge chambers, the number of chambers could (in theory, at least) expand threefold. At first, in 1919, this was only meant as a temporary stopgap measure, necessitated by the backlog because of the courts' strike against the Germans in the final months of World War I and the many trials caused by the war's aftermath. France faced like problems after World War II and then also worked with single judges.[72] However, in France the situation soon returned to normal, whereas in Belgium it never did, the provisional measure turning into a permanent one, with the turning point being a 1985 Act which made the single judge the ordinary judge and which also introduced single judges into the courts of appeal, panegyrics of the collegiate administration of justice in lawbooks and political speeches notwithstanding. In fact, the decision to choose for the single judge was a purely financial one, as at the time (and still today) no one denied that justice would be better served by chambers of three judges.[73] Yet, no one really protested either, though in 1992 parliament expanded somewhat the number of cases in which a chamber of three judges is competent.[74] Still, it is sad that both in France and in Belgium the authorities seem to think of the ordinary courts only when costs need to be cut.

2.6. *Conclusion*

Despite some differences, France and Belgium have in common that they have abandoned the ideals of the Revolution, even though they have both largely stuck to its structures. The highest courts have regained power; the specialised courts have taken on more importance; professionalisation has triumphed over democratisation; the judges have won their freedom from parliament and government, and so on. In short, having grown out of the Revolutionary court system, today's Belgian and French courts with their preference for hierarchy, specialisation, professionalisation and independence have become almost the antipodes of their revolutionary predecessors. If not for its unbridled chaos, it is as if the Old Regime is back and the Revolution has never been. One can only wonder whether this reassertion of the old pattern was inevitable.

71 Perrot 2004, p. 92-93.
72 Farcy 1992, p. 45.
73 Nandrin 1989, p. 97-111.
74 Cf. Lemmens 1992, p. 57.

3. Rejecting the Revolution: the Netherlands

The history of the court system in the Netherlands shows that what happened in France and Belgium was anything but preordained. Strange enough, however, by rejecting many principles of the Revolution, the Dutch have, albeit without intending to do so, managed to preserve more of its ideals.

3.1. *The Dutch Judicial System before the End of the 20th Century: an anti-Revolutionary Mentality Hiding behind French Forms*

The Netherlands started with the same judicial system as France and Belgium, as they had also been a part of France under Napoleon. However, this happened later than in Belgium. One might have expected the Batavian Revolutionaries, who had been inspired by events in France, or Napoleon's brother who later became king, to copy the French,[75] but they did not. Instead, in 1809 there was even an original Code of judicial institutions and procedure in the Kingdom of Holland, which was to remain without effect, as Napoleon annexed the Netherlands in 1810; and shortly thereafter the judicial system was cast in the French mould.[76] Already three years later the Netherlands regained their independence and it might well have been possible that the country would have overhauled its judicial system to have one which would fit better with Dutch traditions.[77] However, this was no longer possible when the Netherlands were united with Belgium in the United Kingdom of the Netherlands in 1815, as the Belgians by then had become accustomed to (and even enamoured of) the French institutions. True, in 1827 an Act reorganised the court system, but, under Belgian pressure, the French model was largely left intact with a four-layer hierarchy, consisting of courts (*kantongerecht, arrondissements-rechtbank, provinciaal gerechtshof* and *Hoge Raad*) which resembled their French counterparts. On 1 February 1831 the new system was to come into effect, but by then Belgium had seceded, so that there the French system remained. In the Netherlands the 1827 Act was revised, but the 1835 Act and the new judicial system which finally was established in 1838, still remained faithful to the French example.[78]

However, structures do only tell one part of the story and concentrating on them in this case obscures the differences in mentality between the French Revolution and the Dutch. Absent was the distrust of the professional lawyer (and its consequences, like elected judges, the preference for conciliation, the idea that the Court of Cassation was a watchdog, and so on).[79] Consequently, the 1835 Act abolished the trial by jury[80] and the commercial courts.[81] The Revolution allowed

75 See in general about Dutch law and institutions in the period 1795-1810: Moorman van Kappen & Coppens 1997; Hallebeek & Sirks 2006.

76 Van Boven 1990.

77 Cf. Moorman van Kappen 1998, p. 54-66.

78 Cf. Brenninkmeijer 2006, p. 53.

79 Van Boven 1990, p. 277.

80 Bossers 1987.

the commercial courts to survive because their judges were elected non-lawyers, whereas for the Dutch that was exactly the reason to abolish these courts. Likewise, the *Hoge Raad*, the Dutch equivalent of the Court of Cassation, only slowly gained acceptance.[82] In short, the outlook of the Dutch judicial system might have been French, but its mentality was not.

3.2. *The Recent Reforms: the Goal of Simplification almost Completely Realised*

There have been many plans for a reform of the court system in the Netherlands, but most of them were unsuccessful. An exception was an 1875 Act which abolished some appeal courts, but apart from that it is striking that from the end of the 19th century the number of specialised courts started to grow.[83] However, in 1971 the Minister of Justice set up a study group to prepare a general reform. Five years later a commission was appointed to elaborate upon its ideas and government accepted most of the proposals which this commission made in 1989. The main goal was the integration of all existing courts into one unitary structure, which would handle civil, criminal and administrative cases, with in principle two instances and with the possibility of an appeal to Cassation. This amounted to a three-level hierarchy with only one type of courts at each level and the abolition of all specialised courts.[84]

Needless to say, such a complete overhaul could only be realised in stages. The first one, making the *arrondissementsrechtbanken* (district courts) competent for administrative cases, was completed in 1994 and could take place without too much trouble, even though many specialised administrative courts were abolished. The second stage was only realised in 2002 and saw the reforms running into trouble, as it foresaw the abolition of the *kantongerechten* (subdistrict courts), the local courts which were the equivalent of the justices of the peace in Belgium or in France (before 1958). As in other countries, these local courts were popular because of their accessibility and resistance against their abolition was great. In the end, government and parliament had to make a major concession. The *kantongerechten* have indeed disappeared, but within the *arrondissementsrechtbanken* there will still be a special section, called *kanton*, which will handle the cases which used to come before the former *kantongerechten* and effort has also been made to preserve the best elements of the more accessible procedure before these courts. Moreover, the *arrondissementsrechtbank* will still have a residence in all the places which used to have a *kantongerecht*.[85] It is clear from this that a steep price was paid for the integration of the *kantongerechten* in the *arrondissementsrechtbank*. The third stage of the reforms did not just run into trouble, it has failed completely. It had to reform the last instance in administrative cases, but in 2004 the decision was taken to wait with this part of the

81 Klomp 1998, p. 24-28.
82 Cf. Kortmann 1990, p. 417-419.
83 See for this and for history of the Dutch judicial system in general, Holthöfer 1993, p. 15-53.
84 Seidel 1990, p. 94-97; Bovend'eert 1994, p. 155-162.
85 Stein & Rueb 2005, p. 12-13.

reforms and, consequently, the highest administrative courts still exist in some kind of limbo.[86]

Even though the overhaul of the judiciary system was not an all-out success, the situation in the Netherlands today is completely different from the French Revolution. Yet, the Dutch have been more faithful to the Revolution's ideals than the French and the Belgians. The Revolution wanted deprofessionalisation and simplification. The former never really took root in the Netherlands, but in France and even more in Belgium it has gradually become less important. As to simplification, however, the Dutch have even gone further than the Revolution would have thought. Hence, the paradox is that the Dutch by rejecting the Revolution saved more of it than France and Belgium, who have betrayed it by preserving it.

3.3. *It could have happened in Belgium too: the Dreams of Krings and the Interuniversity Centre for Judicial Law*

The history of legal reform is mostly a history of failure and only seldom one of success, though when the latter is achieved it can be so overwhelming that everything is swept away by it. The Netherlands are not remarkable because of the plans the Dutch had for reform, but because of the success they had. Similar schemes were hatched in France,[87] but most of all in Belgium. In fact, the Belgians had the plan for one *arrondissementsrechtbank* (for Dutch speaking Belgians even the name was the same one as in the Netherlands) already in 1964. The then commissioner for judicial reform, Van Reepinghen, had an assistant-commissioner, Krings, who convinced him to propose the abolition of the court of first instance, the *conseil des prud'hommes* and the commercial court. The unitary *arrondissementsrechtbank* would then take their place. This proposal had logic on its side. After all, in some places there were no specialised courts and yet justice, assured by the court of first instance, still ran its usual course without problems. As has been written above, this proposal was not accepted and the specialised courts even could strengthen their position in the 1967 Judicial Code. An *arrondissementsrechtbank* was established, but it was only a very meagre shade of what Krings had wanted, a court which would only judge disputes of jurisdiction between the court of first instance and the specialised courts. Lobbying by special interest groups had won the day against the wish for a simplified court system.[88]

The dream of a unitary court remained alive and it made a come-back in the mid 1990's. In 1993-1995 several lawyers, among them the then president of the International Association for Procedural Law, M. Storme in his final lecture at the University of Ghent, called for a unitary court.[89] Politicians did not remain unaware

86 De Haan 2005, p. 215-220.

87 The discussion there is still going on, see e.g. Van Lang *et al.* 2005, p. 1760-1786.

88 One can read Kring's own words about this in Krings 2003, p. 169. See also Cambier, p. 262-278.

89 Storme 1995, p. 68. See also Storme 1995a, p. 125. For the others, see: Moeykens 1992, p. 145; De Corte 1995, p. x-xi; Van Orshoven 1995, p. 19-44; Van Orshoven 1994-1995, p. 897-908.

of this and at the request of Minister of Justice De Clerck the Interuniversitary Centre for Judicial Law wrote a note about the establishment of the courts and tribunals and their members (most of it was written by its Antwerp member Laenens).[90] The Centre went even further than Krings in 1964 and pleaded for an *arrondissementsrechtbank* Dutch style, which would also be competent in administrative cases, though the Centre was ahead of the Dutch when it also planned to integrate the justice of the peace in the *arrondissementsrechtbank,* though with a place apart in order to preserve the justice of the peace as such within the structure of the *arrondissementsrechtbank* (The Dutch later had to adopt a similar solution.) and there would also have to be guarantees for a good geographical distribution. The Centre was very much concerned about that, because the last thing it wanted was a 'mastodon court'.

Initially, the prospects looked good for the Centre's proposal, as, at the time it was drafted, the mind of public opinion in Belgium was very much on the Dutroux scandal[91] which had made it clear to everyone that a reform of the police and the courts was urgently needed. Politicians of all parties agreed that an integration of the courts of first instance could be one of the remedies for the ills of the administration of justice in Belgium.[92] Yet, not much happened thereafter, in spite for some renewed calls for and articles about an *arrondissementsrechtbank*[93] and in 2004 a study undertaken at the request of Minister of Justice Onckelinkx only mentioned the arguments against a '*mega- arrondissementsrechtbank*'.[94] The awkward term already indicates that the Centre has failed to convince opponents that the last thing it wants is a mastodon court. This may also be because the Centre's proposal itself has never been made public, so that outsiders have not been confronted with the text itself, which is an admirable document taking the edge off its opponents' arguments, but with a few summaries,[95] which, however good they are, cannot do

90 This document has not been published. I have consulted it in the form of a fourteen pages fax sent by Jean Laenens (with thanks to my colleague P. Taelman for providing me with a copy).

91 Dutroux was a paedophile who had abducted and murdered several young children. Due to police and judicial bungling he was caught too late to save most of his victims, which enraged the Belgian public and even led to the greatest demonstration ever in the country, the so-called White March, in 1996. When Dutroux, the people's arch-enemy number one, managed to escape briefly in 1998, two ministers of the federal government resigned and the most important democratic political parties concluded an agreement about a reform (called Octopusagreement because there were eight of them) (see for more details, e.g. Laenens & Storme 2000).

92 *Parlementaire stukken, Senaat,* 1997-1998, No. 1-994/2, Bijlage 3, *Krachtlijnen inzake de hervorming van de gerechtelijke organisatie.* See also the standpoints of some political parties reported in *Parlementaire Documenten, Kamer van volksvertegenwoordigers,* 2004-2005, No. 1571/001, 27 January 2005, 8 note 1. Cf. also a 1999 memorandum by the association of Flemish jurists (Laenens 1999 (see <http://www.vlaamsejuristenvereniging.be/memovjv.htm>, last consulted 20 March 2007)).

93 De Corte 1998, p. 377-382; Storme 2005a, p. 149; Van Orshoven 2003, p. 115-118.

94 Erdman & De Leval 2004, p. 88.

95 Baeteman 1998, p. 377-382; Duquesne 1999, p. xviii-xix (without any reference to the original document).

justice to the original document.[96] (It deserves to be on the reading list of anyone in the world who plans the reform of courts). One may wonder whether this really matters, as resistance against reform is highest amongst the judges of the special courts, who like to preserve their autonomy at the cost of an overall less efficient judicial system. After all, if they really want to see the original text, it is not that hard to get hold of it, but it is much easier to ridicule its caricature than to convincingly refute its arguments.

Nevertheless, in January 2005 a member of parliament, Fons Borginon, submitted a bill about the horizontal integration of the courts and tribunals at the levels of first and second instance.[97] His proposal amounts to the establishment of an *arrondissementsrechtbank*, of which the current courts will become sections, but, apart from losing their autonomy the current courts will continue to exist with their special characteristics (e.g. two lay assessors in the commercial and labour sections) and they will remain situated in their current residences. This proposal does not go as far as the one by the Centre (for example, the *arrondissementsrechtbank* will not be competent in administrative cases), but it could be a major step towards a greater reorganisation of Belgium's judicial organisation, if it will ever be enacted...

3.4. *Conclusion*

The French Revolution wanted a deprofessionalisation and a simplification of the court system. With hindsight the former, however laudable in theory, is not very practical. Justice is too important to be left to amateurs. Simplification, however, is still worth fighting for and both the Dutch system and the Belgian reform plan show how it can become a reality. True, the Netherlands have not been able to completely realise their reforms and the Belgians are, for now, only trying to achieve something, but that should not stop other countries from trying to follow their example.

96 Hence also other proposals for reform (Jassogne 2000, p. 16).

97 *Parlementaire Documenten, Kamer van volksvertegenwoordigers*, 2004-2005, No. 1571/001, 27 January 2005.

Bibliography

Alvazzi del Frate 2005
Alvazzi del Frate, P., *Giurisprudenza e référé législatif in Francia nel periodo rivoluzionario e napoleonico*, Turin: Giappichelli, 2005.

Association française pour l'histoire de la justice 1993
Association française pour l'histoire de la justice, *Epuration de la magistrature de la Révolution à la Libération: 150 ans d'histoire judiciaire*, Paris: Association française pour l'histoire de la justice, 1993 (*Histoire de la justice*, VI).

Baeteman 1998
Baeteman, G., 'Een voortgezette hervorming van de rechterlijke macht?', *Tijdschrift voor privaatrecht*, XXXV, 1998, p. 377-382.

Bancaud 2002
Bancaud, A., *Une exception ordinaire. La magistrature en France, 1930-1950*, Paris: Gallimard, 2002.

Bancaud & Robert 2001
Bancaud, A. & Robert P., 'La place de la justice en France: un avenir incertain', in: Robert, P. & Cottino, A. (eds), *Les mutations de la justice. Comparaisons européennes*, Paris: Harmattan, 2001, p. 184-185.

Baudoin 1997
Baudoin, L., *Cent ans au service de la justice consulaire*, Paris: Hervas, 1997.

Beauthier 1999
Beauthier, R., 'La lente conquête d'une suprématie. L'exemple de l'organe de cassation de l'Ancien Régime au XIXe siècle', *Revue de droit de l'ULB*, XX, 1999, p. 7-99.

Benat-Berger 2003
Benat-Berger, F., 'La réforme de 1958. La suppression des justices de paix', in: Petit, J.-G. (ed.), *Une juridiction de proximité: la justice de paix 1790-1958*, Paris: PUF, 2003, p. 225-247.

Bossers 1987
Bossers, G., *Welk ene natie die de jurij gehad heeft en ze weder afschaft*, Delft: UVA, 1987.

Bourdon 1942
Bourdon, J., *La formation de la magistrature sous le Consulat décennal (an VIII-X)*, Paris: Rodez, 1942.

Van Boven 1990
Van Boven, M., *De rechterlijke instellingen ter discussie. De geschiedenis van de wetgeving op de rechterlijke organisatie in de periode 1795-1811*, Nijmegen: Universiteit Nijmegen, 1990.

Bovend'eert 1994
Bovend'eert, P.P.T., 'Herziening van de Nederlandse rechterlijke organisatie. Een rechtsvergelijkende beschouwing', *Tijdschrift voor bestuurswetenschappen en publiekrecht*, XLIX, 1994, p. 155-162.

Brenninkmeijer 2006
Brenninkmeijer, A., 'Judicial organization', in: Chorus, J. *et al.* (eds.), *Introduction to Dutch law*, The Hague: Kluwer, 1999, p. 53-61.

Cadiet & Jeuland 2004
Cadiet, L. & Jeuland, E., *Droit judiciaire privé*, Paris: Litec, 2004.

Van Caenegem 1992
Van Caenegem, R., *An historical introduction to private law*, Cambridge: Cambridge University Press, 1992.

Cambier 1968
Cambier, C., 'Principes de l'organisation judiciaire', *Annales de droit*, XXVIII, 1968, p. 262-276.

Chauvaud 1995
Chauvaud, F., *Le juge, le tribun et le comptable. Histoire de l'organisation judiciaire entre les pouvoirs, les savoirs et les discours (1789-1930)*, Paris: Anthropos, 1995.

Commaile 1989
Commaile, J., 'Les tribunaux de famille sous la Révolution', in: Badinter, R. (ed.), *Une autre justice. 1789-1799*, Paris: Fayard, 1989.

De Corte 1995
De Corte, R., 'Voorwoord', in: Schoenaerts, B. & Lamiroy, M. (eds.), *De Belgische justitie. Een Kafkaiaanse nachtmerrie. Analyse & remedie*, Ghent: Mys en Breesch, 1995, p. vii-xx.

De Corte 2000
De Corte, R., 'Eenheidsrechtbank naar af?', *Juristenkrant*, 2000/5, p. 2.

Cottereau 1987
Cottereau, A. (ed.), *Les prud'hommes XIXe-XXe siècles*, Paris: Les Éditions ouvrières, 1987.

Crubaugh 2001
Crubaugh, A., *Balancing the scales of justice. Local courts and rural society in Southwestern France, 1750-1800*, Philadelphia: Pennsylvania State University Press, 2001.

Dahlmanns 1982
Dahlmanns, G., 'Belgien', in: Coing, H. (ed.), *Handbuch der Quellen und Literatur der neueren Europäischen Privatrechtsgeschichte*, III/2, Munich: Beck, 1982, p. 2585-2601.

Dahlmanns 1982a
Dahlmanns, G., 'Frankreich', in: Coing, H. (ed.), *Handbuch der Quellen und Literatur der neueren Europäischen Privatrechtsgeschichte*, III/2, Munich: Beck, 1982, p. 2491-2505.

David 1974
David, M., 'L'évolution historique des conseils de prud'hommes en France', *Droit social*, février 1974, p. 3-21.

Demars-Sion 2005
Demars-Sion, V., 'Une expérience d'arbitrage forcé: les tribunaux de famille révolutionnaires', *Revue historique de droit français et étranger*, LXXXIII, 2005, p. 385-420.

Depoortere 1999
Depoortere, R., *Les cours d'appel en Belgique et leurs prédécesseurs en droit 1795-1999. Compétences et organisation. Production et conservation des archives*, Brussels: ARA, 1999.

Dhondt 2002
Dhondt, L., *Verlichte monarchie, Ancien Régime en revolutie: een institutionele en historische procesanalyse van politiek, instellingen en ideologie in de Habsburgse, de Nederlandse en de Vlaamse politieke ruimte (1700/1755-1790)*, Brussels: Ara, 2002, 5 vols.

Van Dievoet 1943
Van Dievoet, E., *Het burgerlijk recht in België en Nederland van 1800 tot 1940. De rechtsbronnen*, Antwerp: De Sikkel, 1943.

Dubois 2000
Dubois, B., *Les Conseils des prud'hommes au XIXe siècle. Entre Etat, patrons et ouvriers: les linéaments de la justice de travail (1806-1868)*, Lille, 2000 (unpublished doctoral thesis, Lille II).

Duquesne 1999
Duquesne, A., 'La restructuration de l'organisation judiciaire', in: Materne, J. & Misson, L. (eds.), *Pour une justice nouvelle. Propositions de réforme*, Diegem: Kluwer, 1999, p. xi-xx.

Elliott & Vernon 2000
Elliott, C. & Vernon, C., *French legal system*, Harlow: Longman, 2000.

Fettweis 1961
Fettweis, A., *Eléments de l'organisation judiciaire*, Liège: Presses universitaires de Liège, 1961.

Erdman & De Leval 2004
Erdman, F. and De Leval, G., *Justitiedialogen*, Brussels: FOD Justitie, 2004.

Farcy 1992
Farcy, J.-Cl., *Guide des archives judiciaires et pénitentiaires*, Paris: CNRS, 1992.

Franssen, Van Loon & Delrue 1997-1998
Franssen, G., Van Loon, F. and Delrue, S., 'Evolutie van de procesvoering voor de vredegerechten in Vlaanderen (1796-1990)', *Rechtskundig weekblad*, 1997-1998, p. 1241-1246.

Gadeyne 1997-2001
Gadeyne, G., *De rechtbank van eerste aanleg (en voorlopers)*, Brussels: ARA, 1997-2001, 2 vols.

Gilissen 1983
Gilissen, J., 'L'ordre judiciaire en Belgique au début de l'indépendance', *Journal des tribunaux*, 1983, p. 565-574 & p. 585-596.

Van Goethem 1997
Van Goethem, H., 'La Belgique sous l'annexion à la France, 1795-1813: l'acceptation des nouvelles institutions judiciaires et du droit français', in: Dauchy, S. *et al.* (eds.), *Auctoritates. Xenia R.C. Van Caenegem oblata: law making and its authors*, Brussels: KVAB, 1997, p. 289-300.

Gouron 1996
Gouron, A., 'Jurisprudence de la Cour de Cassation et arrêts de règlement', in: Gouron, A, *et al.* (eds.), *Europäische und Amerikanische Richterbilder*, Frankfurt: Klostermann, 1996, p. 53-82.

Gridel 1994
Gridel, J.-P., 'A propos d'un éventuel retour du juge de paix: réminiscences prospectives', *Recueil Dalloz*, 1994, *Chronique*, p. 29-30.

De Haan 2005
De Haan, P., 'Compromisvoorstel integratie rechterlijke macht. Naar een verdeling van de hogere bestuursrechtspraak over de gerechtshoven', *Nederlands tijdschrift voor bestuursrecht*, 2005, p. 215-220.

Hallebeek & Sirks 2006
Hallebeek, J. and Sirks, A., *Nederland in Franse schaduw. Recht en bestuur in het koninkrijk Holland (1806-1810)*, Hilversum: Verloren, 2006.

Halpérin 1987
Halpérin, J.-L., *Le tribunal de cassation et les pouvoirs sous la Révolution*, Paris: LGDJ, 1987.

Halpérin 1990
Halpérin, J.-L., 'Le tribunal de cassation sous la Révolution (1790-1799)', in: Association des Magistrats et Anciens Magistrats de la Cour de Cassation (ed.), *Le tribunal et la cour de cassation*, Paris: Litec, 1990, p. 25-51.

Halpérin 1996
Halpérin, J.-L., 'Le juge et le jugement en France à l'époque révolutionnaire', in: Jacob, R. (ed.), *Le juge et le jugement dans les traditions juridiques européennes. Etudes d'histoire comparée*, Paris: Montchrestien, 1996, p. 233-256.

Heirbaut 2005
Heirbaut, D., *Hadden/hebben de Belgische ministers van justitie een civielrechtelijk beleid*, Mechelen: Kluwer, 2005.

Hilaire 1989
Hilaire, J., 'La Révolution et les juridictions consulaires', in: Badinter, R. (ed.), *Une autre justice. 1789-1799*, Paris: Fayard, 1989, p. 243-266.

Van Hille 1972
Van Hille, P., *De gerechtelijke hervorming van keizer Jozef II*, Tielt: Veys, 1972.

Holthöfer 1993
Holthöfer, E., *Beiträge zur Justizgeschichte der Niederlande, Belgiens und Luxemburgs im 19. und 20. Jahrhundert*, Frankfurt: Klostermann, 1993.

Humbert 1995
Humbert, S., 'Des apaiseurs aux juges de paix: une continuité en Flandre', in: Dauchy, S., Humbert, S. & Royer, J.-P. (eds), *Le juge de paix*, Lille: Centre d'histoire judiciaire Lille II, 1995, p. 5-30.

Humbert 1997
Humbert, S., 'Les élections des juges de paix dans le département du Nord (1790-an 11)', in: Rousseaux, X. & Lévry, R. (eds.), *Le pénal dans tous ses états. Justice, états et sociétés en Europe (XIIe et XXe siècles)*, Brussels: FUSL, 1997, p. 351-369.

Ithurbide 1970
Ithurbide, R., *Histoire critique des tribunaux de commerce*, Paris: LGDJ, 1970.

Janssens 1997
Janssens, R., 'Het Hof van Cassatie van België. Enkele hoofdmomenten van zijn ontwikkeling', *Legal history review*, XLV, 1977, p. 95-116.

Du Jardin 2001-2002
Du Jardin, J., 'Voltallige zitting voor een eenduidige interpretatie van het recht', *Rechtskundig weekblad*, 2001-2002, p. 649-676.

Jassogne 2000
Jassogne, C., 'La spécialisation et la mobilité des magistrats', *Journal des tribunaux*, 2000, p. 16-17.

Jugnot 1998
Jugnot, G., *Histoire de la justice française*, Paris: Litec, 1998.

Klomp 1998
Klomp, R., *Opkomst en ondergang van het handelsrecht*, Nijmegen: Ars Aequi, 1998.

Kortmann 1990
Kortmann, T., 'Twee eeuwen cassatie', *Rechtsgeleerd magazijn Themis*, IX, 1990, p. 417-419.

Krings 2003
Krings, E., 'Les travaux du commissaire royal à l'occasion de la réforme judiciaire', in: *Mélanges offerts à Silvio Marcus Helmons*, Brussels: Bruylant, 2003, p. 159-173.

Laenens 1999
Laenens, J., *Memorandum van de Vlaamse Juristenvereniging t.a.v. de federale formateur*, 1999, consulted on: <http://www.vlaamsejuristenvereniging.be/memovjv.htm> (last consulted 20 March 2007).

Laenens & Storme 2000
Laenens, J. and Storme, M. (eds.), *Dans l'encre de l'Octopus*, Brussels: Bruylant, 2000.

Lafon 2001
Lafon, J., *La Révolution française face au système judiciaire d'Ancien Régime*, Geneva: Droz, 2001.

Van Lang *et al.* 2005
Van Lang, A. *et al.*, 'Débat sur l'avenir du dualisme juridictionnel', *L'actualité juridique. Droit administratif*, 2005, p. 1760-1786.

Lecocq & Martinage 1983
Lecocq, P. and Martinage, R., 'L'inamovabilité de la magistrature française dans les constitutions au XIXe siècle et son application', in: Vanderlinden, J. *et al.* (eds.), *Liber amicorum John Gilissen*, Antwerp: Kluwer, 1983, p. 215-248.

Lemmens 1992
Lemmens, P., 'Rechterlijke organisatie', in: Lemmens, P. & Storme, M. (eds.), *Het vernieuwd gerechtelijk recht. Eerste commentaar bij de wet van 3 augustus 1992 tot wijziging van het Gerechtelijk Wetboek*, Antwerp: Kluwer, 1992, p. 49-70.

Lemonnier-Lesage 1999
Lemonnier-Lesage, V., *Les arrêts de règlement du Parlement de Rouen. Fin XVIème-XVIIème siècles*, Paris: Panthéon Assas, 1999.

Lemosse 1990
Lemosse, M., 'La Cour de cassation au dix-neuvième siècle', in: Association des magistrats et anciens magistrats de la Cour de cassation (ed.), *Le tribunal et la cour de cassation*, Paris: Litec, 1990, p. 53-70.

Logie 1998
Logie, J., *Les magistrats des cours et tribunaux en Belgique 1794-1814. Essai d'approche politique et sociale*, Geneva: Droz, 1998.

Logie 1998a
Logie, J., 'Les tribunaux de commerce dans les départements réunies', in: Leroy, A. (ed.), *Influence du modèle judiciaire français en Europe sous la Révolution et l'Empire*, Lille: ANRT, 1998, p. 67-79.

Métairie 2004
Métairie, G., *La justice de proximité. Une approche historique*, Paris: PUF, 2004.

Michielsen 2004
Michielsen, J., *The 'nazification' and 'denazification' of the courts in Belgium, Luxembourg and the Netherlands*, Maastricht, Maastricht University Press, 2004.

Miersch 2000
Miersch, M., *Der sogenannte référé législatif. Eine Untersuchung zum Verhältnis Gesetzgeber, Gesetz und Richteramt seit dem 18. Jahrhundert*, Baden-Baden: Nomos, 2000.

Moeykens 1992
Moeykens, F., 'Enkele kritische beschouwingen bij de nieuwe procedureregels vanaf 1 januari 1993', *Tijdschrift voor Brugse rechtspraak*, 1992, p. 145-162.

Montazel 1998
Montazel, L., *Entre fait et droit: histoire d'un pouvoir judiciaire. Les techniques de la cassation civile en France et en Allemagne au XIXème siècle*, Frankfurt: Klostermann, 1998.

Moorman van Kappen 1998
Moorman van Kappen, O., 'Les conceptions des rédacteurs de la constitution néerlandaise de 1814 sur la réforme judiciaire', in: Leroy, A. (ed.), *Influence du modèle judiciaire français en Europe sous la Révolution et l'Empire*, Lille: Université de Lille, 1998, p. 54-66.

Moorman van Kappen & Coppens 1997
Moorman van Kappen, O. and Coppens, E. (eds), *De Bataafse omwenteling en het recht*, Nijmegen: GNI, 1997.

Nandrin 1989
Nandrin, J.-P., 'Le juge unique en Belgique. Quelques jalons historiques d'une révolution tranquille', *Revue interdisciplinaire d'études juridiques*, XXIII, 1989, p. 97-111.

Nandrin 1992
Nandrin, J.-P., 'Eclairage historique. De l'homme "de bien" au juge professionnel ou l'histoire ambivalente d'un désenchantement', in: Benoit, G. *et al.* (eds.), *Compétences des juges de paix et des juges de police*, Bruges: Die Keure, 1992, p. 19-38.

Nandrin 1995
Nandrin, J.-P., *Hommes et normes. Le pouvoir judiciaire en Belgique aux premiers temps de l'indépendance (1832-1848)*, Louvain-la-Neuve: unpublished doctoral thesis, 1995 (for a summary see *Revue belge d'histoire contemporaine*, XXV, 1994-1995, p. 252-262).

Nandrin 1995a
Nandrin, J.-P., 'La justice de paix en Belgique de 1830 à 1848. Les raisons et les effets d'une professionalisation', in: Dauchy, S., Humbert, S. & Royer, J.-P. (eds.), *Le juge de paix*, Lille: Centre d'histoire judiciaire Lille II, 1995, p. 155-166.

Nandrin 1997
Nandrin, J.-P., 'Les nominations judiciaires en Belgique en 1832. Une entreprise de légitimation d'un jeune état indépendant', in: Rousseaux, X. & Lévy, R. (eds.), *Le pénal dans tous ses états. Justice, états et sociétés en Europe (XIIe et XXe siècles)*, Brussels: FUSL, 1997, p. 405-429.

Nandrin 1997a
Nandrin, J.-P., 'Justice de conciliation, proximité et carte judicaire de 1830 à nos jours. Une comparaison franco-belge', *Revue interdisciplinaire d'études juridiques*, XXXVIII, 1997, p. 85-102.

Nandrin 1998
Nandrin, J.-P., *La justice de paix à l'aube de l'indépendance de la Belgique (1832-1848). La professionnalisation d'une fonction judicaire*, Brussels: FUSL, 1998.

Nandrin 1998a
Nandrin, J.-P., 'L'acte de fondation des nominations politiques de la magistrature. La Cour de cassation à l'aube de l'indépendance belge', *Revue belge d'histoire contemporaine*, XXVIII, 1998, p. 153-202.

Van Orshoven 1994-1995
Van Orshoven, P., 'Administratieve rechtbanken? Ja of nee. Pleidooi voor een jurisdictioneel monisme', *Rechtskundig weekblad*, 1994-1995, p. 897-908.

Van Orshoven 1995
Van Orshoven, P., 'Spanning tussen norm en doel. Een voorbeeld uit het administratief contentieux', in: Van Gerven, W. *et al.* (eds.), *De norm achter de regel. Wet, doel en algemene rechtsbeginselen. Hommage aan Marcel Storme*, Ghent: Kluwer, 1995, p. 19-44.

Van Orshoven 2003
Van Orshoven, P., 'Wat we zelf beslechten, beslechten we beter! Enkele krachtlijnen voor een Vlaams gerechtelijk decreetboek', in: Taeymans, M. (ed.), *Defederalisering van justitie*, Ghent: Larcier, 2003, p. 115-118.

Payen 1997
Payen, P., *Les arrêts de règlement du Parlement de Paris. Dimension et doctrine*, Paris: PUF, 1997.

Payen 1999
Payen, P., *La physiologie de l'arrêt de règlement du parlement de Paris au XVIIIe siècle*, Paris: PUF, 1999.

Pene Vidari 1998
Pene Vidari, G., 'Les tribunaux de commerce en France et en Italie aux XVIIIe et XIXe siècle', in: Bouineau, J. *et al.* (eds.), *Hommage à Romuald Szramkiewicz*, Paris: Litec, 1998, p. 403-423.

Perrot 2004
Perrot, R., *Institutions judiciaires*, Paris: Monchrestien, 2004.

Rousseaux 1999
Rousseaux, X., 'Une architecture pour la justice. Organisation judiciaire et procédure pénale (1789-1815)', in: Rousseaux, X. *et al.* (eds.), *Revolution and criminal justice. French models and national traditions (1789-1830)*, Paris: Harmattan, 1999, p. 37-58.

Rousseaux & Nandrin 1993
Rousseaux, X. & Nandrin, J.-P., 'Le personnel judiciaire en Belgique à travers les révolutions (1780-1832). Quelques hypothèses de recherches et premiers résultats', in: Arnould, M. *et al.* (eds.), *Le personnel politique dans la transition de l'Ancien Régime au nouveau Régime en Belgique (1780-1830)*, Kortrijk: UGA, 1993, p. 13-69.

Rousseaux & Tixhon 2004
Rousseaux, X. & Tixhon, A., 'Les statistiques judiciaires belges (1830-2000)', in: Heirbaut, D., Rousseaux, X. & Velle, K. (eds), *Histoire politique et sociale de la justice en Belgique de 1830 à nos jours*, Bruges: Die Keure, 2004, p. 163-183.

Rousseaux & Weber 2004
Rousseaux, X. & Weber, D., '*Les politiques pénales en Belgique*', in: Heirbaut, D., Rousseaux, X. & Velle, K. (eds), *Histoire politique et sociale de la justice en Belgique de 1830 à nos jours*, Bruges: Die Keure, 2004, p. 63-102.

Van Royen 1989
Van Royen, H., *De herstructureringspogingen van de rechterlijke macht in België: de vredegerechtsomschrijvingen*, Hamme: Harry van Royen, 1989.

Royer 1979
Royer, J.-P., *La société judiciaire depuis le XVIIIe siècle*, Paris: PUF, 1979.

Royer 2001
Royer, J.-P., *Histoire de la justice en France de la monarchie absolue à la République*, Paris: PUF, 2001.

Royer, Martinage & Lecocq 1982
Royer, J.-P., Martinage, R. & Lecocq, P., *Juges et notables aux XIXe siècle*, Paris: PUF, 1982.

Scholl 1956
Scholl, S., 'De Gentse werkrechtersraad, de oudste van België (1810-1859)', *De gids op maatschappelijk gebied*, XLVII, 1956, p. 1047-1080.

Seidel 1990
Seidel, J., 'Herziening van de rechterlijke organisatie in Nederland', *Tijdschrift voor bestuurswetenschappen en publiekrecht*, XLIV, 1990, p. 94-97.

Van Soest 1988
Van Soest, J., *De Hoge Raad der Nederlanden: 1838-1988: een portret*, Zwolle: Tjeenk Willink, 1988.

Stein & Rueb 2005
Stein, P. & Rueb, A., *Compendium van het burgerlijk procesrecht*, Deventer: Kluwer, 2005.

Storme 1995
Storme, M., *Ik die bij de sterren sliep en 't haar der ruimten droeg. De metabletica van het procesrecht*, Gent: Mys en Breesch, 1995.

Storme 1995a
Storme, M., 'Slotrede', in: Lemmens, P. & Storme, M. (eds.), *Vertrouwen in het gerecht*, Diegem: Kluwer, 1995, p. 123-126.

Storme 2005
Storme, M. (ed.), *De Hoge Raad voor de Justitie na vier jaar gewogen*, Brugge: Die Keure, 2005.

Storme 2005a
Storme, M., 'Slotrede', in: Linsmeau, J. & Storme, M. (eds.), *Het gerechtelijk recht. Waarom en waarheen*, Brugge: Die Keure, 2005, p. 145-150.

Szramkiewicz 1995
Szramkiewicz, R., 'Les tribunaux de commerce: une longue histoire dans la justice économique', *Justices. Revue de droit processuel*, I, 1995, p. 7-14.

Terlinden 1918
Terlinden, C., 'La magistrature belge sous l'occupation allemande. Souvenirs d'une guerre. Août 14-octobre 18', *Belgique judiciaire*, 1918, p. 1169-1182 & p. 1201-1225.

Tixhon 1999
Tixhon, A., 'Contrôler la justice, construire l'état et surveiller le crime au XIXe siècle. Naissance et développement de la statistique judiciaire en Belgique (1795-1901)', *Revue belge d'histoire contemporaine*, LXXVII, 1999, p. 965-1001.

Velle 1999
Velle, K., 'De materiële en territoriale bevoegdheid van het vredegerecht in België (1850-1940): een bijdrage tot de politieke geschiedenis van justitie', *Standen en landen. Nieuwsbrief*, VI, 1999, 8-21.

Verwoerd 1982
Verwoerd, J., 'Gerechtelijke reorganisatie in veranderd perspectief: België, de bondsrepubliek Duitsland en Nederland', *Tegenspraak*, 1982, p. 330-345.

Vincent *et al.* 2003
Vincent, J., Guinchard, S., Montagnier, G. & Varinard, A., *Institutions judiciaires. Organisation. Juridictions. Gens de justice*, Paris: Dalloz, 2003.

Vuye 1998
Vuye, H., 'Justitie morgen: de toekomst van de vrederechters in een breder perspectief', *Tijdschrift van de vrede- en politierechters*, 1998, p. 413-438.

Warlomont 1959
Warlomont, R., 'Les idées modernes de Joseph II sur l'organisation judiciaire dans les Pays-Bas autrichiens', *Legal history review*, XXVII, 1959, p. 269-289

Witte 1981
Witte, E., 'Het Belgische ambtenarenparlement, 1831-1848', *Revue belge de philologie et d'histoire*, LIX, 1981, p. 828-882.

M. Petrak

PRIVATE OR PUBLIC JUSTICE? MODERN DISPUTES ON THE ORIGIN OF CIVIL PROCEDURE IN ROMAN LAW

1. Introduction

The aim of this paper is to analyse the most important modern attempts to reconstruct the origin and development of civil procedure - particularly in ancient Roman law - and try to answer the vexed question of whether the earliest Roman civil procedure is one type of *private justice* or whether it has the characteristic features of *public justice* from its inception.

As a starting point, it is important to note that the theory that arbitration, i.e. the most important embodiment of *private justice*, is the original and the oldest form of civil procedure is commonly encountered in contemporary civil procedural law scholarship. In order to understand the basic features of this theory and its significance for contemporary civil procedural law, we shall briefly, *exempli gratia*, make some observations regarding the origin and development of civil procedure in the classic Croatian work in this discipline - *Građansko parnično procesno pravo* (*The Law of Procedure in Civil Litigation*) by Professors Siniša Triva and Mihajlo Dika, which is especially influenced by contemporary Italian and German doctrine.

At the very beginning of this book, in analysing the forms of protection of private rights, Triva and Dika give a brief overview of the development of the various forms in which legal protection is given.[1] In the opinion of the authors, the protection of private rights has not always been regulated by law. Initially, protection was provided only by means of private and unregulated *self-help*: 'An individual would undertake the measures he considered to be adequate and applicable in realising his presumed right'.[2] In the next stage of development, individuals were obliged to cooperate and eventually started to settle their disputes by means of agreements. Their disputes were settled by a third person in whom both parties had confidence. This person assumed the role of a chosen judge or

1 Triva & Dika 2004, p. 9 *et seq.*

2 Triva & Dika 2004, p. 9.

arbitrator by whose decision the conflicting parties would voluntarily abide. Eventually, the state sanctioned this form of the *private justice*, yet in subsequent stages of development, it gradually 'imposed on everyone an organised judicial apparatus, thus replacing private protection with organised state protection'.[3] However, this transition from *private justice* to the system of *public justice* did not take place 'overnight'; rather it was a long historical process. The transition period was characterised by a combination of elements of private arbitration and state legal protection. In this context, authors emphasise the Roman system of legal protection where:

> 'in the first stage, the dispute was settled before the state judicial organs *(in jure)* with the purpose of formulating the content of hypothetical legal protection while in the second stage the admissibility of the request for legal protection was decided before a chosen judge in whom the parties had confidence *(in judicio)*'.[4]

Following the transitional period, the system of state legal protection prevailed and in the final stage of development the state 'also took over the enforcement of its decisions'.[5]

According to this reconstruction of events, the initial process emerged when *self-help* was superseded as a mode of protection by private arbitration which was then in turn replaced by the protection provided by the state judiciary. *Self-help – private justice – public justice* are therefore the successive stages in the development of legal protection.

However, it must be emphasised that the theory that *private justice* in the form of arbitration was the earliest type of civil procedure did not originally emerge and develop within the field of civil procedure scholarship. Rather, it developed within modern Roman law scholarship in response to complex issues regarding the origin and development of Roman civil procedure and was adopted by other legal disciplines from there.

2. Private Justice as the Origin of Roman Civil Procedure?

The father of the theory of *private justice* in the form of arbitration as the earliest type of civil procedure was the famous Austrian Romanist Moriz Wlassak (1854-1939) whose works, written during the first quarter of the 20th century, gave this theory a systematic treatment. The following statement by Wlassak perhaps best describes the essence of his research on the origin of Roman civil procedure: 'My goal was and still is to create a firm foundation for the thesis that Roman civil procedure originated from arbitration (*Schiedsgericht*)'.[6] Taking Wlassak's statement as a starting point, it is not difficult to understand why his studies on the origin and

3 Triva & Dika 2004, p. 10.
4 Triva & Dika 2004, p. 10.
5 Triva & Dika 2004, p. 10.
6 Wlassak 1904, p. 139: 'Mein Ziel war und ist es, eine haltbare Grundlage zu schaffen für die These: der römische Privatprozeß hat seinem Ursprung im Schiedsgericht'.

development of Roman civil procedure eventually became known in Roman law scholarship as *Schiedsgerichtstheorie*.[7]

2.1. *Private Arbitration as the Primary form of Roman Civil Procedure?*

According to Wlassak's analysis of the origin and development of Roman civil procedure, *self-help* was the primary form of dispute resolution. In the subsequent historical phase, the parties to a dispute agreed, on the basis of a contract, to entrust the resolution of their dispute regarding a certain right to an unbiased third party. Wlassak was of the opinion that in this manner, *self-help* had been replaced by *private justice* in the form of arbitration.[8] Further historical development of this procedure moved in the direction of *public justice*. It was characterised by the state gradually assuming control over private arbitration litigation, i.e. private arbitration litigation becoming subject to control by the state judiciary. This phenomenon can be clearly perceived in the basic structures of *legis actio* and formulary procedures, i.e. in their bipartite division into proceedings before the state magistrate or *praetor* (*in iure*) and proceedings before a chosen judge (*apud iudicem*).[9] Wlassak calls this form of procedure 'semi-state procedure' (*der halbstaatliche Prozeß*).[10] One could also define it as *semi-public justice*. However, according to Wlassak, the contractual basis of the procedure as its oldest element could still be recognised at this stage of development. The contractual basis of the procedure was recognised by Wlassak in the act of *litis contestatio*. Generally speaking, few sources referring to *litis contestatio* in the *legis actio* procedure have been preserved. From these it may be seen that the act of *litis contestatio* took place before a magistrate, i.e. *praetor* (*in iure*) in such a way that the parties to the dispute would call in several Roman citizens to witness the presentation of the matter in dispute (*lis*)[11] so that later, if necessary, they could testify in the proceedings *apud iudicem* regarding the dispute between the litigants.[12] Based on these facts, Wlassak contended that *litis contestatio* was essentially a contract between the litigants made before the *praetor* and in the presence of the

7 Kaser & Hackl 1996, p. 29 *et seq.*; Talamanca 1987, p. 6.

8 See e.g., Wlassak 1889, p. 54 *et seq.*; Wlassak 1917, p. 222; Wlassak 1921, p. 247: Wlassak 1924, p. 147 *et seq.*

9 For a general discussion of the basic characteristics of *legis actio* procedure see Talamanca 1987, p. 4 *et seq.*; Kaser & Hackl 1996, p. 34 *et seq.*; Honsell, Mayer-Maly & Selb 1987, p. 506 *et seq.* all with references an to extensive bibliography; for a general discussion of the origin, structure and basic characteristics of the formulary procedure see Talamanca 1987, p. 25 *et seq.*; Honsell, Mayer-Maly & Selb 1987, p. 524 *et seq.*; Kaser & Hackl 1996, p. 151 *et seq.*, with detailed references to an extensive bibliography on these issues.

10 Wlassak 1921, p. 247.

11 The very name *litis contestatio* was given due to the presence of witnesses in the process of presenting the disputed matter (*contestari litem*); Kaser & Hackl 1996, p. 75 *et seq.*

12 In his analysis of the *legis actio* procedure, *Gaius* does not mention the act of *litis contestatio* but one definition of the term '*contestari litem*' is preserved in *Festus*' extracts from the dictionary of rare words (*De verborum significatu*) by the grammarian *Verrius Flaccus: 'Contestari litem dicuntur duo aut plures adversarii, quod ordinato iudicio utraque pars dicere solet: "Testes estote"'*; see Lindsay 1913, s.v. *contestari litem*, 50.

summoned witnesses. In this contract, the litigants set forth the matter in dispute, chose a judge (*iudex*) to settle their dispute and agreed to abide by his decision. The contractual contents of *litis contestatio* were particularly discernible in the structure of the formulary procedure which was devoid of the strict formalism of the preceding period.[13] In the last stage of development of Roman civil procedure, i.e. in the period of *cognitio* (extraordinary) procedure, there was no bipartite division of the procedure and no contractual appointment of a *iudex*. The *iudex* became a state official who conducted a unified procedure, from filing a civil suit to pronouncing a judgement. Therefore, according to Wlassak, the introduction of the cognition procedure marked the introduction of a pure state procedure, i.e. a system of *public justice* as such.

This interpretation is based on an assumption of the 'strict gradual development' (*streng stufenmaßige Entwicklung*) of Roman procedure. As we have seen, the stages of this development were as follows: 1) *self-help*; 2) *private justice* in the form of arbitration; 3) *semi-public justice*; and 4) purely *public justice*. Wlassak's reconstruction of the origin and development of Roman civil procedure had a significant impact on the study of Roman law during the first half of the 20th century and virtually became *communis opinio doctorum*.[14]

In Croatian studies of Roman law, Wlassak's views were followed in particular by Marijan Horvat's early works. This may be easily recognised in Horvat's *Savremeni nazori o postanku i značaju dvodiobe rimskog privatnog procesa* (Contemporary Opinions on the Origin and Significance of the Bipartite Division of Roman Civil Procedure) from 1938, a detailed synthesis of scholarly thoughts on the development of Roman civil procedure at the time.[15]

However, Wlassak's theory also had a fundamental impact beyond the sphere of Roman legal studies. Some important authors believed that the stage of *self-help* was replaced by *private justice* in the form of arbitration as the primary type of legal procedure in other ancient legal cultures as well such as in ancient Babylonian and ancient Greek law.[16]

13 Wlassak 1889, p. 59 *et seq.*; Wlassak 1920, p. 9 *et seq.*

14 Koschaker, Rabel, Biondi, Mazeaud, Betti, Heuss, Bozza, Carreli, etc. followed Wlassak's interpretation; for bibliographical data of the works of these and other subsequent authors see Broggini 1957, p. 7, fn. 14.

15 See: Horvat 1938, p. 149 *et seq.*; Eisner & Horvat 1948, p. 541 *et seq.*

16 For ancient Babylonian law see Lautner 1922; for ancient Greek law see Steinwenter 1925. It is worth mentioning that Steinwenter came to the conclusion that private arbitration litigation represented the original form of the ancient Greek procedure. Such a conclusion was based on an analysis of the court scene depicted on Achilles's shield which Homer described in the Iliad, Canto 18, verses 497-508. According to Steinwenter's interpretation, the person called *istor* mentioned in these verses, whom the parties to the dispute had turned to, was actually a private arbitrator. Therefore, according to this author, the court scene was likewise an archaic confirmation of the correctness of the theory of private justice in the form of arbitration as the oldest type of legal procedure; see Steinwenter 1925, p. 36 *et seq.* The authors who have analysed this court scene recently (e.g. H.J. Wolf, G. Thür), have, for valid reasons, abandoned the *Schiedsgerichtstheorie* as an interpretative paradigm of the archaic Greek procedure; see *amplius* Thür 1998, p. 432 *et seq.* On the Romanist criticism of this theory see *amplius infra* § 2.3).

Moreover, it is important to emphasise in this context that, as we have seen, contemporary civil procedure scholarship also followed Wlassak's paradigm of the origin and development of civil procedure. This is very obvious from *inter alia*, the aforementioned brief overview of the development of the various forms of legal protection by the Croatian authors Triva and Dika.[17]

2.2. *Litis Contestatio as the Contractual Basis of Roman Civil Procedure?*

The validity of the theory of *private justice* in the form of arbitration as the oldest type of Roman civil procedure basically depends on one key issue: can we really regard the *litis contestatio* of the *legis actio* procedure as representing – in its essence – a formal act of a contractual nature and is it a direct descendant of those primary contracts on private arbitration which supplanted *self-help*?

The first Romanist who presented this thesis *in nuce* was the famous German lawyer Rudolph von Jhering (1818-1892). In his opinion, briefly outlined in the first part of his epochal work *Geist des römischen Rechts*,[18] the origins of legal procedure among the archaic Romans were completely different from all other civilisations. Some peoples had initially transcended *self-help* and settled the disputes in their communities by resorting to the supernatural powers of their deities in the form of different types of trials by ordeal, prophecies, casting lots and so on. Others had replaced *self-help* by appointing authorities to settle disputes in their communities. In both cases, the parties to the dispute had to appear before the court of some superior authority, either divine or human, i.e. before one form of *public justice*. Jhering, however, was of the opinion that this had not been the case during the archaic Roman period. The Romans differed from all other peoples in having transcended the *self-help* stage by introducing the following types of *private justice*: a contractual form of resolving legal disputes (*'vertragsmäßige Entscheidung der Rechtsstreitigkeiten'*) through the institution of a defence judge, i.e. an arbitrator (*Schiedsrichter*) or an extrajudicial oath taking.[19] Therefore, Jhering argued that the original procedural form of settling disputes in ancient Rome had been arbitration as a type of *private justice*. Parties to a dispute would enter into a contract to appoint an arbitrator. They did not submit themselves to an arbitrator as some sort of public authority but rather voluntarily bound themselves to abide by his decision based on a private contract. According to Jhering, this primary contractual form of settling disputes as a vestige of former purely *private justice* was also preserved in the solemn forms of *legis actio* procedure. While Jhering regarded private arbitration as having already been placed under state jurisdiction in the *legis actio* procedure, it was possible to recognise the contractual basis of the entire procedure in the act of *litis contestatio*. As we have already stated, it may be concluded based on the small number of existing sources dealing with *litis contestatio* in *legis actio* procedure, that this act took place before a *praetor* (*in iure*) in such a manner that the parties to the

17 See *supra* § 1; cf. also Juhart 1961, p. 1 *et seq.*; Ude 1980, p. 41.

18 See Von Jhering 1878, p. 108 & p. 167 *et seq.*

19 Von Jhering 1878, p. 167.

dispute summoned several Roman citizens to serve as witnesses when the matter in dispute was presented (*lis*) so that in the subsequent proceedings *apud iudicem*, they could, if necessary, testify as to what the matter being disputed between the parties actually was.[20] On the basis of the aforementioned sources, Jhering argued that *litis contestatio* was, in essence, a contract entered into by the parties to the dispute before the *praetor* and in the presence of the summoned witnesses. In this contract, the parties would define the matter in dispute, chose a judge (*iudex*) to settle their dispute and agree to abide by his decision.[21] Based on Jhering's analysis, we may conclude that the contract by which the judge was chosen was the oldest element of *legis actio* procedure. Jhering was of the opinion that *private justice* in the form of arbitration had been agreed upon by means of such contracts as the oldest procedural form for settling disputes in ancient Rome. Over time, however, private arbitration came under the control of the public authorities. This historical development can be demonstrated mainly by the fact that litigation was divided into two parts. In the first historically more recent part of the procedure conducted before the *praetor* (*in iure*), the magistrate would examine whether all the prescribed preconditions for rendering legal protection had been fulfilled.[22] If this were the case, the parties would, with the *praetor's* consent, choose a judge who rendered a judgement in the second stage of the procedure (*apud iudicem*). According to Jhering, the latter originated directly from private arbitration, as the oldest Roman form of litigation. Jhering believed that the state had taken over private arbitration without changing its basic features.[23] In such a way, the earlier private arbitrator was replaced by a *iudex* chosen from an official list of judges (*album iudicum*); yet his role remained unchanged. However, in contrast to a private arbitrator, the judgement of the *iudex* was authorised by the state due to the extremely important role of the *praetor* in the entire procedure.

Jhering's understanding of the act of *litis contestatio*, as a contract for private arbitration replacing *self-help* was, as we have seen, adopted and elaborated by Wlassak as a sort of Archimedean point for his reflections on the origin and development of Roman civil procedure from which his theory of private arbitration as the original form of civil procedure (*Schiedsgerichtstheorie*) was derived.

It has already been pointed out that there are very few direct sources on *litis contestatio* in the *legis actio* procedure. On the basis of the most important one, *Festus'* previously cited interpretation of the concept '*contestari litem*', we can see clearly only that the parties to the dispute summoned several Roman citizens to witness the presentation of the matter in dispute.[24] According to the prevailing interpretation of *Festus'* fragment among 19th century Roman law scholarship, the witnesses appeared before the *praetor* only at the very end of the *in iure* proceedings in

20 *Festus'* interpretation of the concept *contestari litem, supra* note 11.

21 Von Jhering 1878, p. 168 *et seq*.

22 Since the oldest *legis actio* procedure was, as we have said, conducted in a strictly formal way, the *praetor* had to observe quite closely as to whether the parties were fully abiding by the prescribed procedural ritual.

23 Von Jhering 1878, p. 172, fn. 73.

24 *Festus'* explanation of the concept *contestari litem, supra* note 11.

response to a joint ritual invitation by the parties: '*Testes estote*!' Therefore, prior to Wlassak's work, the prevailing view was that *litis contestatio* referred only to the act of summoning the witnesses before whom the content of the previous hearing was then recapitulated as the final stage of the *in iure* proceedings. In this way, the witnesses were in a position to testify, if necessary, in the *apud iudicem* proceedings as to what the matter in dispute between the parties was.[25] However, as we have already seen, Wlassak interpreted the concept of *litis contestatio* in this oldest form of *legis actio* procedure (*legis actio sacramento*) in a much broader way. According to him, the summoning of the witnesses was merely one phenomenon accompanying the procedure. The essence of *litis contestatio* consisted in the solemn appearance of the witnesses before the *praetor*, whereby the parties presented the matter in dispute and agreed that their dispute would be settled by a chosen judge, whose decision they would abide by.[26] On the basis of this interpretation, Wlassak drew the conclusion that *litis contestatio* actually represented a contract between the parties to the dispute, concluded before the *praetor* and the witnesses *via* the strict forms of the oldest *legis actio* procedure. By means of this contract, the matter in dispute was presented and a judge was chosen to settle the dispute. However, the contractual nature of *litis contestatio* is not easily recognisable in the solemn forms of *legis actio* procedure. The very nature of *litis contestatio*, according to the aforementioned author, can fully be recognised only in the formulary procedure, purged of the strict formalism of the preceding period. Wlassak argued that, regardless of the formal aspects, the content of this contract had always been the same. Moreover, this interpretation of *litis contestatio* was also crucial to understanding the oldest stage of Roman legal procedure, i.e. that which had preceded the emergence of *public justice* as the state judicial authority. For if *litis contestatio* were a procedural contract between the parties, presenting the matter in dispute and choosing the judge by whose decision they would abide, then it would have the same content as a private arbitration contract. According to Wlassak's historical reconstruction, it could be concluded that *litis contestatio* developed from private arbitration contracts, and that the Romans, prior to the emergence of the *legis actio* procedure, had settled their disputes through *private justice* in the form of arbitration as the primary type of legal procedure. Private arbitration was placed under the control of the state judiciary in the *legis actio* procedure as the nucleus of an emerging system of *public justice*. This explains how the phenomenon of a bipartite division of the procedure emerged, whereby the first part was conducted before a state magistrate (*in iure*) and the second before a judge chosen by the parties (*apud iudicem*).[27] Following Wlassak's deductions, it can be concluded that the bipartite structure of *legis actio* and formulary procedure represent the transitional stage in the development of Roman

25 This interpretation was first developed in 1827 by a Swiss Romanist (F. Keller) in Keller 1827 and it eventually became generally accepted; see e.g. Kaser & Hackl 1996, p. 291.

26 See e.g., Wlassak 1889, p. 81 *et seq.*; cf. Eisner & Horvat 1948, p. 556, fn. 2; Kaser & Hackl 1996, p. 291 *et seq.*

27 See Wlassak 1889, p. 69 *et seq.* & p. 81 *et seq.*; cf. Eisner & Horvat 1948, p. 556, fn. 2; Kaser & Hackl 1996, p. 291 *et seq.*

civil procedure between the former order of *private justice* and the future system of *public justice*.

2.3. *Criticism of the Theory of Private Justice as the Origin of Roman Civil Procedure in Modern Studies of Roman Law*

As we have already said, Wlassak's theory of *private justice* in the form of arbitration as the primary form of Roman civil procedure (*Schiedsgerichtstheorie*), which was based mainly on his interpretation of *litis contestatio* as a procedural contract, dominated the Romanist literature of the first half of the 20th century. From there it penetrated to other disciplines as well, above all civil procedure scholarship.

However, in the course of the 1940s and 1950s, significant Romanist works, published by Kaser and Biscardi, completely refuted this thesis on the contractual character of *litis contestatio* in *legis actio* procedure. Contemporary Romanist discussions of *litis contestatio* have been based on the insights of these authors.[28] According to the current prevailing interpretation, *litis contestatio* in *legis actio* procedure consisted of solemn acts of the parties to the dispute before the *praetor* and the witnesses whereby the matter in dispute was defined.[29] There are, in fact, a number of arguments related to both form and content that run counter to Wlassak's interpretation and these are advanced today to deny the contractual character of *litis contestatio* in *legis actio* procedure. From the formal point of view it has been argued that the solemn acts making up *litis contestatio* did not correspond

28 See Kaser 1944, p. 126; Biscardi 1953, p. 461 *et seq.*; Biscardi 1955, p. 1 *et seq.*

29 See Kaser & Hackl 1996, p. 75 *et seq.* As we have already said (*supra* note 25), older Romanist doctrine, following Keller, held that the witnesses appeared before the *praetor* only after the parties had mutually and ritually summoned them: '*Testes estote*'. The witnesses were thus called at the very end of the proceedings *in iure*, in order that the content of the hearing could be restated before them. Therefore, according to this view, only the final stage of the proceedings *in iure* constituted an act of *litis contestatio;* see e.g. Keller 1827, p. 1 *et seq.*; Eisner & Horvat 1948, p. 556, fn. 2. Contrary to this older interpretation, the prevailing opinion among Romanists today is that several Roman citizens of legal age (*Quirites)* were summoned as witnesses in advance, at the very beginning of the proceedings *in iure*, in order to be present during the entire solemn acts by the parties to the dispute (e.g. vindication, counter-vindication, etc.) in presenting the disputed matter (*lis*). However, the ritual exclamation '*testes estote*' was directed to the Quirites by the parties to the dispute only at the end of the proceedings *in iure,* thereby binding them to their legal duty to testify about what they had seen and heard (cf. Lex XII Tab. 8, 22 where it is prescribed that a witness to an act, who later refuses to testify about it, is punished by being made *inprobus intestabilisque*). It is worth mentioning that this reconstruction has been made on the basis of some content-related similarities with Gaius, Inst. 2, 104, which concern the making of a testament *per aes et libram.* The testator summoned five Roman citizens of legal age to be present at the ritual of composing a solemn testament, yet only at the end of this ritual, i.e. with the final words of the nuncupative act, would he solemnly bind those five Qurites to be the witnesses to his testament: '*... itaque vos Quirites, testimonium mihi perhibetote*' (cf. Kaser & Hackl 1996, p. 76, fn. 40; on the original meaning of the nuncupative act see *amplius* Noailles 1949, p. 300 *et seq.* Bearing all these facts in mind, it should be emphasised once again that *litis contestatio* in *legis actio* procedure consisted of the litigants' solemn acts before the *praetor* and the witnesses in presenting the matter of the dispute.

to any known Roman contractual forms and that in earlier times, there was no general concept of a contract under which such an act could possibly be subsumed.[30] In terms of content, it is completely disputable whether the choice of a *iudex* formed part of *litis contestatio* or not. Moreover, the question arises of whether there was even the possibility for the parties to choose a judge in *legis actio* proceedings. Thus, for example, the Croatian Romanist Horvat, in his work entitled *Deux phases du procès romain* of 1959,[31] abandoned Wlassak's interpretation of the origin and development of this procedure, thus also significantly revising his own former views.[32] Horvat emphasised that there had been no room in *legis actio* procedure for any agreement among the litigants regarding the choice of a judge. For, as was obvious from Gaius' statements on *legis actio per iudicis arbitrive postulationem*, the plaintiff made a request to the *praetor* (*postulatio*) in a strictly prescribed form, whereupon the *praetor* would assign (*datio*) the judge.[33] Gaius also mentions this idea of assigning a judge in connection with *legis actio sacramento*.[34] The plaintiff's unilateral request is completely incompatible with any notion of the contractual appointment of a judge. Moreover, it is obvious that the *praetor* had the final word in assigning the judge and that the *datio iudicis* constituted first and foremost an act of the *praetor's* authority.[35] Bearing all of this in mind, we may conclude, in accordance with all of the existing sources, that *litis contestatio* in *legis actio* procedure did not by any means represent a contract between the parties to the dispute. Thus there was no historical connection between *litis contestatio* and its ostensible predecessor, the private arbitration agreement. This statement refutes the entire theory of *private justice* in the form of arbitration as the original type of Roman civil procedure (*Schiedsgerichtstheorie*). Therefore, the *legis actio* procedure cannot be regarded as a form of 'semi-state procedure' or 'semi-public justice' in which private arbitration was placed under the control of the state judiciary. This also refutes Wlassak's interpretation of the origin of a bipartite division in *legis actio* procedure. Finally, if *litis contestatio* was not a procedural contract, then there is no proof whatsoever for the statement that private arbitration represented the oldest procedural form for settling disputes in ancient Rome, one which, at some point in time, had replaced *self-help* and was in turn later transformed into the *legis actio* procedure, thus becoming partially 'state controlled'. Based on these arguments, Romanists gradually abandoned Wlassak's views during the second half of the 20th century.[36] The original Roman civil procedure was decidedly not *private justice* in

30 See Kaser & Hackl 1996, p. 79.

31 Horvat 1959, p. 163 *et seq.*; Horvat 1958, p. 137 *et seq.*

32 On Horvat's earlier views see *supra* § 2.1.

33 See Gaius, Inst. 4, 17 where it is said that the plaintiff, were the defendant to deny his claim, was obliged to direct the following words to the *praetor*: '*Quando tu negas, te praetor iudicem (sive arbitrum) postulo uti des*' ('Since you have denied, I request of you, *praetor*, to assign a judge/or arbitrator/').

34 See Gaius, Inst. 4, 15, where we find expressions like 'iudex daretur', 'dabatur iudex', or 'quam iudex datus esset'.

35 Horvat 1959, p. 139 *et seq.*: cf. Kaser & Hackl 1996, p. 79.

36 Cf. Talamanca 1987, p. 6 & p. 22 *et seq.*; Kaser & Hackl 1996, p. 29 *et seq.* & p. 79 *et seq.*

the form of arbitration whose partial 'state control' - i.e. control by the emerging apparatus of *public justice* - had subsequently given birth to the *legis actio* procedure.

3. Public Justice as the Origin of Roman Civil Procedure?

Proceeding from this Romanist criticism of the nature of *litis contestatio*, it is not difficult to conclude that, as a result, Jhering's basic insight that the origins of ancient Roman civil procedure were completely different from those of other ancient peoples' - a claim on which Wlassak's *Schiedsgerichtstheorie* was later based - also becomes highly questionable. According to Jhering, as we have already emphasised, only the Romans had transcended the stage of *self-help* by introducing *private justice* in the form of the contractual settlement of legal disputes ('*vertragsmäßige Entscheidung der Rechtsstreitigkeiten*'), whereas all other ancient peoples had abandoned *self-help* by introducing one or the other kind of primary *public justice*: either turning to the supernatural powers of their deities in the form of various types of trials by ordeal, prophecies, casting lots, and so on, or empowering certain authorities to settle disputes in their community.

Jhering's thesis and Wlassak's theoretical interpretation based on it undoubtedly represent extremely lucid and inspired attempts to explain the origin and development of Roman civil procedure. However, we believe that their explanations are inconsistent with archaic Roman reality as we shall try briefly to elaborate on the following pages of this paper.

First of all, it must be emphasised that Wlassak's theory of private arbitration as the oldest form of Roman civil procedure (*Schiedsgerichtstheorie*) was completely based on Jhering's theory of *self-help* (*Selbsthilfetheorie*). The core of this theory, as presented in the first part of Jhering's capital work entitled *Der Geist des römischen Rechts*,[37] consisted of the propositions that *self-help* was the primary form of settling disputes and that *self-help* had been supplanted by private arbitration. Consequently, it is not difficult to conclude that Jhering's *Selbsthilfetheorie* was based on the presumption that, in the pre-state era, there existed a situation of struggle of all against all, unhindered by any rules. Therefore, according to Jhering, the primary source of law resided neither in divine revelation nor in the will of the state but was to be sought in primordial physical power, in the power of the individual.[38] In archaic times, only from power (*vis*) could law (*ius*) emerge, with *self-help* as the primary form of the protection of rights. At that time an individual only had those rights that he could obtain and maintain through the strength of his own body (*Faustrecht*). Therefore, the only law that existed was the law of the stronger (*Recht des Stärkeren*), until the *self-help* phase was replaced by the contractual settlement of legal disputes. Therefore in turn, *private justice* in the form of arbitration was the oldest type of civil procedure. It must be mentioned here that in the later editions of the aforementioned work, Jhering emphasised that his overview of the genesis of Roman civil procedure, based on the idea of transcending *self-help* via the

37 See Von Jhering 1878, p. 108 et *seq*. & p. 167 *et seq*.
38 Von Jhering 1878, p. 107 *et seq*.

contractual settlement of legal disputes, represented only a hypothetical construction of legal prehistory (*'eine hypotetische Construction der Urzeit'*). Jhering expressly stated that his observations did not refer to that historical period in which the *iurisdictio* of the *praetor* as a function of *public justice* most certainly did not derive from the contractual will of the parties to a dispute but rather was assigned to him.[39] However, we do not find such reservations in the many later proponents of the theory of *self-help*, beginning with Wlassak,[40] who completely superimposed Jhering's hypothetical construction upon archaic Roman reality.

Since it is our intention to prove that the *Selbsthilfetheorie* and the *Schiedsgerichtstheorie* based thereupon are, as 'hypothetical constructions', quite inapplicable when analysing the origin of Roman civil procedure, we must briefly analyse the philosophical foundations of these theories. First of all, Jhering's construction of the 'zero point' of history when there was a state of struggle of all against all and the power of the stronger represented the sole law, obviously drew upon the naturalistic theories of the second half of the 19th century, primarily on Darwinist evolutionary hypotheses. Jhering transferred Darwin's principle of selection, i.e. the idea that only the fittest survived in a merciless and continual struggle for life, into the sphere of law (*Kampf ums Recht*), taking it as one of the basic starting points for his philosophical and legal observations. His legal thinking thus took on the contours of a sort of 'social Darwinism'. In this respect, Jhering's theses on the genesis of the law and legal procedure, as presented in his work *Der Geist des römischen Rechts* obviously stemmed from the aforementioned Darwinist paradigm.[41] However, by projecting the conclusions of natural science onto social reality, Jhering simultaneously lent a new form to some much older philosophical concepts containing analogous ideas. Here we are referring primarily to the ideas of the English philosopher Thomas Hobbes (1588-1679) according to whom the primary, i.e. natural human state (*status naturalis*) was a struggle of all against all (*bellum omnium in omnes*).[42] Prior to the emergence of the state, there reigned only the law of self-preservation and egoism. Every individual had a natural right to all things which obviously resulted in numerous conflicts. However, the fear of death and destruction gradually forced individuals to end this struggle. Hobbes was of the opinion that it was a basic law of nature and a general rule of the mind that everyone would strive for peace. However, this state of peace could only be achieved by creating state authority. Therefore, reason itself demanded the creation of the state which came into being on the basis of a social contract in which all individuals renounced a certain part of their natural rights and transferred them to the sovereign authority.[43] Even this slight reference to some of Hobbes' basic ideas

39 Von Jhering 1878, p. 169, fn. 71.

40 On Wlassak's views, see *amplius supra* § 2.

41 On Jhering's social Darwinism see, for example, Wieacker 1967, p. 450 *et seq.*; Wieacker 1969, p. 9 *et seq.* & p. 25 *et seq.*; Wieacker 1973, p. 63 *et seq.*

42 Hobbes used the expression *bellum omnium in omnes* for the first time in his work *De cive* (1, 12) from 1642.

43 On Hobbes's philosophical and political ideas see, for example, McPherson 1986, p. 9 *et seq.*, and the bibliography listed on p. 65.

on the origin of the state will suffice to show how Jhering's thoughts on the origin of Roman civil procedure had been influenced by such philosopheme to a considerable degree. It seems obvious that the *Selbsthilfetheorie* is only one theoretical variation on the thesis of the natural human condition as 'a struggle of all against all'.[44] Moreover, Jhering's thesis that the Romans, unlike other peoples, had transcended the stage of *self-help* in a rational way, i.e. by contractually settling disputes, is obviously nothing else than an application of the concept of the social contract to a discussion of the genesis of Roman civil procedure. In support of this statement, we must mention that in his *Der Geist des römishen Rechts* Jhering also advocated the view that a social contract had been the basis for the creation of the state.[45] Therefore we may conclude that Hobbes' concept of the social contract constituted the deepest philosophical root of Wlassak's theory of *private justice* in the form of arbitration as the earliest type of Roman civil procedure (*Schiedsgerichtstheorie*).

On the basis of a detailed analysis, we have already established that the latter theory, according to which *self-help* was replaced by *private justice* in the form of the contractual settlement of disputes, does not correspond to historical reality.[46] What then is the status of the other tenets of which the theory of *self-help* consists? Leaving aside the most recent scientific insights that completely challenge the Darwinist paradigm,[47] as well as the question of whether such a paradigm may be applied to an analysis of interpersonal relations,[48] we shall confine ourselves to the conclusion that this picture of the hypothetical 'zero point' of history where total chaos and anarchy reign and wild individuals wander around brandishing sticks, desperately struggling for survival, is utterly ahistorical. There are simply no sources and no evidence on the basis of which one might establish that even in prehistory such primordial and 'natural' conditions existed, characterised by the absence of any community, authority or rules or in which naked physical strength was the only law, and *self-help* the only protection.[49] The evidence we possess on Palaeolithic peoples, thanks primarily to the discovery of their cave drawings, has shown that

44 On Hobbes philosophical and political tenets as the forerunners of Jhering's *Selbsthilfetheorie* see Staszkow 1963, p. 86 *et seq.*; cf. also Kaser 1951, p. 27 *et seq.*

45 See Von Jhering 1878, p. 209 *et seq.* & p. 216 *et seq.*

46 See *supra* § 2.3.

47 See, for example, Lings 1991.

48 Having analysed the (in)applicability of the Darwinist paradigm in analysing the oldest Roman legal rules, the Roman and civil law scholar from Göttingen, Okko Behrends, rightly emphasised that 'the legal rules valid among people are something completely different from the stereotypes of animal behaviour acquired by natural selection'; Behrends 1982, p. 73, fn. 57.

49 For example, even Eisenhart, in his work *Statum naturalem Hobbesii ex corpore iuris civilis profligatum et profligandum* from 1744 categorically stated in connection with Hobbes' idea of the natural conditions that '*statum illum generis humani quem Hobbesius fingit nunquam fuisse*' ('the state of the human race which Hobbes imagined never existed') and that *Hobbesi doctrina veterum iurisconsultorum philosophiae plane contraria* ('Hobbes' doctrine is completely contrary to the philosophy of the ancient lawyers'); cit. according to Staszków 1963, p. 87. The same statements are completely applicable to Jhering's theory of *self-help*. Thus, for example, Behrends, in his work of 1982, noted that this theory was *una construzione puramente astorica*; see Behrends 1982, p. 75; cf. also Broggini 1959, p. 113 *et seq.*; Kaser & Hackl 1996, p. 28 *et seq.*

prehistoric man lived in organised communities bound by numerous commands and religious taboos. In addition, contemporary ethnological discoveries regarding 'primitive' cultures have resulted in similar findings.[50] These facts undeniably speak in favour of the thesis that Hobbes' *status naturalis* or Jhering's stage of *self-help* were only rationalist speculations devoid of any essential compatibility with (pre)historical reality.[51] In any case, this paradigm is, due to its ahistorical nature, inapplicable as a methodological model in attempting to explain the genesis of law and legal procedure just as, for example, was the Marxist utopian vision of an original genteel order, a classless society of free and equal individuals whose decay resulted in the creation of the state as an expression of the class society and an organ of class violence.[52]

As opposed to Jhering and Wlassak, and contrary to the *Selbsthilfetheorie* and *Schiedsgerichtstheorie*, which are based on assumptions regarding the ostensible 'progressiveness' and 'rationality' of the Romans who were apparently the only people capable of transcending the *self-help* stage via freely contracted arbitration as a form of *private justice*, more recent Romanist studies have advocated the idea that the earliest Romans, like all other archaic peoples, were wont to settle disputes in their community by turning to the supernatural powers of their deities, in the form of various types of trials by ordeal or prophecies as a kind of primary *public justice*.[53]

In short, the most persuasive current theory on the topic is that archaic Romans settled their disputes in the form of a judgement of the supreme God (*Iuppiter*), based on the augural rituals (*augurium*) and proclaimed by the Roman king (*rex*) as the organ of *public justice*.[54] This theory is founded on an analysis of the gestual, verbal and symbolic similarities of ritual structures between the act of

50 See, for example, Mayer-Maly 1985, p. 9 *et seq.*

51 It may be correct to say, as has often been emphasised, that Hobbes' construction of 'the state of nature' *(status naturalis)* was only a speculative reflection of the England of his era, which was torn by the civil war (1642-49) and general anarchy and lawlessness; cf., for example, Hampton 1986, p. 5. If we accept this view, we might draw the conclusion that the *status naturalis* was by no means man's primary condition but rather that the very opposite, i.e. the 'anti-evolutionist' view, according to which 'there have been no barbaric conditions which did not result from some collapsed culture', was correct; cit. Schelling 1860, p. 12.

52 Cf. Kaser & Hackl 1996, p. 28 *et seq.*

53 See, for example, Noailles 1949, p. 72 *et seq.*; Broggini 1957, p. 29 *et seq.*; Kaser & Hackl 1996, p. 29 *et seq.*, with references to supplementary literature. It is interesting to note how the idea that the earliest Roman civil procedure originated from trial by ordeal (*Gottesurteil*) as a form of divine *public justice* had also been briefly discussed by Rudolph von Jhering in his incomplete and posthumously published work entitled *Die Vorgeschichte der Indoeuropäer*; see Von Jhering 1894, p. 436. Unfortunately, Jhering did not have time to develop this idea in more detail or to incorporate it into his theory of the origin and development of Roman civil procedure. This idea might have encouraged him to revise some of the basic theses presented in his *Der Geist des römischen Rechts,* above all his view that the Romans, unlike some other peoples, had not transcended *self-help* by turning to the supernational powers of their deities in the form of various trials by ordeal, prophecies, casting lots, i.e. by introducing the religiously based order of *public justice*, but rather by means of *private justice* in the form of contractual settlement of legal disputes (*vertragsmäßige Entscheidung der Rechtsstreitigkeiten*).

54 The first Romanist who presented this view as the coherent theory with convincing reasoning was Gerardo Broggini in Broggini 1957, p. 24 *et seq.*

vindicatio in *legis actio* procedure and the solemn act of *inauguratio* of the Roman kings[55] (a very inspirative theme which deserves a separate research).

4. Facit

As we have seen, contemporary studies of civil procedural law still follow the theory of *private justice* in the form of arbitration as an explanatory paradigm for the origin and development of civil procedure.[56] In the opinion of this author, it is time that contemporary civil procedure scholarship abandons this obsolete view on the topic and takes into account more recent Romanist reconstructions of the origin and development of Roman civil procedure, starting from the insight that the religious based rituals of *public justice* represented the very first beginnings of that procedure.

55 On the structural analogies between the ritual of *vindicatio* and the ritual of *inauguratio* see Manthe 1993, p. 69 *et seq.*; Kofanov 1999, p. 382 *et seq.*

56 See *supra* § 2.1.

Bibliography

Behrends 1982
Behrends, O.,'La mancipatio nelle XII Tavole, IURA', 33 *Rivista internazionale di diritto romano e antico*, 1982, p. 46-103.

Biscardi 1953
Biscardi, A., 'La *litis contestatio* nella procedura *per legis actiones*', in: *Studi in onore di V. Arangio-Ruiz*, III, Naples: Jovene, 1953, p. 461-472.

Biscardi 1955
Biscardi, A., 'Esquisse d'une critique de la *litis contestatio*', 33 *Revue historique de droit français et étranger*, 1955, p. 1-19.

Broggini 1957
Broggini, G., *Iudex arbiterve, Prolegomena zum Officium des römischen Privatrichters*, Cologne/Graz: Böhlau 1957.

Broggini 1959
Broggini, G., 'Vindex und Judex. Zum Ursprung des römischen Zivilprozesses', 76 *Zeitschrift der Savigny-Stiftung für Rechtsgeschichte, Romanistische Abteilung*, 1959, p. 113-148.

Eisner & Horvat 1948
Eisner, B. & Horvat, M., *Rimsko pravo (Roman Law)*, Zagreb: Nakladni zavod Hrvatske, 1948.

Hampton 1986
Hampton, J., *Hobbes and the Social Contract Tradition*, Cambridge: Cambridge University Press, 1986.

Honsell, Mayer-Maly & Selb 1987
Honsell, H., Mayer-Maly, Th. & Selb, W., *Römisches Recht*, Berlin: Springer, 1987.

Horvat 1938
Horvat, M., *Savremeni nazori o postanku i značaju dvodiobe rimskog privatnog procesa (Contemporary Opinions on the Existence and Significance of the Bipartite Division of Roman Civil Procedure)*, 64 Mjesečnik Pravničkog društva (Law Society Paper), 1938.

Horvat 1958
Horvat, M., *O dvodiobi u najstarijem rimskom civilnom procesu (On the bipartite division of the oldest Roman civil procedure)*, 8 Zbornik Pravnog fakulteta u Zagrebu (Collected Papers of the Faculty of Law in Zagreb), 1958, p. 137-150.

Horvat 1959
Horvat, M., 'Deux phases du procès romain', in: *Droits de l'antiquité et sociologie juridique. Mélanges Henri Lévy-Bruhl*, Paris: Sirey, 1959, p. 163-169.

Von Jhering 1878
Von Jhering, R., *Geist des römischen Rechts auf den verschiedenen Stufen seiner Entwicklung*, Leipzig: Breitkopf & Härtel, 1878.

Von Jhering 1894
Von Jhering, R., *Die Vorgeschichte der Indoeuropäer*, Leipzig: Breitkopf & Härtel, 1894.

Juhart 1961
Juhart, J., *Civilno procesno pravo FNRJ (Civil Procedural Law of the FPR Yugoslavia)*, Ljubljana: Univerzitetna založba, 1961.

Kaser 1944
Kaser, M., 'Zum Ursprung des geteilten römischen Zivilprozessverfahrens', in: Wilcken, U., San Nicolò M. & Steinwenter, A. (eds.), *Festschrift für L. Wenger*, Vol. I, Munich: Beck, 1944, p. 106-128.

Kaser 1951
Kaser, M., 'Vom Ursprung des römischen Rechtsgedankens', in: Moschetti, G. (ed.), *Atti del Congresso internazionale di diritto romano e di storia der diritto in Verona, 1948, II*, Milan: Giuffrè, 1951, p. 19-36.

Kaser & Hackl 1996
Kaser, M. & Hackl, K., *Das römische Zivilprozeßrecht*, Munich: Beck, 1996.

Keller 1827
Keller, F., *Über Litis Contestation und Urteil*, Zurich: Gessner, 1827.

Kofanov 1999
Kofanov, L., 'Il ruolo del collegio degli auguri nell'elaborazione del diritto romano arcaico', in: Piro, I. (ed.), *Règle et pratique du droit dans les réalités juridiques de l'antiquité*, Catanzaro: Rubbettino, 1999, p. 380-388.

Lautner 1922
Lautner, J., *Die richterliche Entscheidung und die Streitbeendigung im altbabylonischen Prozeßrecht*, Leipzig: Weicher, 1922.

Lindsay 1913
Lindsay, W.M. (ed.), *Sexti Pompei Festi de verborum significatu quae supersunt cum Pauli Epitome*, Lipsiae: Teubner, 1913.

Lings 1991
Lings, M., *Ancient Beliefs and Modern Superstitions*, Cambridge: Quinta Essentia, 1991.

Manthe 1993
Manthe, U., 'Stilistische Gemeinsamkeiten in den Fachsprachen der Juristen und Auguren der Römischen Republik', in: Zimmermann, K. (ed.), *Der Stilbegriff in den Altertumswissenschaften*, Rostock: Universität Rostock, Institut für Altertumswissenschaften 1993, p. 69-74.

Mayer-Maly 1985
Mayer-Maly, Th., *Gedanken über das Recht*, Vienna/Cologne/Salzburg: Böhlau, 1985.

McPherson 1986
McPherson, C.B., 'Introduction', in: Hobbes, T., *Leviathan* (Penguin Classics), London: Penguin Books, 1986, p. 9-64.

Noailles 1949
Noailles, P., *Du Droit sacré au Droit civil. Cours de Droit Romain Approfondi 1941-1942*, Paris: Sirey, 1949.

Schelling 1860
Schelling, F.W.J., *Philosophie und Religion, Sämtliche Werke*, I, 6, Stuttgart/Augsburg: J. G. Cotta'scher Verlag, 1860.

Staszków 1963
Staszków, M., '*Vim dicere* im altrömischen Prozeß', 80 *Zeitschrift der Savigny-Stiftung für Rechtsgeschichte, Romanistische Abteilung*, 1963, p. 83-108.

Steinwenter 1925
Steinwenter, A., *Die Streitbeendigung durch Urteil, Schiedspruch und Vergleich nach griechischem Rechte*, Munich: Beck, 1925.

Talamanca 1987
Talamanca, M., s.v. 'Processo civile (diritto romano)', in: *Enciclopedia del diritto XXXVI*, Milan: Giuffrè, 1987, p. 1-79.

Thür 1998
Thür, G., 'Artur Steinwenter als Gräzist', 115 *Zeitschrift der Savigny-Stiftung für Rechtsgeschichte, Romanistische Abteilung*, 1998, p. 426-437.

Triva & Dika 2004
Triva, S. & Dika, M., *Građansko parnično procesno pravo (The Law of Procedure in Civil Litigation)*, Zagreb: Narodne novine, 2004.

Ude 1980
Ude, L., *Civilni pravdni postopek in samoupravni sodni postopek (Civil Procedure and Self-governmental Procedure)*, Ljubljana: Univerzitetna založba, 1980.

Wieacker 1967
Wieacker, F., *Privatrechtsgeschichte der Neuzeit (unter besonderer Berücksichtigung der deutschen Entwicklung)*, Göttingen: Vandenhoeck & Ruprecht, 1967.

Wieacker 1969
Wieacker, F., 'Rudolph von Jhering', 86 *Zeitschrift der Savigny-Stiftung für Rechtsgeschichte, Romanistische Abteilung*, 1969, p. 1-36.

Wieacker 1973
Wieacker, F, 'Jhering und der "Darwinismus"', in: Paulus, G., Diederichsen, U. & Canaris, C.W. (eds.), *Festschrift für Karl Larenz zum 70. Geburtstag*, Munich: Beck, 1973, p. 63-92.

Wlassak 1889
Wlassak, M., 'Die Litiskontestation im Formularprozeß', in: Leipziger Juristenfakultät (ed.), *Festgabe der Leipziger Juristenfakultät für B. Windscheid zum 22. Dezember 1888.*, Sonderabdruck, Leipzig: Duncker & Humblot, 1889.

Wlassak 1904
Wlassak, M., 'Der Gerichtsmagistrat im gesetzlichen Spruchverfahren', 25 *Zeitschrift der Savigny-Stiftung für Rechtsgeschichte, Romanistische Abteilung*, 1904, p. 81-187.

Wlassak 1917
Wlassak, M., *Anklage und Streitbefestigung im Kriminalrecht der Römer*, Vienna: Akademie der Wissenschaften, 1917.

Wlassak 1920
Wlassak M., *Anklage und Streitbefestigung, Abwehr gegen Phillip Lothmar*, Vienna: Akademie der Wissenschaften, 1920.

Wlassak 1921
Wlassak, M., *Der Judikationsbefehl der römischen Prozesse*, Vienna: Akademie der Wissenschaften, 1921.

Wlassak 1924
Wlassak, M., *Die klasische Prozeßformel*, Vienna: Akademie der Wissenschaften, 1924.

D. Čepulo

MODERNITY IN SEARCH OF TRADITION: THE FORMATION OF THE MODERN CROATIAN JUDICIARY 1848-1918*

Modern European social and legal systems were formed during the 'long 19th century' from 1780 to 1918. Basic structures, ideas and cultural patterns formed at that time are still embedded in today's reality. This article reconstructs the basic features of the formative period of the modern Croatian judiciary. It was shaped mainly on the basis of Austrian laws but adaptation of these laws depended mostly upon political factors. The old-fashioned judiciary was turned into a rational structure but it has not developed as an autonomous institution.

1. The Postulates: Legal Culture and Legal Tradition

The contemporary harmonization of law raises the question of cultural differences that affect the implementation of rules. Integrative tendencies have complementary and differentiating polarity in national and regional cultures as determinants of different identities within transnational frameworks. Understanding the application and internalization of legal rules by professional lawyers as well as by other individuals as potential or actual actors in the legal process depends upon a variety of factors, the cultural legal matrix being among the most important.

However even the definition of legal culture is a problem. Different approaches point to principal values, institutional models, legal education and legal ideas that influence the formation of legal consciousness and the behaviour of lawyers and other individuals. These and other factors as well as their roles in constituting legal culture still remain to be discussed. Legal culture can be conceptualized at various levels of abstraction (regional, national or sub-national) that do not exclude speaking about a plurality of legal cultures in a single framework. The subject may also be approached through various institutional or social units such as parliaments, governments, courts, faculties of law, works of

* This research was undertaken in the framework of the research project *The Croatian Legal Culture in a European Context: Tradition and Modernization*, supported by the Ministry of Science, Education and Sports of the Republic of Croatia.

theoreticians and judges, families etc. Research may target a variety of issues such as identification of the factual concept of law or understanding the rule of law in a certain society, foreign influences to a particular legal system, content of legal education and its role in shaping legal discourse, different procedural styles in the courts and their origins in various connected units such as the former Yugoslav federal republics, today's independent states etc. Surely the concept of legal culture opens complex questions and offers a variety of avenues to search for answers.[1]

Apart from the challenging complexity or perhaps disturbing heterogeneity related to the question of legal culture, it seems natural that one of the principal roles in defining legal culture belongs to tradition. Legal culture is founded upon relatively stable patterns that have been built and stabilized over a long period of time. The process of building such patterns is necessarily determined by previous development in the broader legal and social environment as well as by changes in the actual environment. Formation of particular elements of modern legal culture thus appears as a process over time, which has been one of the principal methodological tools of modern historical science.[2]

Modern European societies and legal systems were formed during the so-called long 19th century between 1780 and 1918. During this time basic features were established that directly or indirectly determined or influenced development leading up to the contemporary period. In spite of the growing tendency toward harmonization, certain basic structures, ideas, cultural patterns and even important pieces of regulation such as constitutions and civil codes came into being in the 19th century and are still deeply present in contemporary legal and social systems. Whether a challenging burden or a foundation for further development, the heritage of the past that is embedded in contemporary reality can hardly be understood on the basis of ignorance of tradition.[3]

The transition from archaic social systems to modern societies and the formation of modern legal systems occurred in the 19th century through a variety of dynamics. However particular characteristics in each society have certain common features. The emergence of Croatia's modern society and legal system that began in 1848 was part of that process. Even though the Croatian institutions formed at that time do not show continuity with the contemporary period, the process of their formation laid the foundation and strongly influenced further development as well as affected legal culture.

In this text I will briefly present the formative period of the modern Croatian judiciary. In particular, I will look closely at the organization of the judiciary and judicial independence, the influence of exogenous models and certain differences between the laws on the books and law in action. First I will give an outline of Croatian constitutional and legal development up to the present in order to give an impression of the context of the period under examination. The purpose of this

1 See for example: Gessner 1996; Hesselink 2001; Nelken 1997; Nelken 2004, p. 1-28; Teubner 1998, p. 1-32.

2 Burke 1992, p. 151-153. See also Braudel 1980.

3 See for example: Hesselink 2001, p. 72 *et seq.*; Tilly 1997, p. 13 *et seq.*; Watson 2001.

article is to acquaint a broader segment of academics and practitioners with the main formative features of the Croatian judiciary as deeper determinants of the further development.

2. The Croatian Constitutional Framework from the 19th Century to Today

The position of Croatia up until 1918 was characterized by its extensive autonomy in the framework of the Kingdom of Hungary, which had been part of the Habsburg Monarchy since 1526. This autonomy had medieval roots going back to the beginning of the 12th century. The disappearance of the Croatian kingdom at that time was followed by the development of a distinct constitutional position and special institutions in the territory ruled by the Hungarian dynasty. The institution of the *ban* (chief executive official) inherited from the early medieval period and the legislative *Sabor* (Diet) that first appeared in the 13th century were effective up until 1918. Until 1848 Croatian autonomy was substantiated in a set of written and customary rules (*iura municipalia*) but its reach depended upon political conditions as well. The continuity of the autonomous institutions was preserved only in the Kingdoms of Croatia-Slavonia, which made up a single administrative unit. The coastal region of Dalmatia came under the power of the Venetian Republic at the beginning of the 15th century and then became an Austrian province from 1797 to 1918, with an intermediate period of French rule from 1805 to 1813. Apart from that, the Croatian-Slavonian border zone with the Ottoman Empire (Military Border) was under the jurisdiction of Austrian military authorities from the end of the 16th century until 1882, when it was re-united with Croatia-Slavonia. The official names of the territories were the 'Kingdoms of Croatia and Slavonia' and the 'Kingdoms of Dalmatia, Croatia and Slavonia' (also called the Triune Kingdom). In the 19th century - during the formation of the modern Croatian nation - both of these names interchanged with the national denominations 'Croatia' and 'Croatian kingdom'.

The introduction of modern institutions in Croatia-Slavonia began with the abolishment of feudalism by the Croatian Diet in 1848 and continued during a period of false constitutionality and absolutism imposed throughout the Habsburg Monarchy from 1849-60. This was replaced by provisory constitutionalism that ended in 1867 with the Austrian-Hungarian Compromise. This compromise was then followed by the sub-dual Croatian–Hungarian Compromise in 1868. The latter set down a stable constitutional basis of Croatian-Slavonian autonomy in the framework of Hungary but assigned certain control functions to the 'common government' that was in fact under Hungarian control.

Croatian political institutions ceased to exist in 1918 when the unitary Yugoslav Kingdom was established with the Serbian dynasty at the throne. The new state joined regions that had belonged to different legal systems. Large portions of their inherited regulations in civil and criminal law and in procedure as well as judicial organisation remained in force in six different 'legal regions' until legal unification of the country undertaken during the King's dictatorship from 1929 to 1931. The Austrian influence present in large portions of the inherited regulations influenced the new laws as well. The Croatian political identity in Yugoslavia re-appeared as the large autonomous unit of the Bannate of Croatia was formed in 1939. However the Yugoslav state collapsed in 1941. Provisory regimes under German and Italian control were established in the occupied territories, among them the fascist Independent State of Croatia (NDH). In 1943 the Yugoslav resistance movement, which was communist at its core, laid down the political and institutional foundations for the federal organisation of the second Yugoslavia, in which Croatia was to be one of the federal republics.

Federalism was adopted by the Yugoslav constitutions from 1946 to 1974, granting constitutional individuality to the republics. In reality, the federal system was integrated by the power of the Communist Party and by the charisma of its leader, Josip Broz Tito, while the institutional systems of the republics were based on unified models that showed no substantial differences. Still, the factual circumstances as well as cultural and legal cultural differences affected different judicial styles and adjudications in the republics in spite of the same or very similar regulations. Parts of the regulations, such as civil procedure, reflected certain influences of previous rules in spite of the different political context of the communist regime. The political crisis that erupted in the 1980s paved the way to the disintegration of the country. This resulted in proclamations of independence from the former republics, beginning with Croatia and Slovenia in 1990. In 2004 Slovenia became a member of the EU while Croatia became an official candidate for accession and began negotiations in 2005.[4]

3. The Birth of the Modern Croatian Judiciary 1849-1860: Modernisation Imposed from Outside

The Croatian judiciary before the reforms of 1849 was based on manor courts and municipal courts merged with the administration in the districts, counties and towns. The highest court in the territory of Croatia-Slavonia was the Ban's Table. Cassational jurisdiction belonged to the Table of Seven in Hungary.[5] That structure was shaped through historical development basically equal to that in Hungary, but different from that in the Austrian lands directly subjected to the will of the emperor and modified through his reforms. The law applied in the Croatian courts in civil and criminal cases was based on written regulations from Hungary and Austria, decisions of the highest courts, and customary law that was developed from the 16th to 19th centuries.[6] The educational basis for this system was the Royal Academy of Sciences in Zagreb, founded in 1776 when it succeeded the Political-cameral school of 1767. The Royal Academy offered two-year courses of law, theology and philosophy (philosophy was a precondition for enrolment in law and

4 On Croatian history in English and German, see Goldstein 1999; Perić 2005; Steindorff 2001. On the Croatian constitutional and legal history from 1848 to 1918 see Čepulo 2006, p. 47-91. On development of legal education in Croatia see Čepulo 2007.

5 Beuc 1985, p. 305; Lanović 1929, p. 325 & p. 323-332.

6 Beuc 1985, p. 353-354 & p. 355-356.

theology). The role of the institution was important but it was constantly plagued with problems and never reached expected standards. However, the Court did not accept demands for the foundation of the university including the faculty of law.[7]

The situation in the Croatian judiciary in 1848 was described as unbearable. Complaints particularly addressed arbitrary adjudications and slow procedure that could last for decades. These conditions were seen as consequences of archaic regulations and the incompetence of the judges, many of whom did not have formal legal education. Additionally, judges were underpaid and, according to some reports, bribery was common.[8]

However the abolishment of feudalism in 1848 was not followed by reforms of administrative and judicial institutions in spite of the fact that they were largely outdated. The only exception was the abolishment of the manor courts and the provisory transfer of their jurisdiction to the county courts.[9] This change did not halt the deterioration caused by the transition of former urbarial lands into the private ownership of former peasants and the consequential rise in the number of litigations between former landlords and peasants.[10] The reason that the Croatian Diet did not reform old institutions can be explained by the short period of its work (only one month) and its concentration on political issues during the escalation of the Croatian-Hungarian conflict that erupted after Hungary attempted to reduce Croatian autonomy. However, another important reason was that the Croatian reformers at that time did not have a clearly accepted concept of modernization. Another explanation was the archaic social structure of the Croatian political elite, dominated by an uneducated and conservative petty nobility that was not prepared for more radical reform. Defence of Croatian autonomy against the Hungarian pretensions of the previous decades was grounded upon traditional legal principles that focused on the autonomy of the counties that had made them the inner cores of political life. In 1848 such defensive concepts reflected the attitude that the traditional municipal institutions (among them the county judiciary and administration) had an important role in the defence of autonomy, which should be preserved through the application of modern principles to their organisations. This concept was similar to the one that emerged through the Hungarian confrontation with the Habsburg Court. The Croatian-Hungarian conflict and the influence of Austro-Slavic ideas among Croatian liberals was reflected in 1848 through the gradual acceptance of the idea that the traditional institutions were archaic and should be replaced by modern institutions modelled on Austria.[11] However, Croatian disappointment when the king imposed the centralist March Constitution in 1849, abolishing Croatian autonomy, returned reformers to the idea of improving traditional institutions as a basis of autonomy and a bulwark against absolutism.[12]

7 Čepulo 1996, p. 56-65. See also Čepulo 2007.
8 Gross 1985, p. 100.
9 Markus 1996, p. 1-2 & p. 143-145.
10 Čepulo 2006a, p. 2-3 & p. 329; Gross 1985, p. 101.
11 Markus 2000, p. 276-277.
12 Čepulo 2006, p. 56-57; Gross 1985, p. 67-69.

Croatian reformers would not have a chance to apply either of the two ideas, as the abolishment of Croatian autonomy under the March Constitution in September 1849 was followed by its abrogation and the introduction of absolutism that lasted from 1852 to 1860. During the period of direct jurisdiction of the Vienna Court Croatian institutions were replaced by imposed Austrian laws. The Court undertook the same project in all lands within the Monarchy. Its goal was twofold: establishing the grounds for a centralized administration of the large and heterogeneous empire and setting normative preconditions for modernization of the entire Monarchy as a foundation for progress. The reforms that culminated in 1852-54 concerned administrative and judicial organisation, civil and criminal law as well as civil and criminal procedure.

The reforms essentially changed the organisation of the judiciary in Croatia-Slavonia. The municipal judiciary founded on the representative assemblies was abolished and replaced by a centralist organisation of the state courts with cassation competences belonging to the Supreme Court in Vienna. At first the judiciary was separated from the administration at all levels, but in 1853 it was re-joined at the first-instance courts and in the Ban's Table. Judges were appointed by the king. Candidates were nominated by the president of the court with the consent of presidents of the higher courts and the Ministry of Justice. The position of judges was basically equal to that of civil servants without efficient grants of independence.[13] In 1853 German was approved as the official internal language of the administration and the judiciary.[14] Croatian would be restored into official use in 1860. The three-degree structure of urbarial courts competent for litigation between former landlords and peasants existed from 1858 to 1862 when that jurisdiction was transferred to the competent courts.[15]

The judicial structure was amended at the beginning of 1860 when the imperial government established the local lay courts in local communes, which were competent regarding small informal claims. The local courts consisted of laymen elected from members of the local council and presided over by the head of the local council. The local communes that were the institutional precondition for the foundation of these courts were established in 1851. Both institutions, the local communes (*Gemeinde*) that enjoyed a rather high degree of autonomy and local courts (*Ortsgerichte*), were transplanted from the German and Austrian tradition. There were no such precursors in the Croatian tradition that did not know for free local communes grounded on a developed economic basis and partly independent from the local landlords. But in spite of their imported origin, local courts proved to be useful in the poor countryside where the relatively uneducated population brought a large number of small claims.[16]

The new regulations significantly improved the professional outlook for advocates. The Austrian Law on Advocates (*Advocaten-Ordnung*), introduced in

13 Beuc 1985, p. 305-306 & p. 318-319; Čepulo 2006a, p. 330-334.

14 Gross 1985, p. 113.

15 Beuc 1985, p. 313.

16 Zuglia, p. 255-257.

1852, obliged most of the lawyers to pass the bar examination based on the new regulations. These also provided for the obligatory institution of advocates' boards in towns even though they were not autonomous bodies, but were controlled by the *ban* that was empowered to appoint and revoke advocates.[17] The Law on Public Notary Service (*Notariats-Ordnung*) established the previously unknown public notary service.[18] The land-registry, established in 1850, was also an important improvement.[19]

However, the farthest reaching reform was the introduction of the *Allgemeine Bürgerliche Gesetzbuch* (ABGB). It replaced the archaic *Tripartite,* which up until that time had been a central point of the Croatian legal system, and influenced its other parts. The rational concept of the ABGB, based on the principles of Roman law and private ownership, replaced concepts based on the Hungarian and Croatian customary law and feudal type of ownership. The Tripartite had determined legal structures for a very long time and shaped the minds of Croatian legal practitioners. For that reason, this 'improvement' clashed with structures rooted in the Croatian tradition and caused a variety of problems, especially in villages.[20]

An important step was the introduction of the General German Law on Exchange (*Allgemeine deutsche Wechsel-Ordnung*) in 1850 as a provisional regulation, which was already valid in the Austrian lands. It was replaced in 1876 by the Commercial Code, based on the same law, enacted in the Common (Hungarian-Croatian) Diet and valid both in Hungary and Croatia-Slavonia.[21]

The other changes were also important, even though they were not as radical, because of the fact that previous regulations valid in Croatia-Slavonia were mainly based on older Austrian sources. The Law on Civil Procedure (*Die provisorische Civil-Process-Ordnung*), introduced in 1853, was based on the king's edicts of 1781 and 1796. It replaced previous regulations that were established in royal edicts, customs and judicial practice. It remained in force until 1929 when it was replaced by the Law of Civil Procedure based on the Austrian law from 1895. The Law on Civil Procedure was followed by the other procedural laws, the most important of them being the Law on Non-contentious Civil Procedure in 1854.[22]

Criminal law was also changed. The Criminal Law on Crimes, Misdemeanours and Offences (*Strafegesetz über Verbrechen, Vergehen und Übertretungen*) from 1852 replaced rules handed down in the king's edicts and in customary law. It was based on the Criminal Code from 1803, with the exception of rules on criminal procedure that were not included. That law was blamed for being too rigid, conservative and outdated, but it remained in force until 1929 with some changes such as the abrogation of archaic and obsolete provisions.[23] The new Law on Criminal Procedure (*Strafprozess-Ordnung*) from 1852 replaced liberal law from 1850 which

17 Čepulo 2006a, p. 334-336; Bayer 1968, p. 53-55.
18 Čepulo 2006a, p. 336-337.
19 Gross 1985, p. 129 *et seq.*
20 Gross 1985, p. 108-109.
21 Čepulo 2006, p. 59.
22 Čepulo 2006a, p. 337; Gross 1985, p. 109; Zuglia, p. 18, 20 & 22.
23 Bayer 1995, p. 152.

was influenced by the 1808 French Code on Criminal Procedure. The new law was also blamed for its conservative nature, especially because it returned to inquisitorial principles and reduced the rights of indicted persons during investigation. It was nevertheless an improvement compared with the procedural rules in the Criminal Code of 1803 and the king's edicts. That law would be replaced by modern regulations in 1875.[24] Rigid criminal regulations at that time were a reaction to the previous tradition and the absolutist principles of government.

Functional problems within the traditional Croatian judicial institutions and the replacement of the social-political paradigm (abolishment of feudalism) required serious institutional modifications. It was impossible for such extensive reforms based on unified models for the entire Monarchy, not adapted to the local conditions and imposed in the interest of the centre, to take place without serious problems. The traditional institutions were deeply rooted in the consciousness of the people. The reorganization of institutional relations caused serious disorder. In 1849 local authorities begged the government to reform the judiciary but reports after reforms began in 1850-1851 indicate that conditions had worsened.

The reports from that time indicate chaotic conditions within the judiciary, reduced accessibility to the courts, greater arbitrariness and arrogance of judges and increased corruption.[25] The new reform undertaken from 1852 to 1854 only partially repaired these problems and established normative conditions that allowed gradual stabilization of the new structures. The deeper problem of judicial reform was the archaic social structure within the population whose way of life was largely unprepared for such changes. Another problem was the lack of educated professional staff necessary to apply new laws that demanded more skill in practice. This problem was solved on a short time basis with transfers from Austria. However this was not a real solution, as the new staff was not familiar with the language or the local traditions and was not interested in a career in the new environment.[26] The long term solution was improving legal education. The Royal Academy of Sciences was disbanded and the *Facultas iuridica* was replaced by the Legal Academy, offering a three-year course based on the new regulations.[27]

The biggest problems however, were caused by inadequate conceptions and the inflexible implementation of the ABGB that challenged prevailing conservative structures in the villages. The most striking conflict was between the concept of private ownership and the conservative institution of the communal joint family extensively present in the Croatian villages. The communal joint family was based on collective ownership, and principles of strong solidarity and patriarchal relations.[28] The spontaneous process of division of collective property of the

24 On the both laws see: Bayer 1976, p. 6-7; Beuc 1985, p. 313; Čepulo 2006a, p. 334 & p. 337-338.

25 Gross 1985, p. 104-105.

26 Gross 1985, p. 110.

27 Čepulo 1996, p. 65-74.

28 The statistics on communal joint families appeared only from 1880, when their number was significantly reduced. According to the statistics from 1880, 21.5% of the total population in Croatia-Slavonia lived in fully preserved communal joint families while another 44% were →

communal joint family to individual properties under private ownership gradually arose starting in 1848. The introduction of the ABGB, which was based exclusively on the concept of individual private ownership and did not recognize communal ownership, accelerated that process. The large and solidary social units of communal joint families were divided on the initiative of their members or on the grounds of a distress-warrant due to financial debts of a single member. These divisions were becoming a serious social problem. Because of that and as a result of the complex nature of the communal joint family the Ban's Table took the stand in 1857 that the communal joint family was a specific institution regulated by the provisions of public law and that it should not be adjudicated under principles of the ABGB. But that decision of the Ban's Table was revised in 1858 by the Supreme Court in Vienna. The cassational court in Vienna insisted on a strict application of the principles of the ABGB and even denied the legal existence of the communal joint family, which was interpreted as an individual family with a large number of members. The Supreme Court wrote some more moderate decisions in 1859 under pressure from the imperial government. The government was concerned that the previous interpretation exposed villages to the prospect of social catastrophe. However, the fundamental nature of the new decisions did not change and the problem was not substantially eliminated. In fact, the problem of communal joint families could be solved only through special legislation, but the authorities avoided this approach, as it was not clear which principles it should be based on. For this reason the uncontrolled process of dissolution of communal joint families was intermittently stopped by provisory bans starting in 1850. Special regulations for communal joint families would be enacted only in the 1870s and 1889.[29] Throughout that time and in fact even up until the communist period, communal joint families survived in certain Croatian regions in their own parallel legal world, which was based on conservative customary principles different from the laws on the books.[30]

Apart from these and other problems with the implementation of the ABGB it remained in force until 1946 and its concepts have strongly affected the legal consciousness of Croatian lawyers up until the present.

4. Provisory Constitutionality from 1860 to 1868: Stabilization of the New Structures

Absolutism was followed by provisory constitutionality based on two royal edicts in 1860 and 1861 and by the convocation of the provincial Diets that were supposed to elect delegates for the Imperial Council (*Reichsrat*) in Vienna. However, the Hungarian and the Croatian Diets refused to elect their delegates, as this would imply an acceptance of the abolition of their constitutions. Both Diets intended to

former members or in the process of division. However, it seems that the numbers were actually even larger. Pavličević 1989, p. 256 *et seq.*

29 Gross 1985, p. 208-227; See also Prišlin Krbavski 2006, p. 275-315.

30 Prišlin Krbavski 2006, p. 330.

continue the processes that had been halted in 1849 and transform their aspirations for more independence into reality. Their starting positions as well as the outcomes varied, however.

In Hungary laws introduced during the period of absolutism were abolished and the ABGB was replaced with the Tripartite that would remain in force until 1946.[31] Something different happened in Croatia-Slavonia. There the valid laws were seen as an ambiguous part of the absolutist 'package' shaped and imposed in the interest of the centre, but also as an obvious improvement compared with former conditions. For this reason, the absolutist laws were generally accepted as a provisional solution until they could be replaced by new laws of the Croatian Diet. As previously indicated some of the accepted laws remained in force until 1918, 1929 and even as late as 1946, while others were replaced by autonomous Croatian legislation that was again modelled mostly upon Austrian laws.

Because of the lack of modern autonomous legislation, the Croatian Diet undertook intensive drafting of new laws. Among the anticipated projects were a return to the municipal county organisation that also implied a return to the municipal judiciary, the Civil Code based on the ABGB, which also provided for the organisation of civil courts combining the Austrian organisational model with the Croatian municipal tradition, and the Criminal Code that provided for the organisation of criminal courts including jury courts with general competence. The legislative work was never completed, as the Diet was disbanded only seven months after its convocation. Still, the Croatian Table of Seven with cassation jurisdiction was established in 1862 by the king's order, which completed the Croatian judicial organisation.[32]

The Croatian Diet convened again in 1865. However it concentrated on the institutional arrangements of the relations with Hungary and Austria and did not seriously discuss institutional reforms. The Diet was disbanded in 1867 after it had protested against the Austrian-Hungarian Compromise, which was concluded without Croatian participation.

The new Diet elected under Hungarian pressure concluded a sub-dual Croatian-Hungarian Compromise in 1868. It delimitated common and autonomous competences, granting Croatia-Slavonia autonomy in administration, religion, education, and judiciary with its own legislation (the Croatian Diet), the government responsible to the Croatian Diet and its own judicial system. Croatia-Slavonia participated in the Common Diet and central government, but on the factual conditions of Hungarian predominance and symbolic Croatian influence. The central government retained control of Croatian autonomy in order to protect the common sphere against possible infringements, but control was in fact executed in the interest of Hungary.[33]

31 Gross & Szabo 1992, p. 135.

32 Čepulo 2006a, p. 340-343.

33 The most important instruments of influence of the central (Hungarian) government were: a) the *ban* appointed by the king on the proposal of the Hungarian Prime Minister, b) the Croatian delegates participating in the Common Diet with individual votes, making them an insignificant minority, c) the 'Croatian-Slavonian Minister' in the central government being →

In spite of the control mechanisms reserved for the central government the Croatian-Hungarian Compromise set up a stable constitutional framework of Croatian autonomy for the first time after 1848 - and it was an elementary precondition for modernisation.

5. Modernisation in the Autonomous Framework 1873-1875: Improvement on a Liberal Foundation

Institutional reforms in the framework of the Croatian-Hungarian Compromise were possible only after the reformist National Party won the elections for the Croatian Diet in 1872. Ivan Mažuranić, a prominent member of the National Party and lawyer experienced in the central administration in Vienna, was installed as the *ban* and president *ex officio* of the Croatian-Slavonian government. He resigned from the office in 1880 but the period was marked by extensive reforms that were enacted during his administration.

Modernisation was inspired by the necessity that archaic Croatian institutions and absolutist laws be replaced by modern and functional laws that would be based on the models present in developed European countries and adapted to the Croatian situation. The theoretical basis of the reform was the German idea of the *Rechtsstaat*. The reformists' main goal was to modernize the undeveloped country in order to place it among the developed European nations. Adapting institutions that had already been proven in the other countries was seen as an adequate means to do this.[34]

The reforms were related to all issues of autonomous Croatian jurisdiction, but reforming the administration and judiciary was seen as crucial. The situation was still poor in both branches and these branches were perceived as a foundation for other reforms as well as instruments that would secure their efficiency. For this reason, the reform programme, initiated immediately after the National Party came to power, began with reforms of the administration and judiciary.

One of the first and the most important laws in the field of the judiciary was the Law on Judicial Power. The law proclaimed separation of the judiciary from the administration, the principle of judicial independence, life appointment of judges, tenure of judges, the principle of incompatibility and exclusive competence of the Diet regarding the organization of the judiciary etc. The law forbade judicial review of constitutionality, but allowed judicial review of the legality of administrative acts

responsible to the Common Diet, d) the definition of public finances as part of the common competences (45% of the income collected in Croatia-Slavonia was allocated to the Croatian budget and 55% to the common budget), e) the submission to the king of laws of the Croatian Sabor through the central government (the central government could complain to the king that the Croatian laws breached the common competence or violated common interest; the king always settled such disputes by accepting Hungarian arguments and denying to sanction the Croatian laws). On the Croatian-Hungarian Compromise see Gross & Szabo 1992, p. 232-239; Čepulo 2000, p. 117-148; Pliverić 1885.

34 Čepulo 2003, p. 181.

reflecting German and Belgian influences.[35] The law was in fact almost a literal translation of the Austrian fundamental law of 1867, but certain provisions from the Austrian model were omitted. The most important omissions were the grant of a trial by jury in cases of harsh punishment, political crimes and press offences and the grant of procedure before the administrative court in cases of violation of individual rights committed by the administration. The consequences of these omissions were the institutionalization of trial by jury in the form of a special jurisdiction deprived of general competences and the absence of the administrative court from the Croatian legal system.[36] The Law on Judicial Power was proclaimed in 1874 with temporarily suspended provisions on the separation of the judiciary from the administration and a grant of tenure to judges. The reasons for such a solution were twofold. The government wanted to replace incompetent judges with educated ones before granting them life appointment. On the other hand, the government was eager to proclaim the law as soon as possible because, according to some incorrect presumptions, it was a precondition for incorporation of the Military Border into civil Croatia-Slavonia.[37]

The judicial reform was in a way connected with the reform of legal education. In 1868 the Legal Academy was extended to a four year course based on a university programme and in 1874 the university in Zagreb was founded with the Faculty of Law. The new institution was to produce fully educated lawyers with formal degrees that were particularly needed in the judiciary.[38]

The Law on Judicial Power was followed by laws that applied its principles. A special law provided that the president of the Table of Seven was to be elected by the judges of that court instead of the previous *ex officio* presidency of the *ban*.[39] The Law on the Disciplinary Responsibility of Judges, their Reassignments and Retirement, based on the Austrian model, required consent of the judge as a precondition for his reassignment or retirement before a certain age and granted the procedure before the council of judges in cases of his disagreement as well as in disciplinary cases.[40] Another law partially restructured judicial organization by changing the seats of the courts and their jurisdiction in order to improve parties' access to justice and efficiency of the courts.[41] That reform was partly induced by the lack of finances that was one of the main problems of the judicial reforms. The Croatian-Hungarian Compromise defined public finances as part of the common jurisdiction so that Croatia-Slavonia could not execute an autonomous fiscal policy and provide money needed for the reforms. For this reason rational organisation of the judiciary was even more important. The problem of finances was also reflected in the Croatian government's decision that special commercial courts would not be established because of a lack of experience and financial means. The solution was to

35 Čepulo 2003, p. 13; Čepulo 1999, p. 249-252.
36 Čepulo 2006, p. 72, Čepulo 1999, p. 241 *et seq.*
37 Čepulo 1999, p. 241 & p. 247.
38 Čepulo 1996, p. 75-93.
39 Čepulo 1999, p. 254-255.
40 Čepulo 1999, p. 242; Čepulo 2006a, p. 351.
41 Čepulo 2006a, p. 352-353.

widen the competent court jurisdiction in areas of intensive commercial activity to the field of commercial law.[42]

With regard to organization, an interesting issue is the destiny of the Bill on Advocates, enacted in the Croatian Diet in 1875 on the basis of the Austrian model. The law was supposed to replace the outdated regulation from 1852 and provide for establishment of an autonomous bar association and autonomy of the profession. The king refused to sanction that law however, accepting the objection of the central government that it was improper to require Croatian domicile instead of Hungarian citizenship as a prerequisite for practicing law in Croatia. The issue concerned the theoretical and political question of the existence of Croatian citizenship but it also had practical implications, as the law denied Hungarian lawyers not residing in Croatia the right to practise in Croatian courts. The Croatian Diet sent the king's objections to its committee and then ignored the whole project. Thus, the old law from the absolutist period which required a Croatian domicile for practising in Croatian courts remained in force.[43]

But apart from the deputies' great satisfaction with the separation of the judiciary from the administration, they blocked the government's attempt to apply that principle to the local courts. The bill proposed by the government on the basis of the recent Austrian law was turning the local courts into an unobligatory form of mediatory court. The deputies' argument against such change was pragmatic. They stressed the fact that the inexpensive and simple organisation and procedure proved efficient enough in the local courts, which dealt with both uneducated parties and lay judges. The Austrian regulations imposed in 1860 on the local courts defined small claims with an amount that in Croatia-Slavonia exceeded the real meaning of that term. For this reason the local courts in Croatia-Slavonia in fact absorbed a very large number of potential litigations that would otherwise have blocked a judicial system with an inadequate number of courts. The price was lower quality of adjudications in cases which in fact were not small claims. On the other hand the number of appeals against decisions of the local courts was very small indicating primarily that the parties trusted the local authorities. Confronted with such arguments the government drafted a compromise solution that did not change the basic position of the local court, but improved procedure and granted better protection to the parties.[44]

The most important reform as regards criminal legislation was the new Law on Criminal Procedure of 1875 based on the Austrian Law on Criminal Procedure of 1873. The Austrian law was itself based on the French Code of Criminal Procedure of 1808 and was generally acknowledged as a good piece of codification.[45] Unlike its Austrian model the Croatian law did not mention the jury courts. Instead, trial by jury was regulated as a special jurisdiction by three *leges speciales* that were also based on two Austrian laws. However in the Croatian regulations trial by jury was a

42 Čepulo 2006a, p. 359.
43 Čepulo 1999a, p. 81; Čepulo 2006a, p. 357-358.
44 Čepulo 1999, p. 256-257.
45 Bayer 1995, p. 152.

special jurisdiction and the competence of the jury courts was reduced exclusively to crimes and misdemeanours committed by the press. Punishments were regulated by the Law on Press Matters, modelled upon the Austrian regulation. It replaced the repressive *Presseordnung* of 1852 that instituted the administrative seizure of journals, which was possible only through judicial procedure under the new regulation. The only jury court was established in Zagreb and had jurisdiction over the whole of Croatia-Slavonia. The reduced version of trial by jury represented a defeat of the deputies' insistence that the competence of the jury court should be similar to that in Austria and should cover offences in the press, serious crimes and political crimes. The government insisted that Croatian society was neither educated nor experienced enough for such an extensive competence of the jury and that only the level of education in Zagreb showed a sufficient basis for establishing the jury court.[46]

Liberal reforms also reflected on the regulation of punishments. The repressive Criminal Law from 1853 was not replaced. However special laws abolished archaic punishments such as beating and shackles, while other laws established parole and the *Irish system* in penitentiaries.[47] Other changes also occurred to improve the material basis of the judiciary, such as building of the new court palaces and prisons.[48]

Apart from the question of small claims, civil procedure was not given much attention. However one important improvement was the law that made enforcement proceedings more effective.[49] The reasons for such low activity regarding civil procedure can be found in the government's concentration on organizational and public law issues as the main priority, but also in the fact that the recent Austrian legislation was not as attractive a model-law as the Criminal Procedure Code of 1873 had been. Another reason might be that regulation of civil procedure was still not very important in the country because economic activity based on private property was rather low. The main problem in civil courts was still the transition of the 'common' plots of feudal lands into the peasants' private ownership. It was only in 1876 that the conditions for that transition were defined by law, which helped to remove the last remnants of feudalism.[50]

The much larger problem that has already been mentioned was the regulation of the communal joint families' property and its division. That problem was solved to some extent during this period. The first special law on communal joint families was enacted in the Croatian Diet in 1870. The law was based on the liberal view that the communal joint family was an archaic institution that was only loosely conditioned and would soon disappear due to its division. The problems that the law produced were complicated even further by the arbitrary behaviour of local magistrates authorised to execute the divisions. Because of the uncontrolled dissolution of the properties and the increased social instability, the law was

46 Bayer 1940, p. 42-48; Čepulo 2002, p. 178 *et seq.*
47 Čepulo 2006a, p. 358; Gross & Szabo 1992, p. 337.
48 Čepulo 2006a, p. 359.
49 Čepulo 2006a, p. 359-360; Zuglia, p. 19.
50 Gross & Szabo 1992, p. 395-396; Prišlin Krbavski 2006, p. 264-265.

temporarily abrogated and further divisions banned in 1872.[51] The new Law on Communal Joint Families of 1874 allowed their optional divisions in an attempt to balance individual and collective interests and bring more order to the process, but it could hardly be controlled.[52] The problem was alleviated to a certain extent, but it persisted and it was only in 1889 that the question of communal joint families was adequately regulated.

6. Exogenous Interests in the Autonomous Framework: Authoritarian Rule and Reduction of Judicial Independence 1883-1903

Ivan Mažuranić's intensive reforms starting in 1873 coincided with a political crisis in Hungary as the weak central government in Budapest became busy with its own problems. The formation of a stable nationalist government in Budapest in 1875 led to fewer reforms in Croatia. Croatian autonomy was seen as a challenge to the unity of the Hungarian state so reforms that strengthened the Croatian position should be limited. For this reason reform activity lost its impetus after 1875 and the *ban*, Ivan Mažuranić, resigned in 1880. He was succeeded by a moderate pro-Hungarian politician who resigned in 1883, faced with overwhelming opposition from the central government. Still, he was trusted enough to execute the incorporation of the Military Border into Croatia-Slavonia in 1882. Part of that process was the incorporation of the judiciary of the Military Border into the Croatian judicial system. It began with the dissolution of the separate departments competent for the Military Border at the Table of Seven and the Ban's Table as well as at the office of the State Attorney.[53]

The new *ban*, appointed in 1883, was Karoly Khuen-Hédervàry, a Croatian noble of Hungarian origin. He imposed his own policy by the instrumentalization of the National Party and ruled until 1903 in an authoritarian manner, veiled in a constitutional facade. His task was to secure the dualist structure of the Monarchy and Hungarian predominance by ensuring that the Croatian autonomy did not challenge it. Some time after his installation Khuen-Hédervàry prepared the institutional basis for his rule. Among the first and the most important of his projects was the revision of the judicial reforms accepted during the Mažuranić's period.

Already in 1884 grants of judicial tenure in the Law on Judicial Power were suspended for three years and in 1887 for another three years. The Law on Disciplinary Responsibility of Judges, their Reassignment and Retirement was abrogated in 1884 and 'provisionally' replaced by the absolutist Law on the Interior Organisation of the Judiciary of 1853. The latter empowered the *ban* with the authority to reassign judges and to participate in disciplinary proceedings. The principles from that law were made permanent in 1890 in the Law on Personal

51 Gross & Szabo 1992, p. 387-38; Pavličević 1989, p. 219-223.
52 Gross & Szabo 1992, p. 389-390; Pavličević 1989, p. 231-233.
53 Beuc 1985, p. 245 & p. 246; Čepulo 2006a, p. 364.

Relations, Official Duties and Disciplinary Responsibility of Judicial Clerks.[54] These revisions neutralized the main grants of judicial independence, exposing judges to the direct influence of the government.

Apart from that, jury trials were suspended for three years in 1884 and for another two years in 1887, enabling more efficient persecution of the press. The government argued that trial by jury had lost its meaning because all cases prosecuted by the state attorney ended in acquittal. On the contrary, the opposition insisted that trial by jury was necessary as a grant of objectivity in a country where there were no guarantees of judicial independence. Some majority deputies bitterly criticized trial by jury as a populist form of justice and supported the government's idea that in the future jury trials could be abolished and compensated by increasing the number of lay assessors in the competent courts.[55] Instead, lay assessors were completely removed from adjudication in 1888. The government justified this solution by referring to tendencies in other European countries as well as dissatisfactory experiences.[56] Some changes of the Law on Criminal Procedure undertaken at the same time reduced the number of judges in the county courts to odd-numbers and gave the state attorney the right to access the minutes of judicial sessions closed to the public.[57] All amendments were taken from the Austrian legislation but the opposition attacked the government, objecting that the changes made it easier for the government to influence the court. The opposition also complained that the government revisions were concentrated on the more repressive parts of Austrian legislation while the liberal solutions had been neglected.[58]

Trial by jury was reinstated in 1890 but in 1897, following the political crisis of that year, the competence of the jury court was reduced. The jury court, seated in Zagreb, was deprived of jurisdiction for misdemeanours brought by citizens. These actions were transferred to the jurisdiction of county courts. The amendment made access to court easier, but it also opened the door for state officials appearing as private citizens to sue their critics in the press. These procedures were held before single judges who had been divested of the guarantees of judicial independence since 1884.[59] Jury trials were suspended again in 1903, this time without time limit, after an outburst of large anti-governmental demonstrations in Zagreb.[60] Jury trial would be reinstated only after the new government was installed in 1907.

In 1884 and 1886 the organisation of the judiciary was firmly established and did not undergo significant changes until 1918. These changes primarily affected the organisation of the judiciary in the territory of the former Military Border, which was brought into full accordance with the civil judiciary in Croatia-Slavonia. These

54 Čepulo 2006a, p. 366 *et seq.*; Čepulo 2003, p. 66 & p. 67-68.
55 Čepulo 2000a, p. 964-965.
56 Čepulo 2000a, p. 965-966.
57 Čepulo 2006a, p. 367; Ljubanović 1994, p. 245 *et seq.*
58 Čepulo 2006a, p. 368.
59 Čepulo 2000a, p. 966-969.
60 Čepulo 2002, p. 186-189; Čepulo 2000a, p. 969.

changes could be seen in the restructuring of the judicial organisation as a whole, with the establishment of eleven new county courts in 1886.[61]

One important regulation was the new Law on Communal Joint Families of 1889, based on the idea that this traditional institution which guarded social stability should be kept alive. The law introduced certain new restrictions to the division of communal joint families, allowing the process of division to continue in a socially acceptable manner. The law was abrogated by the communist authorities in 1945.[62]

7. Re-liberalisation of the Croatian Judiciary 1906-1917

Khuen-Hédervâry left Croatia in 1903 when he was appointed president of the Hungarian government. His leave opened more space for the new democratic parties to participate in the government (Croatian-Serbian Coalition in 1906-1907 and 1917-1918). Democratic tendencies in Croatia and Hungary could be seen in the moderate re-liberalisation of Croatian institutions, but further reforms were halted due to internal political crisis and international tensions on the eve of the First World War.[63]

An important event at that time was the foundation of the Association of Croatian Judges in 1907. The Association was based upon the Austrian model and supported by the respective Austrian association. Its main goal was to improve the professional position of judges, but in spite of these efforts the Law on Personal Relations, Official Duties and Disciplinary Responsibility of Judicial Clerks of 1890 was not revised. The king declined to give legislative sanction to the law enacted by the Diet even though its grants of judicial independence were still below those of 1874.[64] The institutional channels of the *ban*'s influence on judges were limited in 1917 when the 1890 Law was revised. But even then the principle of the separation of the judiciary from the administration was not re-established and the regulation remained below the standard set in 1874.[65]

The revision of jury trials was more successful. The new Croatian government reinstated jury trials immediately after coming to power in 1906 and established the second jury court in the town of Osijek in 1907. It is possible that the government's intentions were more ambitious. The government indicated that some repressive parts of the regulation of trial by jury were not removed because of a fear that they would be blocked by the central government and because such regulations were still necessary in the transition period from repressive regulation to the freedom of the press.[66]

There were also attempts to reform the Civil Code and civil procedure. These attempts reflected changes in Austrian and Hungarian legislation regarding the

61 Čepulo 2006a, p. 365-367.
62 Čulinović 1956, p. 151-155; Prišlin Krbavski 2006, p. 330.
63 Šidak *et al.* 1968, p. 213 *et seq.*
64 Čepulo 2006a, p. 374-376.
65 Čepulo 2003, p. 67-71.
66 Čepulo 2002, p. 189-190.

amendments of the ABGB and enactments of the new laws on civil procedure in Austria (1895) and Hungary (1911).[67] The discussions on reforming civil procedure were stopped with the First World War. The draft of the Civil Code prepared in 1917, consisting of the adoption of the amendments of the ABGB and certain orders of the Austrian government, was not enacted due to the breakdown of the state.[68]

8. Conclusion: Modernization and Judicial Independence in the Context of Centre – Periphery Relations

The process of modernisation of the Croatian judiciary can best be presented through an approach based on centre-periphery relations. This best follows the reforms undertaken from 1873 to 1880, but its features can be observed in the other periods as well.

The reforms in Croatia-Slavonia were based upon Austrian laws and supported by the Austrian-based legal education that itself reflected certain influences of more developed models (German, French, and Belgian). Croatian legislation did not offer its own principle of organisation for the judiciary, but rather depended upon imported Austrian models that were adapted to the Croatian environment. Austrian laws were transferred to the autonomous Croatian legislation after a certain delay. Apart from the modifications necessary to adapt Austrian regulations to the situation in Croatia, particularly regarding the social structure, the broader institutional framework and lack of financial resources, the Austrian models usually lacked certain liberal characteristics related to the position of the individual in administrative and criminal procedures. That approach was partly induced by the central government in Budapest, which was resistant to the reforms in Croatia-Slavonia in general, and their liberal content in particular as a means of strengthening the Croatian autonomy. Scepticism of the Croatian political elite regarding the ability of the undeveloped Croatian society to accept more liberal reforms was another reason. But apart from such restrictions and the lack of financial means, the reforms from 1873 to 1880 set rational normative grounds that included grants of judicial independence in general compliance with the tendencies of the time.

However, grants of judicial autonomy did not develop into stabilized factual patterns. Instead conditions deteriorated due to the abrogation of the principle of judicial tenure that was replaced in 1884 by empowering the government to reassign judges and intervene in disciplinary proceedings. This and some other changes in criminal proceedings neutralized the liberal essence of the reforms from the previous period. The political context of these changes was authoritarian rule veiled in a constitutional facade from 1883 to 1903, which subjected the Croatian political scene to strict control in the interest of the Budapest and Vienna centres. Later re-liberalization of the various parts of the regulation, including a limitation of

67 Čepulo 2006a, p. 376; Zuglia, p. 22.
68 Gavella 1993, p. 339 *et seq.*

the government's influence on the judiciary in 1917, improved conditions. However conditions still remained below the standards set in 1874.

This paper reveals certain deeper cultural and structural determinants of the process by which the modern Croatian judiciary was formed. It indicates that the process of modernizing the judiciary in Croatia-Slavonia depended upon the influence of external centres. In other words Croatia-Slavonia was in a peripheral position. It was peripheral to West European centres that generated ideas and institutional models that were accepted elsewhere. These influences were transferred through the Austrian legislation and doctrine that was used as a direct model or source country. This legal-cultural influence intertwined with Croatia-Slavonia's political dependency upon Vienna, which was largely expressed in the initial phases of the modernization up to 1868. Later changes show how the influence of the Budapest political centre strongly affected modernization in the autonomous framework. Budapest's role was by and large restrictive, tending to diminish the political subjectivity of its autonomous political unit. This was reflected in the tactics of Croatian reformers and the narrower content of liberal reforms, while the principal changes undertaken in the authoritarian political framework intentionally avoided judicial autonomy.

The Croatian-Slavonian judiciary was formed during the 19th century as a rational structure on the basis of Austrian regulations. It has developed through various phases and did not follow a linear line of progress. It did not develop and stabilize as an independent institution due to the absence of normative and factual preconditions. For this reason it has not played a role in shaping the legal culture typical for a judiciary in developed countries, which is among the principal supports in the process of forming the rule of law.

Bibliography

Bayer 1940
Bayer, V., *Problem sudjelovanja nepravnika u savremenom kaznenom sudovanju*, Zagreb: nakl. autora, 1940.

Bayer 1968
Bayer, V., 'Opći povijesni razvoj advokature u krajevima koji danas tvore SR Hrvatsku', *Odvjetnik* 18, 1968, 9, p. 53-55.

Bayer 1976
Bayer, V., 'Stogodišnjica donošenja hrvatskog Zakonika o krivičnom postupku iz 1875. god', *Zbornik Pravnog fakulteta u Zagrebu* 26, 1976, 1, p. 6-7.

Bayer 1995
Bayer, V., *Kazneno procesno pravo - odabrana poglavlja. Knjiga II. Povijesni razvoj kaznenog procesnog prava, ed. D. Krapac*, Zagreb: Ministarstvo unutarnjih poslova Republike Hrvatske, 1995.

Beuc 1985
Beuc, I., *Povijest institucija državne vlasti Kraljevine Hrvatske, Slavonije i Dalmacije*, Zagreb: Arhiv Hrvatske, 1985.

Braudel 1980
Braudel, F., 'History and Social Scienes: The *Longue Durée*', in: Braudel, F. (ed.), *On History*, Chicago: The University of Chicago Press, 1980, p. 25-54 (originally: Braudel, F., *Écrits sur l'historie*, Paris: Flammarion, 1969).

Burke 1992
Burke, P., *History and Social Theory*, Cambridge/Oxford: Polity/Blackwell's, 1992.

Čepulo 1996
Čepulo, D., 'Razvoj pravne izobrazbe i pravne znanosti u Hrvatskoj do 1776. godine i Pravni fakultet u Zagrebu od osnivanja 1776. do 1918. godine', in: Pavić, Z. (ed.), *Pravni fakultet u Zagrebu, knj. 1/1*, Zagreb: Pravni fakultet u Zagrebu, 1996, p. 56-65.

Čepulo 1999
Čepulo, D., 'Dioba sudstva i uprave u Hrvatskoj 1874. godine - institucionalni, interesni i poredbeni vidovi', *Hrvatska javna uprava* 1, 1999, 2, p. 255-257.

Čepulo 1999a
Čepulo, D., 'Pravo hrvatske zavičajnosti i pitanje hrvatskog i ugarskog državljanstva 1868-1918 - pravni i politički vidovi i poredbena motrišta', *Zbornik Pravnog fakulteta u Zagrebu* 49, 1999, 6, p. 795-825.

Čepulo 2000
Čepulo, D., 'Hrvatsko-ugarska nagodba i reforme institucija vlasti u Hrvatskom Saboru 1868-1871', *Zbornik Pravnog fakulteta Sveučilišta u Rijeci*, Supplement 1, 2000, p. 117-148.

Čepulo 2000a
Čepulo, D., 'Sloboda tiska i porotno suđenje u banskoj Hrvatskoj 1848-1918', *Hrvatski ljetopis za kazneno pravo i praksu* 7, 2000, 2, p. 931-932.

Čepulo 2002
Čepulo, D., 'The press and jury trial legislation of the Croatian Diet 1875-1907: Liberalism, fear of democracy and Croatian autonomy', *Parliaments, Estate and Representation* 22, 2002, p. 169-192.

Čepulo 2003
Čepulo, D., *Prava građana i moderne institucije: europska i hrvatska pravna tradicija*, Zagreb: Pravni fakultet u Zagrebu, 2003.

Čepulo 2006
Čepulo, D., 'Building of the modern legal system in Croatia 1848-1918 in the centre-periphery perspective', in: Giaro, T. (ed.), *Modernisierung durch Transfer im 19. und frühen 20. Jahrhundert*, Klostermann: Frankfurt a. M., 2006, p. 47-91.

Čepulo 2006a
Čepulo, D., 'Izgradnja modernog hrvatskog sudstva 1848-1918', *Zbornik Pravnog fakulteta u Zagrebu* 56, 2006, 2-3, p. 325-383.

Čepulo 2007
Čepulo, D., 'Legal education in Croatia from medieval times to 1918: organisation, study programmes and transfers', in: Pokrovac, Z. (ed.), *Juristische Ausbildung in Osteuropa bis zum ersten Weltkrieg* (Studien zur europäischen Rechtsgeschichte, Rechtskulturen des modernen Osteuropa. Traditionen und Transfers, Band III), Frankfurt am Main: Klostermann, 2007 (forthcoming).

Čulinović 1956
Čulinović, F., *Državnopravna historija jugoslavenskih zemalja XIX. i XX. vijeka, I*, Zagreb: Školska knjiga, 1956, p. 151-155.

Gavella 1993
Gavella, N., 'Građansko pravo u Hrvatskoj i kontinentalnoeuropski pravni krug', *Zbornik Pravnog fakulteta u Zagrebu* 43, 1993, 4, p. 335-375.

Gessner, Hoeland & Varga 1996
Gessner, V., Hoeland, A. & Varga, C. (eds.), *European Legal Cultures* (Tempus textbook series on European law and European legal cultures), Aldershot: Dartmouth, 1996.

Goldstein 1999
Goldstein, I., *Croatia: A History*, London: Hurst & Company, 1999.

Gross 1985
Gross, M., *Počeci moderne Hrvatske*, Zagreb Globus: Centar za povijesne znanosti Sveučilišta u Zagrebu, Odjel za hrvatsku povijest, 1985.

Gross & Szabo 1992
Gross, M. & Szabo, A., *Prema hrvatskome građanskom društvu*, Zagreb: Globus, 1992.

Hesselink 2001
Hesselink, M.W., *The New European Legal Culture*, Deventer: Kluwer, 2001.

Lanović 1929
Lanović, M., *Privatno pravo Tripartita*, Zagreb: Tipografija, 1929.

Ljubanović 1994
Ljubanović, V., '120. obljetnica donošenja i sankcioniranja hrvatskog Zakona o kaznenom postupku od 17. svibnja 1875', *Hrvatski ljetopis za kazneno pravo i praksu* 1, 1994, 1, p. 237-262.

Markus 1996
Markus, T., 'Zakonske osnove odbora Sabora Hrvatske i Banskog vijeća 1849. godine', *Časopis za suvremenu povijest* 28, 1996, 1-2, p. 143-145.

Markus 2000
Markus, T., *Hrvatski politički pokret 1848.-1849. godine*, Zagreb: Dom i svijet, 2000.

Nelken 1997
Nelken, D. (ed.), *Comparing Legal Cultures*, Aldershot: Dartmouth, 1997.

Nelken 2004
Nelken, D., 'Using the Concept of Legal Culture', *Australian Journal of Legal Philosophy* 29, 2004, p. 1-28.

Pavličević 1989
Pavličević, D., *Hrvatske kućne zadruge I*, Zagreb: Sveučilišna naklada Liber: Zavod za hrvatsku povijest Filozofskog fakulteta, 1989.

Perić 2005
Perić, I., *A History of the Croats*, Zagreb: Centar za transfer tehnologije, 2005.

Pliverić 1885
Pliverić, J., *Das Verhältnis Kroatiens zu Ungarn*, Zagreb: L. Hartman, 1885.

Prišlin Krbavski 2006
Prišlin Krbavski, D.P., *Vlasničko pravno uređenje alodijalnih i urbarskih zemalja u Hrvatskoj nakon reforme općeg privatnog prava godine 1852/1853* (doctoral thesis defended at the University of Zagreb, Faculty of Law), 2006.

Šidak 1968
Šidak, J. *et al.*, *Povijest hrvatskoga naroda g. 1860-1914*, Zagreb: Školska knjiga, 1968.

Steindorff 2001
Steindorff, L., *Kroatien. Vom Mittelalter bis zur Gegenwart*, Regensburg and München: Verlag Friedrich Pustet, 2001.

Teubner 1998
Teubner, G., 'Legal Irritants: Good Faith in British Law or How Unifying Law Ends Up in New Divergences', *The Modern Law Review* 61, 1998, p. 1-32.

Tilly 1997
Tilly, Ch., *Suočavanje sa društvenom promenom*, Beograd: Filip Višnjić, 1997 (original: Tilly, Ch., *Big structures, Large Processes, Huge Comparisons*, New York: Russell Sage Foundation, 1984).

Watson 2001
Watson, A., *Legal History and a Common Law for Europe. Mystery, Reality, Imagination* (Institutet för Rättshistorisk Forskning. Serien III: Rättshistoriska Skrifter), Stockholm: Institutet for Rattshistorisk Forskning, 2001.

Zuglia
Zuglia, S., *Građanski parnički postupak u Hrvatskoj i Slavoniji. Predavanja.* Zagreb: s.a.

III. Public Justice: Towards Accessible and Efficient Dispute Resolution

Jon T. Johnsen

HUMAN RIGHTS IN THE DEVELOPMENT OF LEGAL AID IN EUROPE: THE POLICY WORK ON LEGAL AID IN THE COUNCIL OF EUROPE AND ITS COMMISSION ON THE EFFICIENCY OF JUSTICE (CEPEJ)*

1. Introduction

Human rights impact on legal aid schemes in many ways. Both the UN Covenant on Civil and Political Rights[1] and the European Human Rights Convention[2] (ECHR) contain specific regulations on the right of the accused to legal assistance in criminal cases. They also make it an obligation for the government to provide the charged with legal assistance and cover the costs when deemed necessary (UN Covenant Article 14 (3) d, ECHR Article 6 (3) c).[3]

My impression from following the international legal aid debate for more than thirty years is that we have put little emphasis on human rights. The focus has been on national systems and government's willingness to establish generous and efficient legal aid schemes. Practical results have also been of more interest than the national peculiarities of the legal frameworks. In contrast, human rights form a global system that might bear on legal aid schemes in many countries.

A timely change took place at the 2005 conference of the International Legal Aid Group in Killarney, Ireland, when Roger Smith presented a paper on the role of the European Union in the development of legal aid, particularly in the countries in Eastern Europe. He also discussed the influence of the European Convention on Human Rights and the judgements from the European Court of Human Rights (ECtHR) in Strasbourg.[4]

* Previously presented at the conference *Transforming Lives: The Impact of Legal Services and Legal Aid*, Belfast 19-21 April 2006 and Law and Society' Association Conference *Law's End(s)*, Baltimore 6-9 July 2006.

1 International Covenant on Civil and Political Rights.

2 Convention for the Protection of Human Rights and Fundamental Freedoms.

3 Other regional human rights instruments probably contain similar provisions, but I have not researched them.

4 Smith 2005.

My intention is to follow up on Smith's commendable initiative. Since the beginning of 2003, I have been involved in the work of the Council of Europe's Commission on the Efficiency of Justice (CEPEJ) as an expert member of the Commission's different working groups. CEPEJ has also carried out some analysis of legal aid systems among European jurisdictions as part of its work, although legal aid has not yet been the focus.

My aim is to discuss human rights as a *driving* force in developing national legal aid schemes in Europe. I do not primarily focus on how legal aid might be used to protect human rights, although these two issues are closely intertwined. I limit my discussion to the European Convention and the European Court of Human Rights.

First, I will summarize some of the major doctrinal principles on legal aid embodied in the Convention and the case law of the Court. They form the legal framework for the impact human rights might have on national legal aid schemes (2).

I will then turn to the policy work of the Council of Europe and summarize the resolutions and recommendations that the Council has issued on legal aid during the last thirty years. These 'soft law' instruments supplement the legal framework embodied in the Convention. The human rights framework on legal aid also forms the background for my analysis of the operation of CEPEJ. I emphasize its attempts at developing reliable European statistics on judicial systems and especially on legal aid (3), and end with comments on the potential CEPEJ has for influencing national legal aid policy in Europe in the coming years (4).

2. The Legal Aid Doctrine of the ECtHR

2.1. *Article 6*

The ECHR is expected to be an effective system. Its guarantees must work in practice. The human rights obligations apply to the state. They must respect and implement the rights granted to the citizen through effective legal mechanisms. Consequently, the citizen's perspective is important in the interpretation of the Convention.

Article 6 (1) of the Convention entitles everyone to a fair hearing 'in the determination of his civil rights or obligations or of any criminal charges against him'. Inherent in the notion of a fair hearing is the idea of contradiction. A party to a trial has the right to be informed about the claim or charge against him and the evidence that supports the claim. A party also has the right to present evidence of his own and to argue his case before the court or other decision-making body. Efficient use of such procedural rights presupposes a certain level of legal competence. Important elements are doctrinal knowledge, ability in legal fact analysis and evidence presentation as well as strategic experience in handling legal claims. Without such expertise, the right to a fair trial might become valueless, depending on the complexity of the matter and the judicial system in question. If a party or an accused should lack the necessary expertise himself or herself, he/she must be allowed representation by persons sufficiently skilled. Lawyers are commonly used. As independent professionals, they sell their services in the market, usually at a high price. As with lack of competence, human rights provisions do not accept poverty as a barrier to a fair trial. States are then obliged to provide a legal representative for free or for a sum that the citizen can afford.

The right to legal representation before the courts, independent of capacity to pay, is explicitly guaranteed in ECHR Article 6 (3) regarding criminal cases. The clause reads:

> 'Everyone is entitled to ... defend himself in person or through legal assistance of his own choosing, or if he has not a sufficient means to pay for legal assistance, to be given it free when the interests of justice so require'.

The wording appears discretionary and leaves many issues open to interpretation. Article 6 (3) labels its entitlements as 'minimum rights' in criminal cases. They must be understood as specifications of the general principle of the right to a fair trial in Article 6 (1). Since Article 6 (1) covers criminal charges as well as civil rights and obligations, the 'interests of justice'-standard is not limited to criminal cases. States must also provide legal aid in civil cases when it is deemed necessary to make the right to a fair trial effective. Since they are referred to as 'minimum rights', Article 6 (1) might be used to expand the rights in Article 6 (3) - including free legal assistance - beyond their wording.

2.2. *Case law*

Few cases on the entitlement to legal aid have been brought before the ECtHR. Still, two principled decisions exist.

Airy v Ireland[5] from 1979 contains important specifications on the right to legal aid. The judgement relates to civil legal aid, but bears on criminal aid as well. Airy wanted a judicial separation from her husband, only obtainable at the Irish High Court. Airy was a low-wage earner and a homemaker with four children and at times on unemployment benefits. She could not afford to pay for legal representation and legal aid was not available. ECtHR accepted that self-representation in the High Court would not be effective, due to the character of the substantive matter, the complexity of the proceedings and Airy's personal capacity. None of the petitioners in the 255 judicial separation proceedings initiated in Ireland in the period 1972-1976 had been unrepresented (§ 20-28).

The decision set the precedent which obliges governments to provide sufficient funding for legal aid according to the following discretionary criteria:

- the importance of the case to the individual (applicant);
- the complexity of the case;

5 Application No. 6289/73.

- the individual's capacity to represent himself;
- the costs and the individual's capacity to carry them.

ECtHR applies the criteria on the concrete circumstances of the complaint. Access to courts is meant to be effective for all citizens, independent of their economy. A violation will be established if the costs appear as an actual barrier against access to court. The judgement does not establish a right to a free trial. The citizen might be expected to carry parts of the court costs if they are adapted to his economic capacity.

Steel and Morris v *the United Kingdom*[6] from 2005 confirms the principles of Airy. Steel - a part-time bar worker - and Morris - a postal worker - had joined London Greenpeace, a small group unconnected with Greenpeace International, promoting environmental issues. The group published a leaflet accusing McDonald's of contributing to 'the starvation of the third world' by 'hungering' for profit, economic imperialism, gross misuse of resources, destroying rainforests, producing unhealthy food using a lot of chemicals, exploiting children as consumers, inhuman slaughtering of animals used in the hamburger production and exploiting young unskilled workers as staff (§ 12). McDonald's sued the applicants for slander.

The proceedings became one of the largest in English history with 313 court days at the first instance and 23 for the appeal hearings, involving 40.000 pages of documentary evidence and 130 oral witnesses, several of them expert witnesses giving evidence on a range of scientific questions. Legal arguments took some 100 days in court. The judgements alone filled more than 1, 100 pages (§ 65).

Although the applicants fulfilled the means test, defamation proceedings were outside the legal aid scheme in England. They were mainly left to represent themselves, while McDonald's used a team of experienced lawyers, and were estimated to have spent more than £ 10 million in legal expenses (§ 58, 68). Although the applicants had been given considerable latitude by the presiding judge, and also had conducted their case 'forcefully and with persistence' (§ 68), ECtHR found that in a matter of such complexity, neither the sporadic help from volunteer lawyers nor the extensive assistance from the judge, could form 'any substitute for competent and sustained representation by an experienced lawyer familiar with the case and with the law of libel ...'. The disparity between the levels of representation 'was of such a degree that it could not have failed ... to have given rise to unfairness, despite the best efforts of the judges at first instance and on appeal' (§ 69). The Court concluded that the denial of legal aid was a violation of Article 6 (1) (§ 72).

The judgements contain important requirements to national legal aid schemes. Generally, states cannot set priorities in a way that conflicts with the individual rights embodied in Article 6. All states have a responsibility to organize their judicial systems in a manner that corresponds to human rights. The wording does not allow for any 'margin of appreciation' or leeway for the Member States if they

[6] Application No. 64186/01.

should want to deviate from the principles laid down by the Court by adopting less comprehensive schemes.

Although the principles laid down in Airy appear discretionary and flexible, they have important consequences for the shaping of legal aid schemes. I will discuss three issues, namely economic limits and contributions, limitations on the scope of legal problems and legal advice.

2.3. *Economic Limits and Contributions*

As mentioned, Article 6 does not lay down a right to free trials, but costs must be adjusted to the economic capacity of the individual. This principle obviously bears upon the framing of both economic limits and contributions. Legal aid cannot be limited only to the poor. If costs become exorbitant, as in *Steel and Morris,* middle income and possibly high-income people might also be in need for public support. If the overall economic limits exclude them, a dispensation system might be necessary.

Alternatively, a legal aid system that demands middle-income people to pay ordinary legal aid costs themselves, might not conflict with Article 6 if it protects against exorbitant costs. For the upper part of the income ladder, contributions might be steep. However, legal aid schemes that only cover costs up to a certain limit, or use percentage contributions without any ceiling, might conflict with Article 6 if costs become high.

2.4. *Limitations on Types of Problems*

Several jurisdictions limit the scope of their schemes either by excluding certain types of legal problems, or by restraining them to selected categories. The *Airy* criteria, however, do not distinguish between different types of legal claims. The main criterion is the problem's importance to the individual, not the legal category.

In *Steel and Morris,* the UK argued in vain that:

> 'states did not have unlimited resources to fund legal aid systems, and imposing restrictions on eligibility for legal aid in certain types of low priority civil cases were therefore legitimate, if such restrictions were not arbitrary' (§ 53).

The Court accepted that a defamation action on average might be of lesser importance to vital personal interests than a claim for legal separation as in *Airy.* However, defamation issues had to be considered according to the *Airy* criteria too. The applicants did not start the defamation proceedings, but acted as defendants to protect their right to freedom of expression. The damage claim, which amounted to £ 100,000 at the outset, would have ruined both applicants. Schemes, that keep certain types of legal problems outside the legal aid coverage, might therefore conflict with Article 6 unless they have sufficient space for dispensations according to the *Airy* criteria.

According to its wording, Article 6 only covers 'civil rights and obligations' and 'criminal charges'. It does not mention rights and duties regulated by administrative law. The Court, however, has gradually expanded the scope of Article 6. Today, its guaranties also apply to public law claims that are parallel to civil rights and obligations. Public approval of private land sale, public licensing of professionals or private business, expropriation and social security are all examples of issues that Article 6 protects.[7] It seems safe to infer that the 'interest of justice' - standard must expand similarly and that the states' obligation to provide sufficient legal aid must cover court proceedings in such administrative matters.

ECtHR interprets the concepts of the convention autonomously - according to its own understanding - independent of the interpretation of punishment concepts in national law or doctrine. According to its case law, 'punishment' and 'criminal' charge have a more comprehensive meaning than in most national codes and doctrines (*Engel and others* v *the Netherlands*).[8] Also sanctions perceived as administrative in national law, might qualify as criminal charges, for example, penalty taxes due to missing tax returns, penalty custom due to neglected reporting to the custom's authorities, denial of conditional release from prison, etc. The Court's autonomous interpretation will also bear on legal aid. If an administrative sanction qualifies as a criminal charge, Article 6 (3) also will apply. Schemes that lack coverage for such proceedings, although 'the interests of justice so require', might therefore risk violating the Convention.

2.5. *Legal Aid outside Trials*

To what extent do human rights oblige states to provide legal assistance outside the courts? Many disputes that end in court might well become resolved otherwise, had the parties had access to legal advice at an early stage, be it by resignation, settlement, conciliation, mediation, arbitration, etc.

We also know that an efficient use of the right to a fair trial presupposes that the decision whether to go to court or not, is an informed one. Most people need expert advice whether to sue or dispute a claim in court. Especially among poor people, many are not capable even to decide properly whether to seek a lawyer's assistance about a legal dispute. A legal aid system that limits itself strictly to court assistance might be criticized for not helping its citizens sufficiently in finding out if they need the protection provided by Article 6.

In *Golder* v *UK*,[9] a prisoner wanted legal advice on whether to sue a guard for defamation. The prison denied him to write to a lawyer. The majority of the ECtHR stated that the entitlement to a fair trial also comprehended a right to make an informed decision as to whether to use this entitlement or not. If a person lacks sufficient means for necessary counselling, legal aid might become a prerequisite for effective access to court, and I would expect the Court to make Article 6 (1) bear upon the issue. However, since the main aim of Article 6 is to protect access to court

7 Møse 2002, p. 298-307.

8 Application No. 5100/71; 5101/71; 5102/71; 5354/72; 5370/72.

9 Series A No. 18 1975.

for claims with merits and not the unfounded ones, governments' obligation to provide access to pre-trial legal counselling might be shaped accordingly.

Most disputes end with solutions other than a court decision, and a decision to sue is often made late in the course of a dispute. Still, most solutions of legal disputes outside the courts are arrived at in the 'shadow' of the court outcome – especially if legal experts are involved. The court alternative appears as the 'last resort'; the options for settlement or alternative dispute resolution (ADR) are compared to the court alternative. If poor people lack access to legal aid at the pre-trial stage, they might be without the opportunity to choose their strategy from an informed evaluation of the alternatives. Making legal aid available only after the court alternative has been chosen might pressure poor people to overuse of the courts. At present, the ECtHR is clogged with complaints on excessive delay in the courts. As we will see, speeding up the case handling is a major challenge both for the ECtHR, the Council of Europe and for European governments. More efficient use of negotiations and ADR will obviously reduce the case volume, and better legal advice systems might facilitate such solutions for people without means. However, better legal aid systems might also increase poor and ordinary people's awareness of their rights, and by that increase clogging in the courts.

States differ significantly in their handling of administrative cases. A complex issue is at what stage in the case handling process the principles of Article 6 come into play. If the state in question has an administrative complaint procedure before the claim can be brought before the courts, it might well happen that the interest of justice requires representation also at the administrative stage.[10]

Criminal cases are processed in a complex chain with many actors and stages, running from the discovery or reporting of the offence, until after the sentence is served and the case closed. While Article 6 requires that courts decide the guilt and punishment, the courts' involvement in investigation and indictment differs significantly between the European jurisdictions. However, many decisions made by the police and prosecution or the accused before the main hearing, might impact significantly on the final outcome. If access to legal counsel is important to the accused in such matters, we might argue that the principles for access to legal aid in Article 6 also apply to investigation and prosecution.

2.6. *Simplifications in Law and Procedures*

When handling delays, the Court has repeatedly stated that 'Article 6 (1) of the Convention imposes on the Contracting States the duty to organize their judicial systems so that they can meet its requirements'.[11] The statement gives Member States freedom to choose different strategies to fulfil their obligations.

An alternative to providing legal aid is to reorganize the judicial system in a way that diminishes the need for legal assistance. Governments might simplify both substantive and adjective law, and educate citizens in legal matters or develop 'do-

10 *Marschner* v *France*. Application No. 51360/99.

11 See as a recent example *Hadjinis* v *Greece* (Judgement of 28 April 2005).

it-yourself'-systems that might diminish the need for professional legal counselling and representation. Many matters might be resolved faster and more inexpensively through ADR. Such strategies might become alternatives for governments to improving their legal aid schemes. However, Article 6 might still demand the states to secure that all persons possess the opportunity to make an informed choice between ADR and courts.

3. The Council of Europe's Policies on Legal Aid

Human rights, as understood by the Court, mainly constitute minimum rights that governments may not violate. States are free to establish better systems, and the Council of Europe often encourages such developments. The Council has launched an ambitious policy strategy for improving the efficiency of European judicial systems on the assumption of voluntary acceptance by the Member States. Strategies concern improvements in both the quality and the speed of courts. They are inspired from the principles of Article 6, but as policy strategies, the convention obligations do not limit them. Any remedy or improvement that might enhance speed and quality in the judicial systems might in theory be analyzed and proposed to the Member States for implementation.

3.1. *Resolutions and Recommendations on Legal Aid*

Since access to legal services might be instrumental in making the entitlements of the ECHR effective, the Council has issued many documents over the years that encourage governments to develop legal aid. Some significant resolutions and recommendations:

- *Resolution 76 (5)* on legal aid in civil, commercial and administrative matters.[12] It recommends that governments grant legal aid to all citizens of Member States and to all residents on an equal footing with its own citizens.

- *Resolution* 78 (8) on legal aid and advice,[13] stating that economic obstacles to legal proceedings ought to be eliminated, and that an appropriate system of legal aid will contribute to that aim. Access to legal advice for the economically weak is of equal importance in the elimination of barriers to access to justice. The resolution has an appendix that spells out principles for the means test and contribution system, the merits test, availability, what sort of legal service a proper legal aid

12 Adopted by the Committee of Ministers on 18 February 1976 at the 254th meeting of the Ministers' deputies. Council of Europe. European Commission for the Efficiency of Justice, *Relevant Council of Europe Resolutions and Recommendations in the field of efficiency and fairness of justice.* CEPEJ (2003) 7 Rev, p. 5.

13 Adopted by the Committee of Ministers on 2 March 1978 at the 284th meeting of the Ministers' deputies. Council of Europe. European Commission for the Efficiency of Justice, *Relevant Council of Europe Resolutions and Recommendations in the field of efficiency and fairness of justice.* CEPEJ (2003) 7 Rev, p. 6-8.

system ought to deliver, a complaint system, and that the government ought to carry the financial responsibility.

- *Recommendation No R (93) 1* on effective access to the law and to justice for the very poor,[14] states that governments should promote actions to make the legal profession aware of the problems of the very poor, promote legal advice service for them and carry the costs, and set up advice centres in underprivileged areas. States should facilitate access to ADR for the very poor and extend legal aid to such methods of conflict solution. They also should extend legal aid for the very poor to all judicial bodies and proceedings, be it civil, criminal, commercial, administrative, social, etc. and to aliens and the stateless habitually residing on the territory of the Member State in which the proceedings take place. The grounds for refusing legal aid before judicial bodies ought to be limited to claims that appear inadmissible or manifestly ill founded, or because the application does not satisfy the standard of being 'in the interests of justice'. States are advised to simplify their procedures for granting legal aid to the very poor, and to consider enabling NGOs to provide representation both before national tribunals and international judicial bodies as the European Commission and ECtHR.

- *Recommendation (2000) 21* on the freedom of exercise of the profession of lawyer.[15] States should encourage lawyers to provide legal service to persons in economically weak positions and ensure that effective legal services are available to them, in particular to persons deprived of their liberty.

- *Recommendation (2001) 3* on the delivery of court and other legal services to the citizen through the use of new technologies.[16] States should provide the text of the law both as enacted and as consolidated in electronic form, readily available to the public. Simple text access to the law database should be free of charge for the public and government should make the electronic base available for the private sector for further adaptation and dissemination.

14 Adopted by the Committee of Ministers on 8 January 1993 at the 484th meeting of the Ministers' deputies. Council of Europe. European Commission for the Efficiency of Justice, *Relevant Council of Europe Resolutions and Recommendations in the field of efficiency and fairness of justice.* CEPEJ (2003) 7 Rev, p. 27-29.

15 Adopted by the Committee of Ministers on 25 October 2000 at the 727th meeting of the Ministers' deputies. Council of Europe. European Commission for the Efficiency of Justice, *Relevant Council of Europe Resolutions and Recommendations in the field of efficiency and fairness of justice.* CEPEJ (2003) 7 Rev, p. 59-63, esp. p. 61.

16 Adopted by the Committee of Ministers on 28 February 2001 at the 743rd meeting of the Ministers' deputies. Council of Europe. European Commission for the Efficiency of Justice, *Relevant Council of Europe Resolutions and Recommendations in the field of efficiency and fairness of justice.* CEPEJ (2003) 7 Rev, p. 84-9, esp. p. 85.

The listing demonstrates that legal aid has been a matter of concern for the Council for more than thirty years. It has used different 'soft law' instruments for improving the legal aid schemes in Europe.

3.2. *European Commission for the Efficiency of Justice (CEPEJ)*

The Council's ambitions concerning the quality of the judicial systems of the Member States have also developed. Recently, it has recognized a need for a general overhaul of the judicial systems of the Member States to ensure that they work according to the Court's present interpretations of the Convention. A major instrument is the establishment of the European Commission for the Efficiency of Justice (CEPEJ). I will now analyze how this initiative might affect legal aid. First, I will describe the construction and general aims of CEPEJ and its work so far, and then analyze more thoroughly what its work might mean to legal aid in Europe.

Although justice improvement has been a significant part of the human rights policies of the Council for a long time, the triggering event for establishing CEPEJ has been the huge backlog of the Court. According to Article 34, any person, NGO or group, who alleges violations of the Convention, may complain to the Court after having exhausted available national remedies. Despite an extensive screening and a recent reorganization of the Court, it has received complaints in tens of thousands each year, resulting in a steady increase in backlogs. According to oral information from the president of the court, L. Wildhaber,[17] the Court had 44.000 incoming cases in 2005, and a caseload of 82.000, of which 72.000 qualified as backlog. They had received over 7.000 complaints more than three years ago.

Analyses showed that the bulk of the complaints related to violations of Article 6 on fair trial, with by far the largest category being violations of the entitlement to trial 'within reasonable time'. It appeared as a detrimental paradox that the Court - designed to be the prime protector of swift trials - was unable to comply with the requirement. The steering bodies of the Council wanted to remedy the problem both by making national remedies against human rights violations more effective, and by removing the causes for the claims by improving the quality and speed of the Member States' judicial systems. They decided to establish a new organ to deal with the challenges.

Resolution (2002)12 (Res2002) 12) established CEPEJ from 2003.[18] Its bodies are:

- a plenary with representatives from all Member States that meets twice a year;
- a bureau with four members elected from the representatives, that function as a board for the Commission;
- 1-3 (or more) working parties with a maximum of six expert members.[19]

17 Presented at the CEPEJ plenary on 7-9 December 2005 and recorded by the author.

18 Adopted by the Committee of Ministers on 18 September 2002 at the 808th meeting of the Ministers' deputies and amended on 19 March at the 832nd meeting of the Ministers' deputies. Council of Europe. European Commission for the Efficiency of Justice, *Resolution Res(2002)12 establishing the European Commission for the Efficiency of Justice (CEPEJ).* CEPEJ/GENERAL (2003), p 1.

The resolution points to the requirements of the Convention, especially Article 5 on the right to liberty and security, Article 6 on the right to a fair trial, Article 13 on the right to an effective remedy against human rights violations and Article 14 that prohibits discrimination in the enjoyment of human rights. It outlines four major tasks for CEPEJ, namely to improve access to justice and the efficient functioning of the courts, secure the status and role of the legal profession, improve the administration of justice and management of the courts, and the use of information and communication technologies.

Legal aid is accentuated as one main vehicle for access to justice. Legal advice and assistance both for the defence against criminal charges and for the determination of civil rights and obligations shall be available 'when the interests of justice so require'. Special reference is made to the resolutions and recommendations summarized above and to recommendations on the use of ADR, especially on mediation.[20]

The working methods of CEPEJ are:

- examine results achieved by the different judicial systems by using common statistical and evaluation methods;
- define problems and areas for improvements and exchange views on how the European judicial systems work;
- develop better tools for analyzing judicial systems and models for improving them that are well adapted to the existing problems in the Member States;
- assisting individual Member States in their request on how to better comply with the human rights requirements;
- suggest, if deemed necessary, that the relevant steering committees of the Council of Europe draft new legal instruments or amendments to existing ones.[21]

CEPEJ might develop indicators, collect and analyze data and define measures and means of evaluation. It might also issue reports containing statistics, best practice surveys, guidelines, action plans, opinions and general comments. The Commission might establish collaboration with a research group and invite qualified persons, specialists and NGOs for exchange, arrange hearings and create networks of professionals working in the justice area. CEPEJ will not be a supervisory or monitoring body, which means that independent control of the Member States' fulfilment of their human rights obligations on efficient justice is outside its scope. Improvements presuppose voluntary acceptance and collaboration from the states. Data - for example on unrepresented poor parties in trials - might, however, suggest that human rights obligations are violated.[22]

19 European Commission for the Efficiency of Justice (CEPEJ), *Rules of procedure (CEPEJ/ GENERAL (2003) 3)*, p. 3.

20 *Res(2002)* 12 article I.1.i, cf. appendix 2 (*CEPEJ/GENERAL (2003) 3*), p. 3 & p. 8.

21 Article 2 (1) of appendix 1 to *Res (2002) 12 (CEPEJ/GENERAL (2003) 3)*, p. 5.

22 *Res(2002)* 12 article 2 (2) & 3 (*CEPEJ/GENERAL (2003) 3)*, p. 5-6.

CEPEJ is not a specialized legal aid organization. Legal aid reform is part of a broader strategy that also targets other parts of the justice systems. A general understanding of how it operates is crucial when analyzing its legal aid work.

CEPEJ's mandate expires at the end of 2009. In the next two paragraphs, I will describe CEPEJ's focus on legal aid during its first three years of function. Although improvement of legal aid has been a significant part of CEPEJ's mandate from the start, it has not been the prime target of the work until now. The two main issues were to collect and issue reliable statistics on the main characteristics of European justice systems, and to develop strategies for reducing court delay without reducing judicial quality. The data collection also comprises legal aid indicators, and I will describe them first (3.3). Apparently, legal aid is not a major factor behind delay, or a main remedy against it. However, CEPEJ's ideas of reducing delay also have some implications for legal aid that I will mention (3.4). I will then turn to CEPEJ's focus on legal aid for the remaining years of its mandate (3.5).

3.3. *European Survey*

3.3.1. Method and Purpose

An important part of the work during the first four years has been a European survey of judicial systems in the member countries. A working group developed an extensive questionnaire on public expenditures on courts and legal aid, the judiciary and the courts, court performance, public prosecutors and legal professionals, and sent it to the governments for answering. The research was meant as a pilot study with the aim to develop a statistical tool for measuring and evaluating the performance of the judicial systems as recommended in the mandate of CEPEJ.[23] The findings have been published in CEPEJ: *European Judicial Systems 2002* and cover 40 states that had signed the ECHR. A new study with data from 2004 was published in 2006.[24] It includes 45 States, 44 Council of Europe members and the data for Montenegro (which participated as a part of the Union of States of Serbia and Montenegro). Only Switzerland and 'the former Yugoslav Republic of Macedonia' are missing.

A comparative study of 45 jurisdictions is a demanding task with vast methodological problems.[25] From a researcher's point of view, there are certain peculiarities connected with studies carried out under the auspices of an international organization of governments.

All data in the survey had to be collected through official channels. The ministries and court administrations provided the information and answered the questionnaire. If research or other sources showed differing data, the study had to stick to the official version. Of course, CEPEJ might question the received

23 CEPEJ *European Judicial Systems 2002*, Council of Europe Publishing *(CEPEJ 2005)*, p. 9-10.

24 CEPEJ *European Judicial Systems.* Edition 2006 (2004 data), CEPEJ Studies No 1. Council of Europe *(CEPEJ 2006)*.

25 The author was a member of the working group that supervised the first study.

information in private, but as an international body of governments, CEPEJ cannot publicly denounce or disregard information it has received from its Member States.[26]

The judicial systems in Europe differ significantly both in structure and in the conceptualization of its elements and functions. National statistics differ similarly. The huge variations meant that the respondents perceived the bulk of questions differently, and that the answers and statistical information on the same question often related to entities in the respective judicial systems that were not directly comparable. Using a functional approach by describing certain essential functions in the judicial systems and requesting information about them independent of the national structure and conceptualization, often led to 'blank' answers, since the national statistics lacked entities that corresponded to the functional description in the questionnaire.[27] To remedy the problems, CEPEJ organized meetings with the national reporters,[28] and issued lengthy instructions on how to fill in the questionnaire.[29]

The statistics presented in the first report still had severe validity problems. Due to its character of a pilot study, the working group at a certain point decided not to ask the Member States for further corrections even when it had strong indications that a misunderstanding might make the reported data misleading. Improving data quality as part of the revision process of the 2006 report seemed a better strategy than putting more efforts into improving the 2002 data.

The questionnaire therefore underwent a major revision before the collection of the 2004 data. The data quality of the 2006 report has improved significantly.[30] It advises against comparing the 2002 data with the 2004 data.[31]

As an international body of independent states without monitoring tasks, CEPEJ also felt reluctant to present data in a way that might be conceived as a ranking of the states. Therefore, the reports mainly present statistics alphabetically according to the nation's name. Some are also presented according to numeric value. Comments are sparse, mainly limited to what can be read directly from the tables and figures. CEPEJ has not tried to analyze the immense variations. The main justification is fear that such analysis might easily amount to criticism of several states. The variable quality of the data presented also might lead to severe misjudgements of the findings. From a scientific point of view, such a presentation appears unsatisfactorily, and the alphabetical presentation makes it difficult to read the essential information from the tables and figures. CEPEJ has, however, encouraged everyone interested to make their own analysis of the findings and the

26 See *CEPEJ 2005* appendix 3, p. 106-108 for a description of the methodological issues, and appendix 4, p. 109-119 for a listing of variations in counting and computing of the data received. *CEPEJ 2006* contains the methodology discussion on p. 7-15 and in Chapter 15 Appendix, p. 156-216.

27 *CEPEJ 2005*, p. 12-13.

28 *CEPEJ 2005*, p. 15.

29 See *CEPEJ 2005*, p. 90-205 and *CEPEJ 2006*, p. 9-11 & p. 156-216.

30 *CEPEJ 2006*, p. 9-10.

31 *CEPEJ 2006*, p. 13.

intention is to make the data set downloadable from the Internet free of charge, making it possible for everyone to make their own analysis.[32]

Due to the vast methodological problems described above, one might ask if the European survey-project is too ambitious. Earlier studies using statistical methods for international comparisons of legal aid have been vulnerable to the criticism of whether they actually compare the same phenomenon. I agree with the criticism and have instead advocated a qualitative approach.[33] Many aspects of the CEPEJ study underpin such a criticism.

Still I find the CEPEJ study interesting, able to provide data of value, also on legal aid. It is a huge enterprise. It comprehends 45 jurisdictions with more than 800 million people. It includes many jurisdictions that have been absent in legal aid research. More than 100 people have been involved in the data collection of the last report.[34]

Since the governments studied have decided to set up CEPEJ themselves and also confirmed the study, their commitment to providing the data asked for was far gréater than in a study conducted by an independent institution like a university or a research institute. Not only will the governments put more effort into providing data only available for internal use, there is reason to believe that governments, if necessary, also will develop new statistics to meet the needs of CEPEJ and contribute to the building of a common European statistics on judicial systems. One major goal of CEPEJ is to develop better statistic tools as a vehicle for the better administration of justice within the Member States. We might suggest that statistics produced for the needs of CEPEJ also might be useful for the governments' internal purposes and for the reform debate. Hopefully, it might initiate more sophisticated analysis and reforms of judicial systems in Europe.

3.3.2. Findings on Legal Aid

The questions on legal aid in the surveys were not many, mainly mapping some basic information about the schemes. The 2004 questionnaire asked about the annual budget spent on legal aid, the means and merits test, court fees, legal expense insurance and distribution of the costs of the case according to the outcome. It had questions concerning internet sites with access to legal texts, case law of higher courts and legal forms. The 2006 questionnaire requested much of the same information as the pilot study. It is, however, reasonable to believe that data quality has been significantly improved. CEPEJ also has developed plans to do the survey at regular intervals, although their status is still uncertain. If they establish a working group on legal aid,[35] this group might also want to develop this part of the European survey.

32 Due to the data quality problems, Internet publication was postponed until the 2004 data was ready. They are now available on the CEPEJ website (<http://www.coe.int/CEPEJ>, last consulted 20 March 2007) (*CEPEJ 2006*, p. 11).

33 See Johnsen & Regan, forthcoming.

34 *CEPEJ 2006*, p. 8.

35 See *infra* § 4.5.

Arguably, the selection of questions appears somewhat arbitrary, since CEPEJ tries both to produce information that might help CEPEJ's own policy tasks, as well as information that is of interest to the general debate.

A listing of the total 2004 public expenditure on courts and legal aid shows tremendous variations. Liechtenstein reports 324 Euros per inhabitant and Monaco 130, while Armenia used 0.70 Euros and Azerbaijan 2 Euros.[36]

Looking specifically into legal aid, of the 45 countries that completed the questionnaire, nine did not report any legal aid budget because they lacked legal aid schemes or did not produce a budget that they could report separately. Expenditures varied enormously among the states that provided figures. While Azerbaijan used 0.003 Euros and Armenia 0.005 Euros per inhabitant, England and Wales spent 58 Euros per inhabitant, while Scotland spent 55.

The legal aid budget made up 1% or less of the court budget in Azerbaijan and Georgia. It made up 2% in Italy, 13% in France, 49% in Ireland and 84% in Norway, while Scotland spent 2.3 times more on legal aid than on courts, only topped by England and Wales that used 7 times more on legal aid than on courts.[37]

If we compare with the GDP, expenditures on legal aid vary between 0.001 and 0.2% of the GDP.[38] Since wealth differs greatly between European nations, we might expect that the costs for a legal aid scheme that satisfy the requirements of the ECHR also differ significantly. However, the cost level is only one of many factors that influence expenditures. Volume also is important. Crime rates influence the need for criminal legal aid, while conflict solution patterns influence the need for civil legal aid, etc.

Information on expenditures on civil and criminal aid respectively, appears far more limited. Only 19 countries were recorded in the 2002 survey. Three of them could not provide the expenditure on criminal cases, and six lacked figures for civil cases. Two countries did not report the number of grants in criminal cases and three could not provide the number of civil grants.

The distribution of costs between the schemes varied widely among the nations that provided figures. Many of them spend most of their budgets on criminal legal aid: Italy and Andorra 100%, Turkey 78%, Norway 66% and Ireland 63%. Others spend most on civil legal aid: Germany 81%, France 76% and Switzerland 59%. Germany with 82 million people and France with 60 million inhabitants only reported a total expenditure on criminal legal aid slightly above the figures of Sweden with 9 million inhabitants and Norway with 4.5 million inhabitants (88 and 81 million Euros against 79 and 74).[39]

The CEPEJ omitted these questions in the 2004 survey, most probably because of the low response. However, they added some new issues. 44 countries responded that they provide legal representation in court cases in criminal matters and 38 in civil matters.[40]

36 *CEPEJ 2006*, p. 36-37, table 6.

37 *CEPEJ 2006*, p. 20-21, table 2 and p. 28-29, table 4.

38 *CEPEJ 2006*, p. 28-29, table 4.

39 *CEPEJ 2005*, p. 24, table 4.

40 *CEPEJ 2006*, p. 44, table 8.

Three out of five countries practice a means test for access to legal aid for criminal cases, while four out of five do so for court representation in civil matters. Some states report a maximum income and property ceiling for criminal cases, and most do so for civil cases.[41] Almost all countries practice a merit's test.[42]

The number of legal aid grants also varies significantly. Croatia provides one grant per 10.000 inhabitants, Turkey 15, Hungary 52, Finland 152, the Netherlands 211, England and Wales 452 and Scotland 802.[43]

The data gathered are rough and basic. I still believe they give an impression of an immense variation in the access to legal aid in Europe. Although the sources of error are vast, one cannot escape the notion that the enormous variation in legal aid funding among European countries also mean that the legal aid offered to the poorer part of the population differs significantly both in volume and quality. A proposition that one will find widespread violations of the entitlement to legal aid embodied in Article 6 in the countries with the poorest funding seems close at hand. The figures strongly suggest that states also prioritize very differently between civil and criminal legal aid.

3.4. *Optimum Time Frames*

The other major field of work for CEPEJ has been delay. A working group developed a document entitled 'A new objective for judicial systems: the processing of each case within an optimum and foreseeable time frame'.[44] The document is labelled a 'Framework Programme'. It contains a wide range of general strategies – labelled 'action lines' – for increasing the speed of European judicial systems. None of them specifically addresses legal aid. Most of them concern time-management systems for court and court administrations. However, if the courts' working methods change, then the tasks for legal aid lawyers also will change, and might affect the content of legal aid schemes. Many strategies proposed in the Framework Programme therefore will bear upon legal aid. I will summarize the most striking ones with a few comments on possible legal aid impacts:

- Better involvement of all actors or players in the court process (action line 7).[45] It means that legal aid lawyers and clients will also meet new demands for participating in the planning of trials.

- Mandatory information concerning foreseeable time frames to the parties involved (action line 7).[46] Legal aid lawyers might experience stricter requirements on their information to clients.

41 *CEPEJ 2006*, p. 47, table 10.
42 *CEPEJ 2006*, p. 48, table 11.
43 *CEPEJ 2006*, p. 45, table 9.
44 *CEPEJ 2004*, 19 Rev 2.
45 *CEPEJ 2004*, 19 Rev 2, p. 13.
46 *CEPEJ 2004*, 19 Rev 2, p. 13.

- Development of procedures requiring the courts and the parties to agree on a time schedule (action line 7).[47] Legal aid lawyers might have to prepare their clients to make them understand the consequences of alternative timetables and decide between them.

- Informed negotiations about the use of ADR (action line 7).[48] To make an informed choice, legal aid clients must understand the difference between the ADR alternatives in question and the ordinary court proceedings.

- Sanctions against abusive processes (action line 8).[49]

- Complaint mechanisms against delay in ongoing matters (action line 12).[50] Legal aid lawyers must master such complaint systems to be able to use them for their clients.

- Higher priority to quality at the first instance than at the appeal level (action line 9).[51] The demands for preparation might increase, also for legal aid lawyers.

- Multi tracking - meaning that cases might be handled and progressed differently by the courts, according to their complexity, importance to the parties, state of emergency, etc. (action line 10).[52] Legal aid lawyers will have to adjust to a more flexible time planning.

- Special attention to the most vulnerable categories of participants in the organization of hearings, with special attention to victims of violent crime (action line 11).[53] Legal aid clients obviously are an important target group for such concerns. Legal aid lawyers ought to be well aware of their client's tolerance for litigation stress to use such remedies efficiently.

- More flexible rules on territorial jurisdiction (action line 13).[54] The remedy will also bear on territorial flexibility in the allocation of legal aid.

- The professional actors (judges, prosecutors, lawyers, bailiffs, etc.), their professional organizations and the users of the courts ought to become more involved in the management of the courts (action lines 14 and 16).[55] If the problems of the poor in the judicial systems are to be addressed properly, both

47 *CEPEJ 2004*, 19 Rev 2, p. 13.
48 *CEPEJ 2004*, 19 Rev 2, p. 13.
49 *CEPEJ 2004*, 19 Rev 2, p. 14.
50 *CEPEJ 2004*, 19 Rev 2, p. 15.
51 *CEPEJ 2004*, 19 Rev 2, p. 14.
52 *CEPEJ 2004*, 19 Rev 2, p. 15.
53 *CEPEJ 2004*, 19 Rev 2, p. 15.
54 *CEPEJ 2004*, 19 Rev 2, p. 16.
55 *CEPEJ 2004*, 19 Rev 2, p. 16.

poor people's organizations and legal aid lawyers must be involved in such processes.

- IT-strategies and information systems ought be introduced or developed on a broad scale (action line 1,[56] action line 5).[57] The development of such systems obviously is important to legal aid. It will mean new demands on the skills of legal aid lawyers, and might open new possibilities for IT-assisted dispute resolution systems also within legal aid.

Although not systematically analyzed, I suggest that the jurisdictions with the most extensive backlogs also have the least developed legal aid systems. We know that the communist ideology put limited emphasis on independent courts and lawyers. Therefore, the former East-block countries have little infrastructures to build on in establishing sufficient legal aid systems.

The huge delay problem, uncovered by the unmanageable number of complaints concerning delay to the Court, probably affects the poor in Europe disproportionately. Traditional judicial systems produce few incentives by themselves for avoiding delay. It is left to the parties involved to put pressure on the system. Pressure presupposes resources, for example the ability to argue or complain formally or informally either in person or through a competent lawyer, mobilizing networks, making public pressure to bear or to pay bribes. Poor people usually have access to less of such resources than the wealthy. If the legal aid system is weak or nonexistent, the effects of delay might become strongly class biased.

Most judicare systems lack proper incentives for private lawyers to prioritize efficiency and help as many clients as possible. They accept cases on a case-to-case basis. A private lawyer, who needs a certain amount of income from legal aid, might well achieve this more comfortably by spending more time on fewer cases. Then the economic incentive to counteract delay and inefficiency might be lacking. In most jurisdictions, legal aid work pays less than ordinary commissions, which makes it unpopular among private lawyers. Insufficient funding might result in substandard legal aid work. When forced to prioritize, we might suspect legal aid lawyers to focus on the material issues before delay, and on quick, informal solutions before full trials.

Contracting and other mechanisms that make lawyers responsible for handling larger groups of cases might counteract such strategies, but few jurisdictions apply them. Another option is salaried offices with the responsibility to serve districts, groups or anyone who qualifies.

[56] *CEPEJ 2004*, 19 Rev 2, p. 10-11.

[57] *CEPEJ 2004*, 19 Rev 2, p. 12.

The Framework Programme states that 'every state is responsible for providing the players in the judicial system with the necessary resources with which to operate' (action line 1).[58] The statement also bears upon legal aid.

3.5. *CEPEJ's Plans for an Expert Group on Legal Aid*

CEPEJ's plans for the remaining part of its mandate, suggest more emphasis on legal aid. According to the 'Medium-Term Activity Programme', access to court is an essential issue when dealing with the efficiency of justice and the application of Article 6 of the Convention. A new working group ought to be established with the objective

> 'to facilitate the access to court to all citizens, without hampering the efficiency of the functioning of the justice system and enabling the smooth application of the instruments and standards of the Council of Europe as regards legal aid'.

As shown, the information in 'European judicial systems; facts and figures' shows significant differences in the way Member States address legal aid. The working group is meant to analyze the situation of legal aid in the Member States and the existing solutions, giving priority to a comparative analysis in order to recommend specific measures to the Member States.[59]

CEPEJ should provide technical assistance upon request to any member of the Council of Europe in developing their judicial systems. It might also function as a catalyst for exchanges between different jurisdictions, and promote ideas of improving justice at seminars, conferences and other suitable events and use its website as a 'clearing-house' for studies and reform ideas. Those tasks will also comprehend legal aid reforms. The main undertaking is to produce viable reform ideas, convey them to governments, interest groups and the public, and assume that the states might adopt them voluntarily.

4. Human Rights Influence on Legal Aid Schemes in Europe

Although 'gentle persuasion' might seem to be CEPEJ's main instrument for stimulating the Member States to carry out judicial reforms, other mechanisms might add to its influence. The Council of Europe is an international body that uses legally binding instruments or 'soft law', and other policy strategies to influence their Member States. Its main bodies consist of representatives of the Member States, which means that major decisions usually build on a broad consensus. While CEPEJ itself is excluded from monitoring the Member States, issue recommendations or use other instruments of international law, it might draft proposals when needed and forward them to other bodies of the Council.

58 *CEPEJ 2004*, 19 Rev 2, p. 10.

59 *CEPEJ 2005 (10), Medium-Term Activity Programme*, p. 9.

Still, ideology and appeal to the self-interests of the Member States are the most common tools. As a human rights-based organization, the Council of Europe has a powerful image as the main promoter of human rights in Europe. All Member States have obliged themselves to the loyal implementation of the Convention and the case law of the Court. Although Member States are free to fulfil their obligations with other means than suggested by CEPEJ, there is reason to believe that countries with deficits in their legal aid systems will be receptive to reform models from CEPEJ. Since the other Member States and the Council back them, implementing these models will minimize the risk for being found in violation of the Convention. In a recent decision on the entitlement to a trial within a reasonable time, the Court made an explicit reference to a statement in the 'Framework Programme',[60] and stated that instituting a system of compensations for violations of Article 6, is not sufficient. Remedies must effectively prevent delay (*Sordino* v *Italy*, § 73 and 74).[61] The reference demonstrates that the Court takes an interest in the work of CEPEJ, and is willing to adhere to it in their judgements. A similar reference to future models for legal aid reform, will obviously add to CEPEJ's importance to the Member States.

The Convention and the case law of the Court might also be used in national courts. Article 13 of the Convention obliges all states to provide an effective legal remedy in national law for securing everyone their rights under the Convention. Legal aid lawyers might allege violations of its provisions on legal aid, both before national courts[62] and - if not successful - before the ECtHR. New judgements on legal aid will develop the case law of the Court and bear upon all 46 Member States.

Governments dislike the Court finding against them. Since the Convention allows individuals to sue, the risk of being found in violation is significantly higher than for most other human rights instruments that do not provide for an individual complaint procedure. Several states prefer to operate with safety margins and change dubious rules or practices as a precaution instead of risk being found in violation of the Convention. These features add weight to the policy recommendations of the Council. Many states - often the small and rich ones - emphasize the development of human rights as an important part of their foreign policy. They are then vulnerable to complaints of not fulfilling them at home.

Legal aid activists might also use the human rights' framework in national debates as arguments for legal aid reform. Such activism might help the national enforcement. Amnesty International might provide a model. As an NGO, they *inter alia* focus on violations of the prohibition against cruel or unusual punishment, the death penalty, persecution and imprisonment without a fair trial, censorship and intimidation of political opponents to the regime in power, etc. They invoke public opinion, pressure groups and other governments to put pressure on the government responsible for the alleged violation. Similarly, pressures to fulfil

60 See p. 16.

61 Application No 36813/97.

62 Or other bodies with the competence to function as a national remedy against violations of the ECHR.

human rights commitments on legal aid might be brought to bear upon governments by activist organizations on legal aid.

Another important enforcement vehicle comes from the accession process for countries wishing to join the European Union. They are all required to meet a set of conditions - the Copenhagen criteria - before they can become members. They must guarantee democracy, the rule of law, human rights and the protection of minorities. The standards applied on the judicial systems are derived from the provisions in the Convention, especially from Article 6. Monitoring reports show that the judicial systems and legal aid schemes of the applicant countries have deficits that they must sufficiently remedy before they can join.[63] Knowing the strong drive of the new states to become part of the European Union, there is reason to believe that the accession process also will facilitate the adoption of reform proposals from CEPEJ.

63 Smith 2005, esp. p. 6-13.

Bibliography

Møse 2002
Møse, E., *Menneskerettigheter,* Oslo: Cappelen Akademisk Forlag, 2002.

Smith 2005
Smith, R., *Old Wine in New Bottles: legal aid lessons and the new Europe*. Paper to the International Legal Aid Group conference, Killarney, Ireland, 8-10 June 2005, also published in *Justice Journal,* vol. 2, 2, 2005 (<http://www.justice.org.uk/publications/listofpublications/index.html>, last consulted 2 April 2007).

A. Grgić

THE LENGTH OF CIVIL PROCEEDINGS IN CROATIA: MAIN CAUSES OF DELAY*

1. Introduction

A functioning justice system is the essential prerequisite of a modern society. However, the inability of the courts to render their decisions promptly in civil cases may be regarded as one of its most common problems.

Article 6 § 1 of the Convention for the Protection of Human Rights and Fundamental Freedoms ('the Convention')[1] guarantees the right to a hearing 'within a reasonable time' to everyone within the jurisdiction of the 46 Council of Europe Member States. However, it is evident that some countries have a tendency to be more successful in ensuring that right than others.

The European Court of Human Rights ('the Court'), as the supervising body of the enforcement of the Convention rights, delivers numerous judgements, each year finding violations of the reasonable time requirement in many Member States. The number of such applications has grown exponentially, in particular during the 1990s.[2]

Problems encountered depend mostly on the specific nature of each country's procedural system, but other factors such as legal history, tradition and mentality should not be underestimated.

In Croatia the right to a hearing within a reasonable time has existed ever since 1991 and the entry into force of the International Covenant on Civil and Political Rights. It was reinforced when Croatia ratified the European Convention on 5 November 1997 and is now embodied in Article 29 of the Constitution.

This paper shall firstly offer a brief overview of the criteria taken into consideration by the Court when deciding length-of-proceedings cases. It shall then

* The opinions expressed in this paper are those of the author and do not necessarily reflect the views of the ECtHR.

1 The European Convention on Human Rights, as the most important Convention adopted by the Council of Europe, entered into force in 1953. To date, it has been ratified by 46 European States, i.e. all with the exception of Belarus.

2 Further in this respect see Uzelac 2004, p. 283-314.

review the Court's case-law in respect of Croatia, identifying some of the structural problems contributing to unreasonable delays in those cases. Finally, the paper shall also analyse the existence of the necessary remedies to solve problems of this kind at the national level.

2. The Court's Criteria

Over the years, the Court has established certain criteria, which it takes into consideration when assessing the length of proceedings in each specific case. To this end, the Court normally uses the following wording:

> 'The reasonableness of the length of proceedings must be assessed in the light of the circumstances of the case and with reference to the following criteria: the complexity of the case, the conduct of the applicant and the relevant authorities and what was at stake for the applicant in the dispute'.

As it will be shown, in assessing the reasonableness of the length of proceedings, the Court has adopted a pragmatic approach; it has never expressed itself *in abstracto* on a 'standard length' for any specific type of proceedings. It has rather adopted an individual approach to each specific case, at the same time developing guidelines to be taken into account. More generally, the Court focuses on establishing whether the period for which the case was pending before each court instance had been used effectively and whether there had been any unjustified periods of inactivity imputable to the authorities.

2.1. *Complexity of the Case*

The first criterion to be considered, the complexity of the case, includes certain legal or factual difficulties which may arise during the proceedings.

The Court has frequently held certain types of cases to be factually complex by nature (such as land consolidation, fraud or taxation cases). For example, in the case of *Wiesinger* v *Austria*,[3] the Court observed '... that land consolidation is by its nature a complex process, affecting the interests of both individuals and the community as a whole ...'.

On the other hand, a certain legal complexity in a case may also arise should there be an ongoing change in legislation or the need to await the outcome of some other parallel proceedings.

In the case of *Todorov* v *Bulgaria*[4] the applicant's civil case had been stayed for almost six years awaiting the outcome of concurrent criminal proceedings. The Court concluded:

> 'It is not the Court's task to determine ... whether the proceedings were ... properly stayed, because, as a general rule, it is for the domestic courts to establish the facts and

3 Application No. 11796/85, judgement of 30 October 1991, § 55.
4 Application No. 39832/98, judgement of 18 January 2005, § 48.

> interpret and apply national law. The Court will not interfere with their rulings unless the applicant succeeds in demonstrating that they acted arbitrarily. Nor can the Court find that a system providing for the dependence of civil proceedings on criminal ones, when they concern the same or related facts, goes per se against the requirements of Article 6 of the Convention. However, the Court notes that after the civil proceedings were stayed, no activity took place in the concurrent criminal proceedings for more than six years ... This delay, which appears unjustified, in turn led to a delay in the civil proceedings'.

Coupled with further delays which occurred after resumption of the civil proceedings, the Court concluded that there had been a violation of Article 6 § 1.

In any event, the complexity of the case alone will rarely be a sufficient reason to justify the unreasonable length of a given case.

2.2. *Conduct of the Applicant*

Another important element the Court shall take into consideration - although rather as a negative presumption - is the conduct of the applicant in the proceedings. As the Court has held on many occasions,

> 'the applicants' behaviour is an objective fact which cannot be attributed to the respondent State and which must be taken into account in determining whether or not the reasonable time referred to in Article 6 § 1 ... has been exceeded'.[5]

So as to avoid liability for the protraction of the proceedings, the applicant

> 'is required only to show diligence in carrying out the procedural steps relating to him, to refrain from using delaying tactics and to avail himself of the scope afforded by domestic law for shortening the proceedings. He is under no duty to take action which is not apt for that purpose'.[6]

Accordingly, the fact that the applicants make full use of remedies available to them under the domestic law cannot be held against them.[7] Furthermore, neither will any delays resulting from a fact beyond the applicants' control be attributable to their conduct.[8]

However, an applicant shall be held liable for a delay in the proceedings in situations when he or she manifestly shows bad faith. Classic examples of such conduct would be moving for adjournment of hearings,[9] repeated groundless requests for withdrawal of the judge assigned to hear the case, failure to attend

5 See, for example, *Wiesinger* v *Austria, supra* note 3, § 57.

6 See *Unión Alimentaria Sanders S.A.* v *Spain*, No. 11681/85, judgement of 7 July 1989, A157, § 35.

7 See *Erkner and Hofauer* v *Austria*, No. 9616/81, judgement of 23 April 1987, § 68.

8 As, for example, in the case of *Lavents* v *Latvia* (No. 58442/00, judgement of 28 November 2002), where the applicant was on several occasions admitted to hospital due to his poor health condition.

9 See *Ciricosta and Viola* v *Italy*, No. 19753/92, judgement of 4 December 1995, A337-A.

hearings or report changes of address,[10] poor coordination between the applicant and the counsel or a refusal to undertake a necessary examination.[11]

2.3. *Conduct of the Competent Authorities*

Pursuant to the Court's case-law, a state can only be held liable for delays imputable to the authorities.

Many Contracting States have claimed that their courts were, for one reason or another, facing an exceptional backlog of cases. In those cases the Court has generally stated that

> 'it [was] for the Contracting States to organise their legal systems in such a way that their courts can guarantee to everyone the right to a final decision within a reasonable time in the determination of his or her civil rights and obligations'.[12]

Under very specific circumstances the Court has accepted a government's argument in this respect. However, this occurred only in cases when the respondent states proved that they had taken, with requisite promptness, remedial action to deal with an exceptional situation of this kind.[13] A temporary backlog, as a consequence of which reasonable steps had been undertaken, will likewise not be in breach of Article 6.[14]

Occasionally, delays may be caused by the wish of a higher court to hear several similar cases together. Such a decision will be tolerated by the Court in so far as it does not cause a substantial delay in one of the proceedings concerned.[15]

2.4. *What is at Stake for the Applicant*

Lastly, the Court will take into account what was at stake for the applicant in the proceedings complained of. The domestic courts may therefore be called upon to expedite a case of certain importance even beyond the time-limits which would otherwise, in a standard case, be deemed acceptable.

In its practice the Court has repeatedly held that certain types of proceedings were of highest importance and should be dealt with with exceptional speed.

The first group of such cases is related to employment disputes, involving dismissals, salary arrears and other employment-related benefits.[16] In such cases

10 See *Mitev* v *Bulgaria*, No. 40063/98, judgement of 22 December 2004.

11 See *Proszak* v *Poland*, No. 25086/94, judgement of 16 December 1997, ECHR 1997-VIII.

12 See, among many other cases, *Frydlender* v *France* [GC], No. 30979/96, § 45, ECHR 2000-VII; *Zwierzyński* v *Poland*, No. 34049/96, § 55, ECHR 2001-VI; *Atanasović and Others* v *the former Yugoslav Republic of Macedonia*, No. 13886/02, § 36, judgement of 22 December 2005.

13 See, for example, *Buchholz* v *Germany*, No. 7759/77, judgement of 6 May 1981.

14 See *Unión Alimentaria Sanders, supra* note 6, § 40.

15 Further to this issue see *infra* § 3.5.

16 See, among many other authorities, *Ruotolo* v *Italy*, No. 12460/86, judgement of 27 February 1992; *Lechelle* v *France*, No. 65786/01, judgement of 8 June 2004.

> '... special diligence [is] required..., regard being had to the fact that the amount the applicant claimed was of vital significance to him and was connected with his professional activity ...'.[17]

Furthermore, the Court often stressed that special diligence was necessary in cases on compensation for accident victims, in particular when death of a family member deprived the applicants of their principal means of financial support[18] or when the case involved particularly grave bodily injury.[19]

Another situation in which particular urgency is called for is when the applicant's health so requires. A good example in this respect is offered by cases concerning persons contaminated by the HIV virus during blood transfusions.[20] In such cases the Court held

> '... that what was at stake in the proceedings complained of was of crucial importance to the applicant in view of the disease from which he is suffering... exceptional diligence was called for in this instance, notwithstanding the number of cases to be dealt with ...'.

The Court has also stressed the importance of a speedy conclusion of cases concerning civil status and capacity.[21] In the case of *Mikulić* v *Croatia*,[22] for example, the Court stated:

> 'In view what was at stake for the applicant in the present case, that is her right to have her paternity established or refuted and thus to have her uncertainty as to the identity of her natural father eliminated, the Court considers that the competent national authorities were required by Article 6 § 1 to act with particular diligence in ensuring the progress of the proceedings'.

Finally, special diligence is particularly called for in childcare cases, including both custody disputes and reuniting children with their parents. The Court stressed on many occasions the importance of a speedy conclusion of such cases stating that:

> 'Proceedings relating to the granting of parental responsibility, including execution of the decision delivered at the end of them, require urgent handling as the passage of

17 See *Doustaly* v *France*, No. 26256/95, § 48, judgement of 23 April 1998.

18 See *Mehmet Özel and Others* v *Turkey*, No. 50913/99, judgement of 26 April 2005.

19 See *Kurt Nielsen* v *Denmark*, No. 33488/96, judgement of 15 February 2000; *Silva Pontes* v *Portugal*, No. 14940/89, judgement of 23 March 1994.

20 See, for example, *X* v *France*, No. 18020/91, judgement of 31 March 1992, A234-C; *A. and Others* v *Denmark*, No. 20826/92, judgement of 8 February 1996.

21 See, among many other authorities, *Bock* v *Germany*, No. 11118/84, judgement of 29 March 1989, A150; *Matter* v *Slovakia*, No. 31534/96, judgement of 5 July 1999.

22 Application No. 53176/99, judgement of 7 February 2002, § 44.

time can have irremediable consequences for relations between the children and the parent who does not live with them'.[23]

3. Length Cases Concerning Croatia and Main Causes of Delay

Since the ratification of the Convention in 1997, the Court has adopted close to a hundred judgements against Croatia (including friendly settlements), out of which approximately 45 concerned excessive length of proceedings. Most judgements in this respect concluded that there had been a violation of the individual's right to a hearing within a reasonable time.[24]

It is furthermore apparent that some 95% of those cases concern the length of civil proceedings or enforcement of a final court judgement.[25] All these factors indicate the existence of systemic problems within the Croatian civil justice system, the reasons for which are numerous and have been the subject of many discussions.[26]

However, in closely studying the Court's length cases examined with respect to Croatia, it is possible to identify several main causes of delay related to the functioning of civil proceedings as such. An overview in this connection is provided below.

3.1. *Successive Remittals*

One of the most common reasons causing simple civil cases to last - in the Court's view - an unreasonably long time are the repeated remittals of a case back to the first-instance court.

The foregoing causes a problem particularly in legal systems such as the Croatian one,[27] allowing for an unlimited number of remittals. The second-instance court reviews the case on appeal and simply quashes the first-instance judgement sending the case back to the lower court for a re-examination. Such practice gives

23 See *Ignaccolo-Zenide* v *Romania*, No. 31679/96, ECHR 2000-I, § 102; *Sylvester* v *Austria*, Nos. 36812/97 and 40104/98, judgement of 24 April 2003; *Monory* v *Romania and Hungary*, No. 71099/01, judgement of 5 April 2005.

24 For judgements which found no violation of this right see *Posedel-Jelinović* v *Croatia*, No. 35195/02, judgement of 24 November 2005 (five years and eight months for three levels of jurisdiction) and *Šoć* v *Croatia*, No. 47863/99, judgement of 9 May 2003 (over four years for one level of jurisdiction, but long periods of delay attributable to the applicant).

25 It would appear from the Court's case-law that criminal proceedings are not often characterised by length problems, mainly due to the short prescription periods (see *Camasso* v *Croatia*, No. 15733/02, judgement of 13 January 2005). The situation is somewhat more complex with regard to administrative proceedings, where unreasonable delays occur quite often, even though the parties have at their disposal an appeal and an action for failure to respond as a means of speeding up those proceedings (see *Počuča* v *Croatia*, No. 38550/02 and *Božić* v *Croatia*, No. 22457/02, both judgements of 29 June 2006).

26 See, among others, Vajić 2001, p. 981-990; Uzelac 2005, p. 1101-1136; Potočnjak 2006, p. 13-30.

27 A problem of this sort has been identified in many other Council of Europe Member States, such as Slovenia, Poland, Hungary, Bulgaria, Ukraine, Romania and Russia.

rise, both in theory and in practice, to an endless cycle of remittals thereby significantly contributing to the overall length of the proceedings.

In its more recent judgements, the Court has addressed the problem as follows:

> 'The Court notes that the decisions were rendered on ... instances and, consequently, cannot conclude that the courts were inactive in the present case. On the contrary, the delay in the present case is caused mainly by the re-examination of the case. Although the Court is not in a position to analyse the judicial quality of the case-law of the domestic courts, it considers that, since the remittal of cases for re-examination is usually ordered as a result of errors committed by lower courts, the repetition of such orders within one set of proceedings may disclose a serious deficiency in the judicial system'.[28]

In the case of *Zagorec* v *Croatia*,[29] in which the applicant's proceedings had been pending since 1992, the first-instance court had given three judgements on the merits. However, all of those judgements were subsequently quashed and remitted by the appellate court, which ultimately resulted in the finding of a violation of the 'reasonable time' requirement.

3.2. *Periods of Inactivity*

Almost without exception the Court will criticise periods of inactivity attributable to the domestic authorities of longer than a few months, irrespective of the reasons causing such lapse of time. These periods are often characterised by the court's failure to schedule any hearings or its laxity in obtaining certain information from other state authorities.

A particularly good example in this respect is offered in the case of *Radoš and Others* v *Croatia*,[30] which concerned the length of several sets of proceedings for payment. In one of the proceedings complained of the competent court had held a hearing on 6 November 1997, only to hold the next one on 2 April 2001. The time that had elapsed between the two hearings was attributable solely to the court for unsuccessfully trying to obtain a criminal case file from another division within the same court.

In another set of proceedings in the same case, the Court had concluded that not a single hearing had been held since the entry into force of the Convention in November 1997 and the rendering of the Court's judgement in November 2002.

[28] See, for example, *Wierciszewska* v *Poland*, No. 41431/98, judgement of 25 November 2003; *Puž* v *Slovenia*, No. 76199/01, judgement of 30 March 2006; *Kukharchuk* v *Ukraine*, No. 10437/02, judgement of 10 August 2006; *Cârstea and Grecu* v *Romania*, No. 56326/00, judgement of 15 June 2006.

[29] Application No. 10370/03, judgement of 6 October 2005.

[30] Application No. 45435/99, judgement of 7 November 2002, §§ 51-52, 89, 96.

3.3. *Court Administration*

Many delays in civil proceedings appear to be the consequence of the poor organisation or malfunctioning of the courts' registries and their work.

3.3.1. Service on the Parties

It is not uncommon for several months to elapse between the adoption of a judgement and its actual service on the parties. In the above-mentioned *Radoš* case, a judgement in one of the proceedings complained of was adopted on 14 October 1999, but only served on the applicant's lawyer on 26 September 2000.[31] In the case of *Antonić-Tomasović* v *Croatia,* the first-instance court gave its judgement in October 2000, only to serve it on the applicant in June 2001.[32]

3.3.2. Obtaining Documents from Third Parties

Another common problem occurs when the court is invited to obtain certain documents or information from another authority, such as for example the State Attorney's Office or the Bureau of Statistics. The reluctance of those authorities to cooperate with the courts is sometimes striking. For example, in the case of *Horvat* v *Croatia*[33] on 22 July 1998 the competent court requested another court to provide information on the legal status of a certain company. On 24 September 1998 the court received a reply containing information on a company other than the one in question. Subsequently, the competent court repeated its request in April 2000.

3.3.3. Sending of Files between Courts

On many occasions delays appear to be caused by the sending of case files from one court to another. In the case of *Nogolica* v *Croatia (no. 2),*[34] it took the first-instance court eight months to forward the appeal and the case file to the appellate court. Subsequently, it took the second-instance court a further 14 months to notice that the case file was lacking the power of attorney for the applicant's lawyer. It then returned the case file to the first-instance court, which obtained the missing document and sent it back in the following three months. The applicant's appeal was decided six months later, that is, almost three years after the appeal had been lodged. The Court criticised these periods, attributing them to periods of inactivity on the part of the domestic authorities.[35]

31 See the *Radoš* case, *supra* note 30, § 25.

32 See *Antonić-Tomasović* v *Croatia,* No. 5208/03, judgement of 10 November 2005, § 16.

33 Application No. 51585/99, judgement of 26 July 2001, §§ 31-32.

34 Application No. 29052/03, judgement of 17 November 2005, §§ 10-11.

35 Another example in this respect is provided in the case of *Fütterer* v *Croatia,* No. 52634/99, judgement of 20 December 2001, §§ 10-12, where it took the court two years to transmit the case to the appellate court, and following a remittal another 17 months to assign the case to a judge and hold a hearing.

In the above-mentioned *Antonić-Tomasović* case, the parties filed their respective appeals against the first-instance judgement in July 2001, including a request for exemption from court fees. The appeals were forwarded to the second-instance court in February 2002. Subsequently, in October 2002 the court returned the case-file to the first-instance court instructing it to decide on the applicant's request for exemption from court fees. The appeals were finally decided in September 2004.[36]

3.3.4. Change of Judges

Certain delays are due to the change of the judges assigned to hear the case. Even though the foregoing may be necessary for the proper administration of justice and, moreover, at times requested by the parties, it should not lead to a substantive delay in the proceedings. In the case of *Delić* v *Croatia*,[37] which concerned the length of several proceedings for payment, the first two sets of proceedings complained of were subject to a six-year delay following the resignation of the judge assigned to hear those cases in 1994. In the case of *Cerin* v *Croatia*,[38] the applicant had requested the withdrawal of the presiding judge in his case on several occasions. He subsequently instituted civil proceedings against the judge and the state resulting in the consequent withdrawal of the judge of his own motion. However, the change of judges assigned to the case had resulted in a delay of one year and nine months, which period had been criticised by the Court observing that: 'It is the normal task of the court in judicial proceedings to decide upon the circumstances which might call for the removal of judges participating in a particular case'.

3.3.5. Other Authorities

Admittedly, the liability for matters of court administration may sometimes lie on other authorities whose cooperation is necessary in matters such as service. In a case which eventually resulted in a friendly settlement, the judgement in the applicant's favour adopted in 1992 had not been served on the respondent company until at least 2003, because it had a business seat in Montenegro.[39]

3.3.6. Conclusion

It transpires from the foregoing that a substantive delay in the proceedings may often be caused by secondary operations, other than the mere work of a judge on a specific case. However, such actions are indispensable for the proper administration of justice. Even though a lot of work still remains to be done in this area, the computerising of the courts and the improvement of the collaboration between

36 See *Antonić-Tomasović*, *supra* note 32, §§ 17-19.

37 Application No. 48771/99, judgement of 27 June 2002, §§ 12-13 and §§ 18-19.

38 Application No. 54727/00, judgement of 15 November 2001, §§ 12-13, § 26 and § 29.

39 See *Bogdanović* v *Croatia*, No. 10993/03, decision of 15 September 2005.

different courts as well as other state authorities may prove to be a step forward in this respect.

3.4. *Conduct of the Proceedings*

It would appear that most cases examined by the Court undergo significant delays because of the hesitancy of the courts in conducting the proceedings. Problems of this sort can arise at any stage of the proceedings, but are most likely to come up before the first-instance court. They are usually manifested in the court's failure, in one way or another, to effectively control the proceedings.

3.4.1. Obtaining Evidence

For example, in the case of *Stojić* v *Croatia,*[40] the first-instance court was entirely inactive over a period of one and a half years because of the applicant's failure to submit the addresses of the witnesses she had proposed to be heard. In this connection the Court observed:

> 'During the period indicated by the Constitutional Court and subsequently by the Government (between 8 March 2001 and 22 November 2002), the court had not been obliged to wait for the applicant's submissions concerning her witnesses because the court itself has the authority to decide how to conduct the proceedings, in particular, which evidence to take and how to evaluate acts or omissions of the parties'.

A fairly specific situation arose in the above-mentioned case of *Mikulić* v *Croatia,* where the applicant had instituted proceedings with a view to having her paternity established. However, the putative father failed to appear on six hearings and refused to undergo the necessary DNA testing on six occasions. In those circumstances, the Court held that no procedural safeguards existed under the domestic law which would have compelled the respondent to comply with the court's order, nor were there any clearly prescribed consequences for the failure to do so. The overall length of proceedings of more than five years, which were still underway at the time of the adoption of the judgement, led the Court to find a violation of both Article 6 § 1 and Article 8 (right to respect for private life) of the Convention.

3.4.2. Obtaining Expert Opinions

Another common problem of first-instance courts is the appointment of experts and obtaining expert opinions, at times crucial for the proper outcome of the case. In the case of *Šundov* v *Croatia,*[41] where the applicant had requested the court to obtain seven additional expert opinions, the Court used a similar argument to the one mentioned above, accepting that:

[40] Application No. 36719/03, judgement of 1 June 2006.
[41] Application No. 13876/03, judgement of 13 April 2006.

> '... the applicant contributed to the protraction of the proceedings, but ..., on the other hand, that the domestic court did not have to grant additional expert opinions every time the applicant had requested it ...'.

Similarly, in the case of *Rajak* v *Croatia*,[42] it took the competent court more than two years to appoint an expert in the case due to the fact that one of the parties had raised an objection as to the impartiality of the expert initially proposed by the court.

3.4.3. Conclusion

Since the 2003 Amendments to the Civil Procedure Act, the Croatian civil proceedings have been characterised by the adversarial hearing, which places on the parties the obligation to provide the court with all relevant evidence concerning their case. However, even in such circumstances the domestic courts are not absolved from ensuring the compliance of the proceedings with the requirements of Article 6 § 1 of the Convention.

Even though the effectiveness of the proceedings was one of the main aims of the 2003 Amendments, from the Court's point of view it is still premature to tell whether and in which areas the new legislation has contributed to the achievement of that goal. In any event, the Court will surely in the future assess those changes with the scrutiny foreseen (required?) by the Convention.

3.5. *Delays before Higher Courts*

The Court's judgements reveal that a substantive delay sometimes occurs before the highest courts in the country. However, as it transpires from its case-law, the Court does not necessarily construe the reasonable time requirement for a highest court of a country in the same way as for ordinary courts.

This difference particularly concerns Constitutional Courts and their specific role as the 'guardian of the Constitution'. In the case of *Süßmann* v *Germany* the Court concluded that the Constitutional Court may sometimes take into account factors other than the mere chronological order in which cases arrive, such as the nature of a case or its importance in political and social terms.[43] In the *Süßmann* case, which concerned a dispute over the level of a supplementary retirement pension affecting many civil servants, the Court found it acceptable that the German Constitutional Court had grouped twenty-four cases raising the same issue and that it had given priority to a series of other urgent cases linked to the German reunification.

The Court applied the same approach in the case of *Gast and Popp* v *Germany*[44] by concluding that: '... while Article 6 requires that judicial proceedings be

42 Application No. 49706/99, judgement of 28 June 2001.
43 See *Süßmann* v *Germany*, No. 20024/92, judgement of 16 September 1996, § 56.
44 Application No. 29357/95, judgement of 25 February 2000, § 75.

expeditious, it also lays emphasis on the more general principle of the proper administration of justice'.

In the case of *Tričković* v *Slovenia*,[45] where the applicant's case concerning a military pension had been pending before the Constitutional Court for less than three years, the Court found no violation of the reasonable time requirement. The delay was found to be justified by the temporary heavy workload of the Constitutional Court as well as the importance of the applicant's case for its future case-law.

The Croatian government have, on the other hand, so far never succeeded in proving an argument of this sort. This is so mainly because the Court has always established other circumstances delaying the proceedings which could not be justified by the specific role or duties of the Constitutional Court within the Croatian legal system. It has already held unacceptable the length of proceedings of four years before one court instance - both the Supreme Court[46] and the Constitutional Court.[47]

A good example in this respect is the case of *Škare* v *Croatia*,[48] where the proceedings had been pending for thirteen years, almost seven and a half of which had passed after the Convention's entry into force in respect of Croatia. During that time it took the Supreme Court two and a half years to decide the applicant's appeal on points of law. Moreover, it subsequently took the Constitutional Court almost five full years to dismiss the applicant's constitutional complaint. As the case had to a certain extent involved legislation concerning transactions with immovable property owned by the former Yugoslav Army, the government claimed that the Constitutional Court had had to resolve individual petitions for review of constitutionality of those laws prior to deciding the applicant's complaint. The Court observed

> '... even assuming that it was necessary to await the outcome of the aforementioned abstract constitutional review proceedings ... before the applicant's case could be dealt with ... the Court notes that it took the Constitutional Court more than two years after the last petition for constitutional review had been refused to put the applicant's case on the agenda, and another nine months to do so after the case had been withdrawn ...'.

3.6. *Enforcement Proceedings*

Another issue the Court was called upon to decide on a number of occasions with regard to Croatia was the length of enforcement proceedings. Ever since the *Hornsby* v *Greece*[49] judgement, which provided that '... enforcement proceedings form an

45 Application No. 39914/98, judgement of 12 June 2001.
46 See *Gudeljević* v *Croatia*, No. 18431/02, judgement of 31 March 2005, see also *Jelavić-Mitrović* v *Croatia*, No. 9591/02, judgement of 13 January 2005.
47 See *Pitra* v *Croatia*, No. 412975/02, judgement of 16 June 2005.
48 Application No. 17267/03, judgement of 15 June 2006, § 28.
49 Application No. 18357/91, judgement of 19 March 1997, ECHR 1997-II.

integral part of the trial referred to in Article 6 § 1 of the Convention ...', the Court has frequently found violations of this right in respect of many Member States.[50]

Enforcement cases are usually quite complex and their protraction is seldom caused by one factor; normally the delay is the consequence of a certain laxity of the authorities coupled with the unwillingness of the enforcement debtor to fulfil the obligation.

This was particularly obvious in several Croatian cases lodged with the Court concerning eviction of illegal tenants. In the case of *Majski* v *Croatia*,[51] after the applicant had instituted proceedings with a view to eviction, the courts acted rather expeditiously in deciding the case and in issuing an eviction order. Subsequently, however, it took the enforcement authorities three and a half years to make the first attempt to evict the tenants. This period was in the Court's view unacceptable under Article 6 § 1.

In a similar case, *Pibernik* v *Croatia*,[52] where the applicant instituted proceedings for disturbance of possession of her flat, the competent courts gave a final decision in her favour only three and a half years later, even though such proceedings under domestic law are to be considered urgent. Furthermore, the applicant obtained an eviction order ten months after having requested it due to what appears to have been the refusal of the presiding judge to endorse the court decision with a certificate of enforceability. Given that the subsequent enforcement of the eviction order lasted for another four years due to many appeals and requests for postponement on the part of the illegal occupants, but also by two Ministries, the Court found a violation of the applicant's right to a hearing within a reasonable time and of the right to respect for her home.[53]

A somewhat unusual situation occurred in the case of *Buj* v *Croatia*,[54] which concerned the registration of the applicant's ownership in the land register as a form of implementation of the decision given in inheritance proceedings conducted after the death of his mother. The competent court that issued the decision gave an order to its land registry division to enter the change of ownership *ex officio* in the public register. In those circumstances the Court interpreted the land registry proceedings as a functional equivalent of enforcement and found Article 6 applicable to the case. Given that the decision acknowledging the applicant's ownership, which became final in 2002, had by the date of the adoption of the Court's judgement not been registered, the Court found a violation of the applicant's right to a hearing within a reasonable time.

50 See, among many other authorities, *Burdov* v *Russia*, No. 59498/00, judgement of 7 May 2002, *Prodan* v *Moldova*, No. 49806/99, ECHR 2004-IV (extracts); *Sharenok* v *Ukraine*, No. 35087/02, judgement of 22 February 2005; *Immobiliare Saffi* v *Italy*, No. 22774/93, judgement of 28 July 1999; *Okyay and Others* v *Turkey*, No. 36220/97, judgement of 12 July 2005.

51 Application No. 33593/03, judgement of 1 June 2006.

52 Application No. 75139/01, judgement of 4 March 2004.

53 Another example in this respect would be the case of *Cvijetić* v *Croatia*, No. 71549/01, judgement of 26 February 2004.

54 Application No. 24661/02, judgement of 1 June 2006.

The limits of the state's liability in enforcement cases, as rightly pointed out in the case of *Omerović* v *Croatia*,[55] would lay in a situation where the enforcement had become impossible due to the fact that a private person did not have the means to settle the debt. However, the State has the obligation to undertake all appropriate steps so as to ensure the prompt execution of final court judgements, irrespective of the subsequent outcome of those proceedings or the financial status of the parties involved.

3.7. *Other Cases where the Length of the Proceedings was a Central Problem*

The Court examined several other cases in which the length of proceedings had been one of the central issues, but which had primarily resulted in a violation of another Convention right.

The first example in this respect concerns cases in which the applicants had claimed damages from terrorist acts basing their claims on former section 180 of the Civil Obligations Act. Namely, the 1996 Amendment to the Civil Obligations Act[56] abrogated that provision and ordered that all proceedings based on it be stayed pending the enactment of new legislation in the matter. The relevant legislation was, however, not enacted until July 2003. In its pilot case on this question, *Kutić* v *Croatia*,[57] the Court held that the prolonged period during which no new legislation had been adopted and which resulted in the applicants' case *de facto* being stayed for more than seven years violated their right of access to a court guaranteed under Article 6 § 1 of the Convention.[58] In those cases, the Court considered that the applicants' length complaint was absorbed by the access-to-court issue.[59]

The Court was also called upon to examine the case of *Karadžić* v *Croatia*,[60] which concerned the abduction of a child, within the meaning of the 1980 Hague Convention on the Civil Aspects of International Child Abduction. In that case the applicant's former partner had taken their son from Germany to Croatia without her consent. She complained about the failure of the Croatian authorities to issue the necessary decisions with a view to returning her son and about the subsequent failure to enforce the final court decision in that respect within a reasonable time. The Court established certain periods of unnecessary protraction before the domestic courts in deciding the case. It further took particular note of the fact that in the period of one and a half years the authorities made only three attempts with a view to enforcing the final decision, none of which were successful. The foregoing

55 Application no, 36071/03, judgement of 1 June 2006.

56 Zakon o izmjeni zakona o obveznim odnosima, *Official Gazette* No. 7/1996.

57 Application No. 48778/99, judgement of 1 March 2002, ECHR 2002-II.

58 A similar situation concerning damage caused by the army and police was found to be in violation of the same provision. The pilot case in this respect was *Multiplex* v *Crotia*, No. 58112/00, judgement of 10 July 2003, followed by approximately 20 cases raising the same issue.

59 Following the *Kutić* judgement the Court has adopted numerous judgements and decisions raising the same issue. As the most recent example, see *Tomašić* v *Croatia*, No. 21753/02, judgement of 19 October 2006.

60 Application No. 35030/04, judgement of 15 December 2005.

had resulted in the applicant being separated from her son for a period of approximately five years. The state was found to have breached its positive obligation under Article 8 of the Convention (respect for family life) and the Court concluded that no separate issue arose in respect of the applicant's length complaint.

The recently adopted judgement in the case of *Vajagić* v *Croatia*[61] also had a length problem at the heart of the applicants' complaints. Namely, the applicants submitted that the unreasonable length of administrative proceedings for determination of compensation for property expropriated in 1976 - caused mainly by constant remittals of the case back to the first-instance authority - violated their rights guaranteed under Article 1 of Protocol No. 1 to the Convention. The Court found a violation of the applicants' property rights, whereas their length complaint under Article 6 was considered not to raise a separate issue.

4. Effective Remedy under Article 13 of the Convention

Article 13 of the Convention requires the existence of an effective remedy at the national level for any Convention right allegedly violated. For a long time, the Court interpreted Article 6 § 1 as *lex specialis* to Article 13, thus requiring no effective remedy for alleged breaches of procedural rights guaranteed under that provision. However, in the case of *Kudła* v *Poland*[62] the Court concluded that developments in the Member States and the ever increasing number of cases concerning the problem of delays in proceedings indicated that there was a need to provide an effective remedy in respect of that issue.

At that time in Croatia practically no remedy existed for the unreasonable length of proceedings. Section 59 (4) of the 1999 Constitutional Court Act provided the possibility of lodging a constitutional complaint if an individual's rights had been 'grossly violated' and if he or she therefore ran the risk of 'serious and irreparable consequences'. The admission of the complaint then depended on the Constitutional Court's discretion. Consequently, as the Court concluded in the *Horvat* judgement,[63] such a complaint offered no avenue of redress for the problem of lengthy proceedings.

Following the *Kudła* judgement, the Croatian parliament enacted the 2002 Amendments to the Constitutional Court Act[64] amending section 59 (4), which went on to become section 63 of that Act. It provided for the possibility of filing a constitutional complaint even before all remedies had been exhausted[65] if the competent court failed to decide the complainant's case within a reasonable time.

61 Application No. 30431/03, judgement of 20 July 2006.

62 Application No. 30210/96, Grand Chamber judgement of 26 October 2000, ECHR 2000-XI.

63 See *Horvat* v *Croatia*, *supra* note 33, §§ 41-45.

64 Ustavni zakon o izmjenama i dopunama Ustavnog zakona o Ustavnom sudu, *Official Gazette* No. 29/2002 of 22 March 2002.

65 Unlike the constitutional complaint under section 62 of the Constitutional Court Act, by which the complainant could argue violation of one or more of his or her constitutional rights, but only after all other remedies had been exhausted.

The Constitutional Court's discretion as to the institution of the proceedings as well as the requirements of 'gross violation' and 'irreparable consequences' had been abandoned. The Constitutional Court could, where it found that the proceedings had indeed exceeded a reasonable time, award the complainant compensation of non-pecuniary damage and order the competent court to decide the case within a certain time-limit. Consequently, on the basis of the clear wording of the provision, the Court ruled in the case of *Slaviček* v *Croatia*[66] that from then on there existed an effective remedy in respect of length of pending proceedings, even before any practice in that respect had been available. It thus became necessary to lodge a complaint with the Constitutional Court prior to addressing the Court in the matter.

Ever since, the Court has closely followed and reviewed the development of the Constitutional Court's case-law in respect of length-of-proceedings cases. In the case of *Šoć* v *Croatia*[67] the Court concluded that the existing remedy was not effective in respect of proceedings that have already come to an end. Furthermore, certain practices of the Constitutional Court were deemed unacceptable under Article 13. This was the case, for example, with the practice of taking into account only the court instance before which the case was pending at the moment of the lodging of the constitutional complaint, rather than assessing the overall length of the impugned proceedings. In the case of *Raguž* v *Croatia*,[68] the Constitutional Court dismissed the applicant's complaint because his proceedings had been pending before the second-instance court for only four days prior to his lodging of the complaint, irrespective of the fact that his case had previously been pending at first instance for some fourteen years.

Similarly, the Constitutional Court was declaring inadmissible constitutional complaints in which the proceedings before the competent court would come to an end after the lodging of the complaint. It based this interpretation on the fact that a complaint under section 63 of the Constitutional Court Act was admissible only while the proceedings complained of were still pending. In the case of *Debelić* v *Croatia*[69] the Court concluded for the first time that such practice was incompatible with Article 13 of the Convention. As a result, in the first half of 2004 the Constitutional Court changed its practice[70] in this respect and continued to examine the length of proceedings complained of irrespective of the fact whether the court before which the case was pending at the time the constitutional complaint was lodged would give its decision in the case.

In respect of the length of enforcement proceedings, the Constitutional Court initially did not consider such complaints as falling within the scope of section 63 of the Constitutional Court Act once an enforcement order had been issued. This was due to the fact that the section relied on implied its applicability only to those cases '… where the competent court fails to give a decision in the case within reasonable

66 Application No. 20862/02, decision of 4 July 2002, ECHR 2002-VII.

67 Application No. 47863/99, judgement of 9 May 2003.

68 Application No. 43709/02, judgement of 10 November 2005.

69 Application No. 2448/03, judgement of 26 May 2005.

70 See the Constitutional Court's decision No. U-IIIA-905/2003 of 5 May 2004, published in the *Official Gazette* No. 58/2004.

time ...'. However, in early 2005 the Constitutional Court changed its practice[71] so as to comply with the Court's case-law in this respect, in particular the principles laid down in the aforementioned *Hornsby* judgement.[72]

Due to the substantive increase in the workload of the Constitutional Court[73] following the enactment of the constitutional complaint as a national remedy for length, by the 2005 Courts Act,[74] the parliament introduced a 'request for protection of the right to a hearing within a reasonable time'. Pursuant to section 27 of the Courts Act, a party to the proceedings lasting an excessively long time shall now first have to address the immediately higher court. Should that court dismiss the party's request, an appeal to the Supreme Court would be allowed. Subsequently, should the party's appeal also be dismissed, he or she would be able to seize the Constitutional Court by lodging a complaint under section 63 of the Constitutional Court Act.[75]

Since the new system of remedies has been in force for a relatively short period of time, the Court has not yet had the opportunity to express its views as to its effectiveness. However, it will be interesting to follow this issue in the future and to see whether the newly appointed task for another 25 Croatian courts will be performed in line with the strict requirements transpiring from the Court's case-law in this respect. Notwithstanding that many Member States introduced similar remedies for length of proceedings, it would indeed compromise the effectiveness of the new Croatian system should the admittedly complicated procedure of complaining about length last an unreasonably long time itself.[76]

5. Conclusion

A good doctor treats the cause rather than the consequence. Strangely enough, the same philosophy applies to length of proceedings.

In its capacity as an international forum, the Court has a limited power of action, particularly taking into consideration its legal basis and the nature of its functioning. Furthermore, it is desirable to have a domestic remedy for situations when the proceedings have lasted an unreasonably long time. However, the need to resort to either of these avenues of redress should be an exception, whereas in Croatia it appears to have become the rule.

71 See the Constitutional Court's decision No. U-IIIA-1128/2004 of 2 February 2005, published in the *Official Gazette* No. 21/2005.

72 See *supra* 3.6 and note 49.

73 By the end of 2005 more than 3.300 length complaints had been lodged; the Constitutional Court has resolved about 1.700 such complaints, finding violations in over 800 cases.

74 Zakon o sudovima, *Official Gazette* 150/2005 of 21 December 2005.

75 If the proceedings are pending before the High Commercial Court, the High Petty Offences Court or the Administrative Court, the request under section 27 of the Courts Act is to be lodged directly with the Supreme Court. If the proceedings are pending before the Supreme Court, a party has the right to lodge a constitutional complaint concerning their length.

76 As has occurred, *mutatis mutandis*, in the context of administrative proceedings, see *Počuča* v *Croatia*, and *Božić* v *Croatia* (*supra* note 25).

Lengthy proceedings are preventing people from having their pecuniary rights acknowledged, their flats recovered, their children found. The consequence of the foregoing may well lead to a denial of justice, should a judgement come too late.

The reasons for these delays, which obviously exist in civil matters much more than in any other type of proceedings, must, at least to a certain extent, be of a structural nature.[77] As has been demonstrated, the existence of certain rules, either in the proceedings themselves or in the internal organisation of the courts, often lead to small delays; when several small delays occur in the course of one set of proceedings that may often result in an excessive overall length of the case.

It would be necessary (and useful) to undertake extensive research with the aim of identifying all the structural problems which unnecessarily protract the proceedings beyond a reasonable time. Only on the basis of such information could one imagine making concrete suggestions with a view to improving the efficiency of civil justice in Croatia.

77 In this respect see the work of the European Commission for the Efficiency of Justice (CEPEJ), whose main aim is the improvement of the efficiency and functioning of justice in the Member States as well as the development of the implementation of the instruments adopted by the Council of Europe to this end. In particular, see the recently adopted CEPEJ Report *Length of court proceedings in the Member States of the Council of Europe based on the case-law of the European Court of Human Rights*. More information is available under <www.coe.int/cepej> (last consulted 20 March 2007).

Bibliography

Potočnjak 2006
Potočnjak, Ž., 'Zaštita prava na suđenje u razumnom roku nakon stupanja na snagu novog Zakona o sudovima', *Hrvatska pravna revija*, April 2006, p. 13-30.

Uzelac 2004
Uzelac, A., 'Accelerating Civil Proceedings in Croatia - A History of Attempts to Improve the Efficiency of Civil Litigation', in: Van Rhee, C.H. (ed.), *The Law's Delay. Essays on Undue Delay in Civil Litigation* (Ius Commune Europaeum, 47), Antwerpen/Groningen: Intersentia, 2004, p. 283-314.

Uzelac 2005
Uzelac, A., 'Efikasnost pravosuđa u europskom kontekstu: usporedba funkcioniranja europskih pravosudnih sustava', *Zbornik Pravnog fakulteta u Zagrebu*, 2005, p. 1101-1136.

Vajić 2001
Vajić, N., 'Duljina sudskog postupka u Hrvatskoj i praksa Europskog suda za ljudska prava', *Zbornik Pravnog fakulteta u Zagrebu*, 2001, p. 981-990.

M.-H. Enderlin
N. Granfelt
S. Seppanen

REFORM IN THE CROATIAN JUSTICE SYSTEM

1. Introduction

Justice reform in Croatia is of great interest to the European Union. The functional efficiency of a legal system is dependant upon the link between 'freedom, security and justice'. Freedom cannot truly exist if a secure environment, supported and guaranteed by a smoothly functioning legal system, is not present.

In the light of its April 2004 candidacy for accession, Croatia entered a process where its judicial reform is measured against three key targets:[1] to ensure respect of democracy and the rule of law for all citizens; to promote a secure environment for the market economy and application of contracts; and finally to guarantee the fair and transparent application and enforcement of both national and EU legislation.

Pierre Mirel, Director of DG ELARG, was quoted as saying, 'the lessons learnt from previous enlargements show the importance of tackling as early as possible cross-cutting issues such as judicial and public administration reform'.[2] This statement was confirmed by the Council decision and accompanying measures concerning the issue of Justice within the context of Bulgaria and Romania's accession to the European Union. Therefore Croatia's accession negotiations should focus on the justice reform within Chapter 23 - Judiciary and Fundamental Rights - and on judicial co-operation within Chapter 24 - Justice, Freedom and Security.[3]

Since 1999, the European Commission has engaged in assistance programmes in order to facilitate the Croatian transition and accession process. The programmes, costing up to € 42 million,[4] include supporting justice reform through, among other

1 Corresponding to the three Copenhagen criteria.

2 Speech of Pierre Mirel, Director DG ELARG, Zagreb 9 May 2006.

3 Chapter 24 'Justice, Freedom and Security' where 'hard acquis' regulates judicial cooperation. Chapter 23 'Judiciary and Fundamental rights' where 'soft acquis' prevails. The emphasis in chapter 23 is less on the legal transposition but rather on the implementation and enforcement of fundamental principles. The acquis covering Justice and Home Affairs includes EU law as well as international conventions.

4 The total allocation of the EU for the Justice and Home Affairs sector in Croatia amounts up-to € 42 Million (covered by OBNOVA, CARDS and PHARE programmes). See European →

things, training judicial staff, reorganizing the court system, developing case management systems, reforming pre-trial criminal proceedings, battling corruption and money laundering, and developing a computerized land register system.

Efficiency of justice can be addressed at many levels; however, this paper will focus on the weight of justice reform in the accession process and issues related to justice reform in Croatia, examined through the perspective of the EU's court restructuring project lead by Finland. Furthermore, this essay will outline the experience and main recommendations for improving efficiency in the Croatian court system, in the light of the Finland project.

2. Accession Process and Reform of Justice

The tools for preparation towards Croatian accession are the same as were used by the EU for the 5th enlargement;[5] however, the weight of justice reform in the accession talks has been increasing, and is of the utmost importance for all Croatian citizens.

2.1. *The Stabilization and Association Agreement has already imposed a Legal Obligation on Croatia*

As a means of regulating issues of Justice and Home Affairs, the European Commission negotiated a Stabilization and Association Agreement (SAA)[6] with Croatia, just as with Romania, Bulgaria and with the ten states admitted as Member States in 2004.[7] Pursuant to their obligation under European law, Article 140 of the Croatian Constitution places the SAA above domestic law. Furthermore, the law governing courts, Article 5, requires Croatian courts to apply international treaties or acts taken in application of international treaties, placing an affirmative duty on the Croatian judiciary to protect the individual rights promulgated by the SAA. Despite this affirmative obligation, it is yet to be seen how the Croatian courts will apply the SAA, as it diverges from the training of its judges, past practice and case law; however, the Croatian application of its first legal link to the European Union will be useful in measuring the nation's progress at implementing and enforcing the EU acquis.

Commission Delegation website <http://www.delhrv.ec.europa.eu> (last consulted 20 March 2007).

5 On the 1st May 2004, Estonia, Lithuania, Latvia, Slovakia, Slovenia, Hungary, Czech Republic, Poland, Malta and Cyprus joined the EU.

6 SAA started its implementation as from 1 February 2005. Title III. Regional cooperation, Article 12 (proposition to cooperate in the field of Justice and Home Affairs), Title VII. Justice and Home Affairs, Article 75 (Reinforcement of the institutions and the Rule of law).

7 During the 1990s, the European Community and its Member States progressively concluded Association Agreements, so called 'Europe Agreements', with ten countries in Central and Eastern Europe. The Europe Agreements provide the legal basis for bilateral relations between these countries and the EU. The European Community had already established similar Association Agreements with Turkey (1963), Malta (1970) and Cyprus (1972).

The SAA gives a framework for discussion about the acquis transposition through sectoral sub-committees and also general Association Council meetings, providing a forum for bilateral discussion in parallel with the negotiations. The first Justice and Home Affairs Sub-Committee met on 30 June 2005, where they discussed justice reform, and where the Ministry of Justice presented the main positions of the justice reform strategy. The strategy includes, among other things: rationalisation of the court network, reduction of backlogs (redistribution of cases within the country from overburdened courts to courts with less workload, transfer of non-disputed cases to public notaries, etc.), training of judges/prosecutors, information and automation of the judicial system, and adoption of the law on legal aid. The second Justice and Home Affairs Sub-Committee convened on 23 November 2006, where the EC and Member States assessed the achievements made during the last year, including the judicial reform strategy adopted by the government in September 2005. Despite some progress, the implementation of the judicial reform strategy is not advancing as smoothly as planned as many short-term measures were postponed (i.e., adoption of the law on legal aid), no definitive action was taken to rationalize the court's network, and neither a concrete timeframe nor a firm budget had been established within which the reform must be implemented.

2.2. *The Use of the Traditional EU Accession/Negotiation Structure*

The *accession criteria* defined and developed during the last enlargement have been applied to Croatia. In 1993, the Copenhagen European Council stated: 'Accession will take place as soon as an associated country is able to assume the obligations of membership by satisfying the economic and political conditions required'. Justice has a key role in the accession criteria as the rule of law is emphasized in all the three Copenhagen criteria.[8] The importance of the rule of law in a democracy is threefold: it ensures its proper functioning, it facilitates the efficient functioning of the market economy by ensuring enforcement of contracts and a level playing field for all economic actors, and finally the rule of law ensures the enforcement of Community legislation.

The Madrid European Council of 1995 highlighted that membership criteria also require that the candidate country must have created the conditions for its efficient integration through the adjustment of its administrative structures. While it is important that European Community legislation is transposed into national legislation, it is even more important that the legislation is implemented effectively through appropriate administrative and judicial structures. This is a prerequisite of

8 There are three criteria on the basis of which applications are assessed: 1. stability of institutions guaranteeing democracy, the rule of law, human rights and respect for and protection of minorities; 2. the existence of a functioning market economy as well as the capacity to cope with competitive pressure and market forces within the Union; 3. the ability to take on the obligations of membership including adherence to the aims of political, economic and monetary union, and to adopt the common rules, standards and policies that make up the body of EU law.

the mutual trust required by EU membership. In 1997, the Luxembourg Council focused also on the institutional capacity to implement Amsterdam Treaty Obligations.

Negotiations were formally opened with Croatia on 3rd October 2005, and the reform measures' progress is monitored through the screening process that started on 20 October 2005. Because each country is evaluated on its own merits, the negotiations offer Croatia the opportunity to demonstrate its ability to complete the necessary reforms and meet all the membership requirements. After a chapter has been screened, the EU Member States decide, upon the Commission recommendations, whether the chapter can be opened for negotiations. The screening process, involving 35 chapters, was completed within one year's time, Chapter 23 on Judiciary and Fundamental rights being the last evaluated in October 2006. Negotiations on individual chapters are scheduled to begin soon, provided that opening benchmarks are fulfilled.

Benchmarking has been used in previous negotiations including the 5th enlargement where benchmarks were successfully used before closing a negotiation chapter or after the closure enumerating conditionalities. The EU requested the candidate countries to provide alignment strategies for several policy areas, while also requesting that each candidate nation demonstrate that it has effectively implemented State Aid rules. In 2005, it was decided[9] to generalise the use of benchmarks, including the introduction of conditions to be fulfilled prior to the opening or closure of a negotiation chapter by establishing an explicit procedure in the negotiating framework.[10] The strategy of using benchmarks builds on lessons learned in the previous enlargement where certain difficulties in implementing the EU acquis were not addressed until a late stage in the process.

2.3. *Is Croatia treated Differently from the 5th Enlargement Group?*

Learning from the previous enlargement, the EC has introduced changes to improve the preparation towards accession.

In fact, Chapter 23, 'Judiciary and fundamental rights', was created in order to separate the political issues from the more technical criteria covered by hard and soft acquis.[11] As such, Chapter 23 has not created new obligations for Croatia; rather, a clear list of directives, regulations, and Council of Europe recommendations facilitate the negotiation and benchmarking exercise. Furthermore, Member States' interest in the negotiation/screening process of Justice and Home Affairs has increased, as for the first time they have been permitted to attend the

9 See 2004 Strategy paper of the European Commission 'Progress in the Enlargement Process' – COM(2005) 561 of 09/11/2005.

10 See Negotiation framework for Croatia – October 2005 <http://europa.eu.int/comm/-enlargement/docs/pdf/st2004_en05_HR_framedoc.pdf> (last consulted 20 March 2007).

11 Often hard acquis is understood as the set of Directives, Regulations and Framework decisions, while soft acquis corresponds to Recommendations, ECtHR and ECJ case law and general principles.

Chapter 23 screening of Croatia and Turkey.[12] The Council's 'Enlargement Group', which meets several days a week, met and discussed the screening reports as well as the progress made in the candidate countries. Increased interest is also reflected by an augmented number of questions sent to the Commission by the Member States on issues relating to court reform, the fight against corruption, political parties' financing, reform of public administration, prosecution of war crimes, and the fight against discrimination.

Had the negotiations with Romania and Bulgaria involved the Chapter 23 procedures, tackling justice reform at the onset of the accession process, the nations' justice systems would be on par with those of the other Member States. Instead the EU has been required to formulate safeguard clauses closely linked to the functioning of the justice system. As such, the Commission could temporarily suspend specific rights with respect to Bulgaria and Romania under the EU laws and standards. For instance, it could enable current Member States to refuse automatic recognition and enforcement of civil and criminal judgements as well as arrest warrants originating in both Bulgaria and Romania.

The negotiation process was also enriched with clearly stated opening benchmarks[13] while only closing benchmarks[14] were used in the past. Opening benchmarks are proposed by the Commission in its screening reports on the various acquis chapters. The Intra-Governmental Conference decides on the benchmarks and the EU Presidency communicates them to the candidate country. Opening Benchmarks are not used in all acquis chapters however closing benchmarks are being laid down in most chapters. Benchmarks for negotiation chapters could refer to the legislative alignment, a satisfactory track record in implementation of key elements of the chapter, the existence of an adequate administrative and judicial capacity, and the fulfilment by a candidate of existing obligations that mirror the EU acquis in the relevant chapter of the SAA.

During the screening of Chapters 23 and 24, Croatia has provided information and indications on their level of law harmonization. While the level of legislative harmonization has progressed fairly well, the implementation and enforcement procedures have been assessed mainly as lacking. The Croatian understanding of the main principles of independence, efficiency, and proficiency is not always sufficiently in line with that of the EU.

Because the opening benchmarks provide Croatia with concrete indications of what is required, the benchmarks will help focus Croatian efforts and facilitate efficient negotiations and preparations. Likewise, the fulfilment of benchmarks will

12 Multilateral session on September 2007 (to explain the EU acquis), bilateral session on October 2007 (Croatia explaining their level of implementation of the acquis). Screening Report which will be the basis for starting negotiation or highlighting opening benchmarks.

13 Benchmarks are conditions laid down by the EU for the provisional closure or where appropriate, for the opening of accession negotiations on individual chapters, i.e. policy areas.

14 Closing benchmarks are proposed in the Draft Common Positions submitted by the Commission to the Council. They are adopted by the Council together with the EU Common Positions upon the opening of negotiations and updated during the negotiations.

provide sound indications to the EU about the state of preparation in Croatia, increasing the transparency of the process, allowing for more effective prioritisation of efforts, and undoubtedly reinforcing the 'own merits' principle, leaving the progress in the hands of each candidate country and its ability to meet all the clear objectives set.

International obligations and regional cooperation issues are linked to the Copenhagen political criteria. The lack of full cooperation with the International Criminal Tribunal for the Former Yugoslavia (ICTY) prevented the EU from opening accession negotiations as envisaged in March 2005. However, it was established on 3 October 2005 that Croatia was fully cooperating with the ICTY. The main issue was the Croatian prosecutors and judges' capacity to prosecute and judge war crimes. The transfer of ICTY cases at different levels (indictment already made, only investigation was conducted, etc) raised many concerns in the judiciary, related to the criminal procedure (validity of testimonies taken via video-link), validity of proofs collected, and the security of the information provided by Member States to ICTY which also required protection under the Croatian system. As a result of this process, the Criminal Procedure Code (CPC) was amended in July 2006 to allow the use of video-link testimony in Croatia from witnesses in third countries.

Therefore, even if there are new tools to prepare and monitor the accession process in the field of Justice and Home Affairs, the Commission is not applying new criteria to Croatia. Negotiations were formally launched in October and all the chapters were screened. The negotiations are not about whether a candidate country will adopt the EU legislation. The rules of the club have indeed to be accepted.

> 'EU law is not negotiable. The sooner Croatia joins the better? Negotiations are about determining how and when this will happen. This will also be the case for Croatia. This is primarily an internal, domestic process as 90 per cent of the negotiations are done at "home"'.[15]

3. Some Issues to be Addressed under the Reform of Judiciary

In parallel to the accession negotiation, the European Commission is monitoring the progress made in the reform of judiciary through the 'Progress Report',[16] 'Peer Expert's Reviews',[17] as well as regular reports. Indeed the Commission has seen the importance of tackling, as early as possible, cross-cutting issues such as judicial and public administration reform as well as fighting corruption. Progress on these issues is first and foremost aimed at improving the everyday lives of citizens by guaranteeing their rights and ensuring that justice prevails. But these reforms are also necessary if candidate countries are to fully benefit from EU policies as Member States and adequately apply EU law.

15 Speech of Pierre Mirel, Director DG ELARG, Zagreb 9 May 2006.

16 Croatia 2006 Progress Report, COM(2006) 649 final.

17 Report of the Justice and Home Affairs Peer Reviews of May 2005 and July 2006.

Chapter 23 'Judiciary and Fundamental rights' is covering the main principles governing judicial independence, impartiality, professional competence, efficiency as well as judicial reform. *Independence* ought to be ensured from the beginning stages, the appointment level; however, the Commission expressed, in various reports, concerns over Croatians' access to the judicial profession. The system in place does not ensure a uniform, objective and transparent assessment of judicial trainees wishing to enter the profession. Judicial appointment is based first on the Ministry of Justice's approval of trainees, where there is neither a uniform training programme nor a competitive exam required before application. Once the Ministry approves a candidate, the State Judicial Council makes judicial appointments based on the opinion of local judicial councils, based on written applications. In addition to a comprehensive judicial appointment process, independence requires that the court be permanent, prohibiting the removal of a judge. New Croatian judges are appointed for a 'probation' period of 5 years, after which they are eligible for life appointments. As a result, the junior judges are the most vulnerable to pressures and external influence. This procedure, allowing for the appointment and possible dismissal of court presidents by the Ministry of Justice has been criticized by EU experts. With the appropriate initial training of court apprentices and better selection procedures, the road would be paved to abolish the system '*à l'essaie*'.

An independent judiciary must be accountable and provide an efficient service, requiring law enforcement offices to work professionally and be publicly accountable for their performance, providing transparency in all forms, and access to justice. Benchmarks for accountability are therefore still needed to evaluate performance on issues such as effective disciplinary proceedings according to clear and pre-established criteria, the establishment of criminal and civil liability rather than almost absolute immunity, an effective code of ethics and rules against conflicts of interests, and an avenue for institutional external complaints such as an Ombudsman. Croatian judges benefit from immunities while public prosecutors do not enjoy such protection. The lifting of immunity can be done by the State Judicial Council (SJC) upon request of the public prosecutor. However, recent practices of the SJC show that they act merely as an investigative body, deciding whether or not there are sufficient elements to initiate a case. Judges should not have immunity from normal criminal prosecution and the role of the SJC should merely be to decide whether to lift immunity, rather than determining the merits of the charge. It should be for the actual investigative judge to decide at a later stage whether the State Prosecutor presented the elements of the crime. In its current form, the SJC's standpoint on criminal procedure prevents the establishment of judicial responsibility. However, with the October 2006 adoption of the Code of Ethics for judges, and with the already expositing Code of Ethics for Prosecutors, it is hoped that a better self-regulating mechanism of the profession will apply.

With respect to access to justice, the adoption of the Law on Legal Aid was announced as a short-term measure in the Strategy of September 2005, to be accomplished within one year. However more than two years after its drafting, the law has not yet been submitted to governmental procedure. Free legal Aid in civil matters is not regulated in Croatia and can only be provided by the bar association through pro bono representation.[18] The bar association has set-up its own criteria for granting legal aid, which among other things requires the applicant to have Croatian citizenship, less than € 350,- income per month and no property. In 2005, the bar association provided legal aid in 488 cases. NGOs can also provide legal assistance but cannot represent the party in front of the court unless their lawyer has passed the bar exam. Finally the parties can also be exempted from court fees (about 3000 cases in 2004).

In its Draft legislation concerning legal aid, the Ministry of Justice has determined that the 'means testing' procedure for beneficiaries of legal aid will be overseen by the State Administration Offices of the various Counties and the City of Zagreb. However, it is not clear how many staff dealing with the legal aid administration will be recruited and trained and when this will happen. There are no indications either whether the premises in the State Administration offices will be found in time. The Ministry of Justice has estimated the preparation for implementation of the law to cost roughly 1.2 MEUR (9 Million Kuna), while the costs for the provision of legal aid is estimated at approximately 1.6 MEUR (12 Million Kuna) for the first year. However, it is difficult to understand how the Ministry of Justice has made this estimate as neither the attorney fees, nor the associations/NGOs costs have yet been negotiated by the Ministry. Furthermore, the bar association substantially increased attorney fees last spring. Therefore, despite the government's commitment to pass the law, there is still a high risk that the budget foreseen for the implementation of the law will be inadequate for both the staffing needs and offices to manage legal aid requests. The European Commission has allocated 1 MEUR to support the legal aid system[19] in Croatia, provided that the government is committed to adopt the Law on legal aid by spring 2007.

The implementation of the Law on Legal Aid is planned to be postponed to possibly 1 January 2008 (depending on when the law is adopted!) in order to allow adequate time for the creation of the appropriate mechanisms, as well as the adoption of by-laws. This means that indigent Croatian citizens will not benefit from legal aid and have access to justice until the end of 2008. The government legislative agenda for legal aid does not seem to be compatible with the requirement of Chapter 23, which expressly requires provisions for offering legal aid (Article 6 of ECHR, Recommendations from the Council of Europe,[20] international conventions as well as the SAA).

The EC has given great attention to the Croatian shortcomings with respect to the reform of justice and the framework of justice together with its functioning. Despite the adoption of the Strategy for the Reform of the Judicial System[21] more

18 Article 21 of the Bar Act.

19 CARDS 2004 'Strengthening the legal aid system in Croatia'.

20 Resolution 76(5) on legal aid in civil, commercial and administrative proceedings. Resolution 78(8) on Legal Aid and Advice.

21 The Strategy was adopted by the government on 22/09/2005 and approved by the parliament after an extended discussion on 10/02/2006.

than a year ago, an action plan has yet to be adopted that would allow for its implementation, with defined benchmarks and a timeframe, financial allocation and the designated responsible authority. However, some progress has been made with the reduction of the case backlog in 2006 which was reduced to 1.2 Million from 1.6 Million in 2005. Furthermore, the President of the Supreme Court has established a monitoring system of old cases (older than 3 years for criminal cases and older than 5 years for civil cases), reducing the number of unsolved cases by 35% in the year since its creation. The analysis of the backlog[22] has triggered a better visibility of its composition and allowed recommendations for better case-handling. It is, however, too early to say whether this reduction of backlog is linked to an increased efficiency of the court system. Nevertheless the average time per category of case was calculated and aided the drafting of new standards for the calculation of judges' workload. The quality of the decisions should also be ensured, and the acceleration of the handling of cases should not merely mean that the more simple cases are solved, while the more complicated ones still require the same lengthy proceedings that often end-up in front of the ECtHR.[23]

4. Finnish Twinning Experience in Croatia and some Recommendations

4.1. *Starting Point of CARDS 2002 project*[24]

The situation in Croatia in the beginning of 2004, when the first Twinning project within the Croatian judiciary began, was characterized by more than 1.300.000 pending cases accumulated during the previous years with the lengthiest and largest number of proceedings plaguing the larger courts, particularly the county and municipal courts in Zagreb, Split, Rijeka and Osijek.

The European Court of Human Rights received 362 complaints against Croatia since April 2002 stemming from the excessive length of its court proceedings.

Croatian courts currently number 266, including the highest courts, unopened courts, and opened courts without staff. Furthermore, as stated in the Progress Report 2006 and the CEPEJ report on the efficiency of justice of October 2006, Croatia has too many inefficiently managed courts.

22 June 2006 statistics collected by the Supreme Court, confirm that execution/enforcement cases are the main problem in 93% of the courts. There are 1.114.019 cases pending but one cannot say that it is all backlog as the average time for judges to make a decision needs first to be established.

23 *Muževič* v *Croatia* (16 November 2006) in which execution proceedings had been pending for more than 8 years and in which the ECtHR not only established a violation of Article 6 ECHR but also ordered the State to finally ensure the execution of a 1996 in-court settlement and a 1999 verdict.

24 EU funded CARDS 2002 Twinning project (1 Million Euro), implemented from February 2004 until May 2006.

4.2. *Project target and progress*

The purpose of the project was to improve the organisation and structure of the Croatian court system, to improve the management of the courts and the exchange of information between the Ministry of Justice and the courts, to increase the efficiency of judicial proceedings, and to support IT development. All these objectives were aiming at shortening the judicial process and decreasing the number of pending cases.

The weaknesses of the Croatian Judiciary, with respect to the organization and structure of the courts, the management of the courts, the information exchange between the Ministry of Justice and the courts, the proceedings, and IT equipment have been reviewed and dozens of recommendations have been made as to how to correct these issues.

The Ministry of Justice and the courts have recognized a majority of their weaknesses and have been receptive to the project recommendations. They have incorporated a number of them into the Overall Strategy of the Judiciary. The Ministry of Justice has also established several working groups for further review and analysis of the recognized problems and employed a number of highly efficient statistical collection methods to assist in the reform.

During the duration of the project the number of pending cases has been reduced, with substantial reductions, e.g. in land registry cases.

4.3. *Organization and Structure of the Croatian Court System*[25]

From late 2004 through early 2005 the project management, together with the Ministry of Justice, prepared a questionnaire for all county, municipal, misdemeanour and commercial courts to collect statistical information to be used as a method of comparison between courts in various domains.

The project management and the Ministry of Justice agreed that the analysis should be based on four main criteria:

1. caseload combined with the number of judges and other staff;
2. population density in a given geographical area;
3. geographical location of courthouses;
4. condition of court buildings (which in the end was not useful since most of the buildings are in a bad or very bad condition).

However, backlog, efficiency, and tradition were not included among the selected criteria.

In the analysis for county and municipal/misdemeanour courts, different limit values were used.

By using the mentioned criteria in examining the municipal courts,[26] the Project's findings included the following. With respect to:

25 Component B of CARDS 2002 Twinning project Reform of the Croatian Court System.

1. caseload: 72 courts failed to meet the criteria, while only 27 satisfied the criteria and 28 fell between;
2. number of judges: 72 courts failed to meet the criteria, while 19 satisfied the criteria and 12 fell between;
3. population: 70 failed to meet the criteria, while 20 satisfied the criteria and 13 fell between;
4. distance: 43 failed to meet the criteria, while 14 satisfied the criteria and 46 fell between.

Despite the lacking performance, the chosen limit values are quite lenient when compared to those used in other European countries. The Ministry of Justice was advised to review the criteria and limit values for concrete actions to be taken.

The project then created the first accurate database, since every court in the nation responded to the survey, with respect to the number of cases, the number of staff, the number of inhabitants within the jurisdiction and the condition of the courthouses.

With 266 courts, including those that are not functioning or are functioning without staff, the ratio of courts versus citizens is approximately 52 courts per 1.000.000 inhabitants. When compared to other European nations, Croatia is one of three countries with a ratio of 50 or more per 1.000.000 inhabitants, while Finland and Hungary have 13 courts per 1.000.000, Moldova has 15 courts per 1.000.000, and Slovenia has 30 courts per 1.000.000.

The Project has delivered recommendations with respect to the court structure in Croatia and proposed guidelines for reducing the number of courts.

The project's recommendations were:
- do not open any new courts;
- close courts without sufficient staff;
- merge municipal and misdemeanour courts;
- further reduce the number of first instance courts;
- reduce the number of county courts and review the possibility to transfer of the jurisdiction of the county courts to appellate courts.

The first two recommendations are based on the fact that the decisions to open new courts are not currently based on an analysis of case inflow, number of inhabitants, etc.

The overall conclusion was that because the Croatian court system is already too extensive and inefficient with too many small courts, any proposal for a further extension would go against all rationale.

By applying the above criteria, the Project ended with the conclusion that a total number of 92 courts was needed in Croatia. The map explaining which courts

26 There were 114 municipal courts in June 2005, out of which 104 had opened and 10 were not yet functioning. In November 2006 there were 107 functioning municipal courts.

would be merged and where the remaining courts would be located can be found on the homepage of the Ministry of Justice.[27]

The above recommendations were presented to the judiciary's most prominent local and international actors during a high level conference on 28 June 2005. During the conference, the President of the Croatian Supreme Court and the Croatian and Finnish Ministers of Justice addressed the leaders of the judiciary concerning the need for judicial reform, while the Resident Twinning Advisor of the Project explained the methods and findings of the Project. The Croatian media dedicated a large amount of favourable coverage to the conference, and against the expectations of the Ministry of Justice, a majority of the courts and media found the project recommendations to be useful and possible to implement.

The Law on Courts[28] gives the Minister of Justice the authority to decide on mergers of various courts (Article 154) and by the end of 2005, the minister had established a working group to rationalize the court network, with the goal of reducing the number of municipal and misdemeanour courts. Members of the working group have been considering the possibility of merging one bigger municipal court with a few smaller municipal courts, in addition to reducing the number of county courts with insufficient caseloads. By the end of the Twinning Project, the Ministry of Justice was planning the merger of misdemeanour courts with municipal courts; however the Supreme Court general session[29] did not approve this plan and suggested instead that the Ministry proceed with a pilot merger of only 8 courts, while also preparing amendments to the Law on Offences. The Supreme Court is of the opinion that it is better to redefine the competence of misdemeanour courts, prior to further merger of municipal and misdemeanour courts.

The working group of the Ministry of Justice works currently on a detailed plan for the rationalisation of the court network, considering mainly the possibility of merging the same type of courts (merging of municipal courts, county courts, commercial courts).

The concrete implementation of a scheme to rationalize the courts should be covered by an Action Plan highlighting the legal changes that are requested (like changes of the Law on Minor Offences and the Jurisdiction of Courts), the financial implications as well as the staff to be reallocated. The Ministry of Justice has committed itself to send such rationalization plan to government by the end of 2006.

5. Conclusion

The perspectives for the future: 2007 will be a decisive year for Croatian justice reform, as the key implementation tools are then expected to be adopted and in place. The reforms include, among other things, decisions on the rationalisation of courts, a new judicial map, the enhancement of an integrated case management

27 <http://www.pravosudje.hr> (last consulted 20 March 2007).

28 OG 150/05.

29 March 2006.

system in a larger number of courts, the revision of access to the judicial profession with the preparation of a new Law on Court Apprentices, a strategy for the reform of criminal procedure preparing a shift of pre-trial investigations to public prosecutors and the police, the enactment of the Law on Legal Aid, track-records of implementation of the strategy on fighting corruption, the adoption of an action plan for minority employment, and the fight against discrimination and xenophobia. For its part, the European Commission is expected to issue its screening report for Chapter 23 by early 2007, outlining the opening benchmarks to be fulfilled during 2007, and to open the negotiations on the judiciary and fundamental rights. The reform of the judiciary is primarily an internal/domestic process, which requires a strong commitment and determination. Managing the process at home is more difficult than the negotiations themselves as the reforms are costly and difficult. Therefore the process can be internally divisive but accession is in the key national interest, and each reform measure is aimed at better and faster justice for the Croatian citizens.

IV. Private Justice: Challenges to the Evolution of Alternative Dispute Resolution

R. Verkijk

MANDATORY MEDIATION: INFORMAL *IN*JUSTICE?[1]

1. Introduction

The aim of this contribution is to look critically at mediation, especially when it is regarded as an alternative to adjudication. In that sense, like arbitration, mediation can be seen as a form of doing 'private justice'. This suggests that mediation is about justice;[2] the title of this contribution hints at the suspicion that *in*justice may well be a result of mediation.

There is extensive literature on mediation, to which the reader is referred.[3] It is therefore not necessary to extensively define and describe mediation all over again. However, for the purpose of creating a basis for the following text some characteristics are worth mentioning. Mediation can be described as the facilitation of a negotiation process by a third party, who is independent and neutral. The process should contribute to the autonomy and self-determination of the parties. A basic concept is that mediation is a voluntary process. This idea can be found in the Proposal for a Directive by the EU on mediation, in the Preamble, sub 9: 'The possibility for the court to refer the parties to mediation should also be covered, *while retaining the principle that mediation is a voluntary process*'.[4] In the UNCITRAL model law on conciliation (which is also about mediation) we find stated: 'The Commission intends that the word "conciliation" would express a broad notion of *a voluntary process* controlled by the parties and conducted with the assistance of a

1 The author would like to thank Tanja van der Meer, Remco van Rhee, Annie de Roo and Alan Uzelac for their comments.

2 On types of justice and the relation between mediation and law, see Nolan-Haley 1996, p. 47-102. She also raises the important question if lawyers should take part in mediation as legal counsel to protect the rights of their clients. See also Genn 2005, p. 17.

3 Like Brown & Marriott 1999 and Genn 2005. For an overview of mediation in Europe, see Mackie *et al.* 2004; *EU Green Paper on ADR* COM (2002) 196, 19.04.2002; for just a few articles with a focus on mandatory mediation: Editor's Note 1990, p. 1086; Winston 1996, p. 187; Boettger 2004, p. 1; Kuhn 1984, p. 733; Wissler 1997, p. 565. For an enumeration of American literature that is critical about ADR, see Menkel-Meadow 1991, p. 1 & p. 3 at notes 3 & 7.

4 *Proposal for a Directive of the European Parliament and of the Council on certain aspects of mediation in civil and commercial matters*, 2004/0251 (COD), October 22, 2004 (italics in text added).

neutral third person or persons'.[5] Finally the literature underlines that mediation is a consensual process, which implies voluntariness.[6]

Mediation is to a large extent adopted by those who are in the legal business[7] and it is often, if not in the first place, seen as a means to resolve legal conflicts. That might lead easily to the treatment of mediation - by lawyers - as if it were a legal phenomenon. But it is not, in my opinion. Compare it to buying a loaf of bread. Despite the fact that the Romans put the label *emptio-venditio* on this transaction, buying a loaf of bread in itself is not a legal concept. Nor is buying a chain of bakeries a legal concept, despite the fact that it is practically impossible to do so without lawyers and sophisticated contracts. That should be kept in mind when comparing mediation with formal legal procedure. The latter *is* a legal concept in itself and has therefore a completely different character.

Mediation is propagated by mediators (who often have not enough cases), their trainers and their organizations (three highly overlapping categories) but also by governments,[8] judges (who often have too many cases), reformers of codes of civil procedure, EU-organizations, the business community and lawyers, as is illustrated by the positive response coming from the CCBE (European Bar Association).[9] All seem to be in favour of trading slow and costly civil procedure for a swift, cheap non-procedure that in some magical way knows no losers but only *win-winners*.

There is but one problem: the demand for mediation is very low. People who have a dispute do not tend to choose mediation to help solve their conflicts. Parties may have several reasons for not using mediation:[10] they do not know enough about it, their attorneys are ignorant about it or they fear that the other party might regard a mediation offer as a sign of weakness. At the early stages of disputes parties themselves are often unwilling to consider the possibility of a compromise.[11] Finally some people simply prefer a black-and-white solution. As a result of these and perhaps other reasons[12] parties rather turn to the courts, despite the relative

5 *Model Law Part 2, no. 32*. The electronic version of the model law is accessible on <http://www.uncitral.org> (consulted September 2006).

6 Like the book by Brown & Marriott 1999, p. 129; or even more explicit (but in Dutch), Brenninkmeijer *et al.* 2003, p. 318. See also e.g. Nolan-Haley 1996, p. 98; Menkel-Meadow 1991, p. 18, fn. 78. Note that until 1 November 2004 CEDR in the UK, a leading organisation in ADR, defined mediation as: '... a voluntary, non-binding, private dispute resolution process in which a neutral person helps the parties try to reach a negotiated settlement', but see also *infra*.

7 Critical about this development is Menkel-Meadow 1991, p. 3 & p. 17.

8 E.g. the letter from the Dutch Minister of Justice of 21 April 2006, *Kamerstukken II* 2005-2006, 29 279, No. 35, p. 5.

9 'The CCBE supports the [European] Commission efforts in order to promote mediation and acknowledges the potential benefit of a Directive in this field' (<http://www.ccbe.org/doc/En/ccbe_position_on_mediation_en.pdf>, consulted September 2006).

10 See the enumeration by Wissler 1997, p. 570.

11 Genn 2005, p. 13.

12 A German judge remarked that parties appear especially reluctant to negotiate when they are insured for the costs of legal assistance or when they receive legal aid, see Althammer 2006, p. 72.

disadvantages.[13] So there exists an efficient way to resolve disputes which - when used - leads to high satisfaction rates with the parties,[14] but they just do not seem to be interested in it. It is as if they do not know what they are missing. And it is that situation which provokes policy makers to make mediation, to some extent, compulsory.[15]

While mediation in its pure essence is described as a voluntary process, it seems that mandatory mediation is becoming widespread. This is recognized in the same documents as mentioned *supra*: see again the EU Directive on mediation (Preamble, sub 9. '*The possibility for the court to refer the parties to mediation should also be covered*, while retaining the principle that mediation is a voluntary process').

This contribution focuses on the following questions:

I. a. what does it mean that mediation is 'mandatory' and
   b. (where) can mandatory mediation be found in Europe?
II. (why) is mandatory mediation problematic?

This article should not be taken as an attack on ADR (or mediation), because that is not what it is. My purpose is to illustrate that mediation and adjudication are different processes with corresponding strengths and weaknesses, advantages and challenges, that are executed with different mindsets. Sometimes this is forgotten as a result of the 'colonization' of ADR by lawyers and legal scholars alike.[16]

2. Mandatory Mediation in Europe

2.1. *Mandatory Mediation*

That mediation is a voluntary process does not prohibit a judge from referring parties to a mediator, as can be deduced from the quote from the EU Draft Directive. Nevertheless, a referral by a judge may in itself lead to a certain compulsion: the parties may feel obliged to follow the judge's directions.[17] Apparently, voluntary and mandatory elements can exist side by side. There is no black and white picture and many situations are imaginable.[18] Therefore, instead of

13 As is found by Genn 1998, and was confirmed in later results, Genn 2005, p. 12; Wissler 1997, p. 565. It was also recognized for example in the Modellversuch '*Güterichter*', Bavarian Ministry of Justice, <http://www.jura.uni-erlangen.de/aber/projektbeschreibung.pdf> (consulted September 2006).

14 E.g. Wissler 1997, p. 568 who also refers to studies which show that mediation produces greater compliance and less relitigation than does adjudication - and to studies that see no significant or long-term differences.

15 Wissler 1997, p. 571; Grillo 1991, p. 1552; yet another possibility is to establish a Mediation Help Line, see <http://www.gnn.gov.uk/environment/detail.asp?ReleaseID=148989&NewsAreaID=2&NavigatedFromDepartment=True> (last consulted 20 March 2007).

16 See Menkel-Meadow 1991, especially her 'apologia' at p. 45.

17 This is sometimes aptly referred to as 'raised eyebrow regulation' or '*sub silentio* pressure'.

18 Cf. Menkel-Meadow 1991, who states 'I believe that until we know more about the effectiveness of settlement-seeking devices, the line should not be drawn between mandatory →

giving a definition of what is 'mandatory mediation', several distinctions will be introduced that may be of relevance here in order to answer the question what mandatory mediation means. It is worth noting that I shall not only take into account whether parties have a legal obligation to cooperate in mediation, but also the psychological effect upon a party when an authority that may influence the outcome of his case, like a judge or a mediator, expresses her wishes.[19]

2.1.1. Distinction 1: What 'Part' of Mediation is Mandatory?

In theory it is easy to distinguish what 'part' of mediation is mandatory. In the first place it can be mandatory to enter *into* mediation. Secondly, there may be some pressure on the parties to cooperate regarding the mediation process and finally, there may be pressure to cooperate to *achieve a result*, more precisely to settle the case.

What it means to enter into mediation is clear. It will be discussed below, as the most important phase in which mediation has been made compulsory. Once parties have started mediation, they may not sabotage it. In the US the notion of 'good faith' has been introduced here. However, the notion is unclear. It may mean something in between *showing up at the mediation table* and *being obliged to really try and settle the case*. In any way this requirement can be considered problematic in at least two ways:[20]

a. it brings a legal element, more precisely a legal obligation, in the process of mediation, and it does so at the cost of 'party empowerment', thereby frustrating one of the main goals of mediation;

b. in legal procedure following mediation you can only discover if a party acted in good faith by disregarding the absolute confidentiality of mediation: in Europe this is illustrated by arrangements in Norway and Italy. This will be discussed later.

The most problematic aspect, by definition located in the final stage of the mediation process, is when it becomes compulsory to reach a settlement. Like the European Commission and the Council of Europe, many have expressed the view that compulsory settlements are not compatible with the *ius agendi*, the right of access to the court. Also, the mediator is legally unable to impose a settlement on the parties; this is why mediation is not arbitration. Therefore, the third kind of pressure - to settle - is officially not on the agenda. I will show later that, unfortunately, we can not dismiss it completely.

and consensual processes. Rather, the line should be drawn between abusive uses of mandatory processes and those used within the bounds of fairness and our existing rules', p. 25.

19 Cf. Ingleby 1993, p. 443; Nolan-Haley 1996, p. 61.

20 Boettger 2004, p. 2

2.1.2. Distinction 2: Who has the Authority to make Mediation Mandatory?

An obligation to start mediation can be retraced to three sources of authority: the law, the judge or the parties themselves. It seems odd that one party can impose mediation on another party, but not if the demanding party simply holds on to existing contractual obligations between the parties. It is becoming more and more commonplace to insert mediation clauses in legal contracts. When they do, people have in advance agreed on mediation. Of course, when they agreed to put a mediation clause in the contract, they were still on speaking terms. Once a dispute arises that is serious enough to consider starting litigation or to invoke mediation, often at least one party has lost his appetite for amicable settlement talks. It is up to his opponent to try to keep him to the contract and paradoxically, to do so he may request the court to make the resisting party cooperate.

The courts in the Netherlands are mainly of the opinion that mediation is a voluntary process so there is no use in forcing either party to enter into mediation, despite the mediation clause. I will come back to that.

The main focus of this contribution is on mediation that has been made mandatory by the law or by the courts and not by the parties themselves. When referring to these potential sources of compulsion, the third distinction attains relevance.

2.1.3. Distinction 3: Grades of Compulsion

Jagtenberg and De Roo distinguish no less than six grades of compulsion.[21] They did not just make them up: they related these grades to the practices that can be found in Europe. I will use this classification to give some examples of different forms of mandatory mediation in Europe (and thereby answer the second part of my first question).

2.2. *Examples of Different Grades of Compulsion in European Justice Systems*

2.2.1. Parties Suggest Mediation

When mediation is truly voluntary in every aspect, when parties choose for mediation without any external pressure at the beginning of mediation or during the process of mediation, there is no compulsion. This might be considered the 'lightest grade' of compulsion. According to mediation ideology, this would be an ideal situation. It is however not utopian. Many mediations have indeed been initiated purely on a voluntarily basis.

21 De Roo & Jagtenberg 2003, p. 50. I owe much of the information about mediation in European countries to their research, yet mistakes in my article have to be considered mine because I selected and added material.

2.2.2. The Court Merely Suggests

An essential feature of this second grade is that the option of mediation will only be examined after the parties have given their consent to do so. We find an example in the French Nouveau Code de Procédure Civile. Article 131-1[22] about *médiation judiciaire* states:

> 'Le juge saisi d'un litige peut, après avoir recueilli l'accord des parties, désigner une tierce personne afin d'entendre les parties et de confronter leurs points de vue pour leur permettre de trouver une solution au conflit qui les oppose'.

It should be realised that in family disputes or labour cases in France a different regime exists which is less permissive - in these cases the judge may impose forms of conciliation or mediation.

2.2.3. The Court Suggests and Explains (the Judge is Committed to Mediation)

The courts show stronger commitment if they not only suggest that mediation might be an option, but also inform the parties on the possibilities and the process of mediation.

In England, when a conflict is brought before the employment tribunal both parties automatically receive information about the possibility that the ACAS (Advisory, Conciliation and Arbitration Service) provides conciliation or mediation service free of charge. If both parties do not respond positively within 28 days, the case will be heard by the judge.[23]

In the Netherlands the situation appears somewhat different from other European countries, because the emphasis has always been on acting more than on contemplating, on practice instead of on rules. Since 2005 court-annexed mediation has been institutionalised after the completion of a 4-year pilot project. In the pilot 973 cases were mediated, in 61% of which a settlement was reached (sometimes only in part) and it has been deemed successful.[24] So far legislation aimed at regulating mediation has not been considered necessary, except in the field of legal aid.[25] That no legislation was needed is partly due to the fact that, except perhaps at the end of the 19th century and a few decades thereafter, it has always been considered an important task for judges to stimulate settlement (unlike English judges, but like in German courts).[26] As from April 2005 cases are screened for their

22 Decree n° 96-652 of 22 July 1996, Article 2, *Official Journal* of 23 July 1996.

23 See <http://www.acas.org.uk/> (consulted September 2006).

24 Combrink-Kuiters, Niemeijer & Ter Voert 2003.

25 *Staatscourant* 25 April 2005, p. 23. In order to stimulate mediation there is financial support; parties can apply for a subsidy for mediation in the same manner as they might for legal aid; Verkijk 2005b, p. 34-40.

26 E.g. Article 19 Dutch *Code of Civil Procedure* 1838: 'The judge may in all cases, in every phase of the proceedings, instruct the parties to appear before him in order to attempt to reach a →

suitability and either court secretaries or the judges themselves inform the parties about the benefits of mediation. Officially there is no pressure on the parties to agree with mediation, but that is not always how parties perceive the suggestion of the judge.[27]

2.2.4. The Court Initiates, No Sanction

This grade of compulsion is defined by the situation in which the judge may initiate mediation or the appointment of a mediator without having obtained prior consent of the parties.

An example is Germany. It is hard to keep up with legislation and proposals in Germany. Since 2001 the judge may propose out-of-court mediation.[28] New proposals are in the making. Possibly in the future the judge may refer the parties to a special mediation judge, a *Güterichter*, whose task it is to try to reach an agreement. In some *Länder* (States) this is already practice:

> 'Es ist der zuständige Streitrichter, der entscheidet, ob er ein Verfahren für mediationsgeeignet hält. In diesem Fall leitet er es zunächst informell an den Güterichter, der Kontakt zu den Prozessvertretern der Parteien aufnimmt. Wenn diese zu einem Schlichtungsversuch bereit sind, wird die Sache auch formell dem Güterichter zugewiesen'.[29]

Article 278 lid 5 *ZPO* (...) (5) now states:

> 'Das Gericht kann die Parteien für die Güteverhandlung vor einen beauftragten oder ersuchten Richter verweisen. In geeigneten Fällen kann das Gericht den Parteien eine außergerichtliche Streitschlichtung vorschlagen. Entscheiden sich die Parteien hierzu, gilt § 251 entsprechend'.[30]

The new paragraph will read as follows: (...) (5):

> 'Für die Güteverhandlung oder für einen sonstigen Güteversuch kann das Gericht die Parteien vor einen beauftragten oder ersuchten Richter oder mit ihrer Zustimmung vor einen Güterichter verweisen. Hält der Güterichter einen Güteversuch für aussichtslos

settlement'. Verkijk 2005, p. 207-212. See also Roberts 1993, p. 459 for a comparison between British and North American courts and p. 461 for new developments in England.

27 Combrink-Kuiters, Niemeijer & Ter Voert 2003, p. 183. For this reason special attention has been paid to the words the courts use when they inform the parties about the mediation scheme.

28 But judges seem hesitant to invoke this article, according to Althammer 2006, p. 69.

29 Quote from a speech by the Bavarian Minister of Justice Beate Merk for the Mediationstag 7-8 October 2005 in Munich, <http://www.justiz.bayern.de/imperia/md/content/stmj_internet/ministerium/ministerium/reden/m_071005.pdf>. For the latest results, see <http://www.beate-merk.de/03_aktuelles/01_presse/pdf/2006_10_06Gueterichter.pdf> (both websites consulted 7 February 2007).

30 *Zivilprozess Reformgesetz* vom 27. July 2001 (BGBl. I S. 1887).

> oder kommt eine Einigung der Parteien in den Fällen des Satzes 1 nicht zu Stande, so wird das Verfahren vor dem Prozessgericht fortgesetzt'.[31]

The main innovation is the introduction of the *Güterichter,* because in his efforts to reconcile the parties their interests are central, not the legal evaluation of the case, while a traditional settlement initiative by the judge will be based on assumptions of a legal nature.[32]

It was mentioned earlier that in France there is more compulsion in family cases to start mediation: a statute of 2002 introduced a form of pressure in the field of parental responsibility. If the parties do not reach an agreement or try mediation, the judge may order (*enjoindre*) them to visit a *médiateur* who will educate the parents on the purpose and nature of mediation:

> 'En cas de désaccord, le juge s'efforce de concilier les parties. A l'effet de faciliter la recherche par les parents d'un exercice consensuel de l'autorité parentale, le juge peut leur proposer une mesure de médiation et, après avoir recueilli leur accord, désigner un médiateur familial pour y procéder. Il peut leur enjoindre de rencontrer un médiateur familial qui les informera sur l'objet et le déroulement de cette mesure'.[33]

2.2.5. The Court Initiates, and Sanctions are Possible

The most prominent example that can be mentioned here is the case of England and Wales, because of the impact of the Woolf-reforms. As far as compulsory ADR is concerned, the story is a bit confusing.[34] At first, Lord Woolf stated that in his opinion ADR should not be made compulsory, but it should only be encouraged.[35] Later he obviously changed his mind: 'Today sufficient should be known about ADR to make the failure to adopt it, in particular when public money was involved, indefensible'.[36]

Litigation in England is however not ruled by quotes from Lord Woolf, but by the CPR he devised and the accompanying rules and practice directions.[37] Under the CPR both the judges and the parties have to adhere to the 'overriding objective of dealing with cases justly'. This stipulates that, amongst other things, the parties are under an obligation to try to avoid the necessity for the start of proceedings.[38]

31 See <http://www.kammergericht.de/Inhalt%20Startseite/mediation_berichte/GesEntwurf_2-11-04.pdf> (last consulted 20 March 2007).

32 Says Minister of Justice Merk, *supra* note 29, p. 7.

33 Article 373-2-10 of the *Civil Code,* inserted by the Law No. 2002-305 of March 4, 2002, Article 5 V, *Journal Officiel* of March 5, 2002.

34 For outsiders, but insider M. Partington also finds that the courts have not been 'wholly consistent in their approach', Partington 2004, p. 100. Cf. John Gatenby, who claims that 'The impact of the CPR in relation to ADR has been uneven', Gatenby 2002.

35 Genn 2005, p. 8. In this paper Genn provides much information on mediation schemes, court orders and other ADR developments in the UK.

36 Genn 2005, p. 9.

37 Much of what is to follow is based on Verkijk 2005a, p. 223-231.

38 Practice Direction – Protocols, Section 4, as already cited (in anticipation) in *Unilever* v *The Procter and Gamble Co.* [1999] 2 All ER 691.

They also have a duty, where appropriate, to consider mediation. To promote this, and to inform the courts of what happened before proceedings are commenced, several 'pre-action protocols' have been developed for different kinds of cases, like personal injury claims and housing disrepair claims.[39] The general Practice Direction on protocols requires parties to comply with the general spirit of the protocols and the overriding objective whatever the subject of the claim.[40]

The failure of parties to consider mediation or other forms of ADR can lead to 'unfavourable' costs decisions, as is illustrated in the Dunnet case.[41] In this case, an appellate judge, when giving permission for the main dispute to proceed to appeal, suggested to the parties that it would be valuable for them to pursue ADR on the present facts. But the defendant (and respondent to the pending appeal) refused to co-operate or even to attend an ADR hearing. The Court of Appeal eventually heard the appeal concerning the merits of the case, which had been in favour of the defendant. It considered that, at least on the present facts, the respondent (and defendant) had been wrong to reject ADR as a potential solution to the dispute.[42] The court took this view even though the defendant had succeeded on the merits of the case at first instance and on appeal. So as to reflect its disapproval of the respondent's neglect of ADR, the court made a costs order which denied that party the right to receive its costs (in both court instances) from the defeated claimant.[43] Denial of costs is a severe sanction. This case illustrates the courts' determination to give ADR a chance to resolve disputes. Cases like this prompted CEDR[44] to change its definition of mediation towards the end of 2004. The new definition is as follows:

> 'Mediation is a flexible process conducted confidentially in which a neutral person actively assists parties in working towards a negotiated agreement of a dispute or difference, with the parties in ultimate control of the decision to settle and the terms of resolution'.

Because they found

39 At present there are eight different protocols. These can be found on the site of the Department of Constitutional Affairs, <http://www.dca.gov.uk/civil/procrules_fin/menus/protocol.htm> (consulted December 2004).

40 Evaluation report 'Further Findings. A Continuing Evaluation of the Civil Justice Reforms', August 2002, obtained from <http://www.dca.gov.uk/civil/reform/ffreform.htm> (consulted December 2004).

41 Or else face the consequences, as is shown in *Dunnett* v *Railtrack plc.* [2002] 2 ALL ER 850. The successful litigant, Railtrack, forfeited a costs order in its favour because it refused to consider the court's suggestion to mediate. See also Andrews 2003, p. 39. In *Hurst* v *Leeming* [2001] EWHC 1051, Leeming escaped (although according to the judge he took a high risk in refusing mediation) but, unfortunately for him, Hurst was bankrupt. See also the main text of *Halsey* v *Milton Keynes General NHS Trust* [2004] 4 All ER 920.

42 The *Dunnet* case, at 14 (*supra* note 41).

43 The *Dunnet* case, at 16 (*supra* note 41), per Brooke LJ, in exercise of the broad discretion concerning costs contained in CPR, Part 44.

44 See *supra* note 6.

> '[t]he old definition (...) overemphasized two features that are seen as less crucial in today's practice. The term voluntary was removed as recent judgments indicate that the courts require parties to behave in a proportionate and responsible manner to settle disputes including the use of mediation. The courts have also recently upheld the enforceability of mediation contract clauses'.[45]

From this and similar cases it may certainly not be concluded that there is a general obligation upon the parties to try ADR before litigating. As another court acknowledged:

> 'The hallmark of ADR procedures, and perhaps the key to their effectiveness in individual cases, is that they are processes voluntarily entered into by the parties in dispute with outcomes, if the parties so wish, which are non-binding. Consequently the court cannot direct that such methods be used but may merely encourage and facilitate'.[46]

It should be mentioned that a year later this same court warned solicitors that they should not lightly advise their clients to refuse mediation;[47] also, another year later, the Civil Procedure Rules were updated so as to further encourage mediation.[48] Notably, 'pre-action protocols' were amended for personal injury (PI) claims to encourage negotiation and mediation, both common ways of dealing with other types of claims. While there has been resistance to mediating PI cases in the UK, the use of mediation is increasing and the success rate in PI cases is said to exceed 90%.

Both from the CPR with its Practice Directions and from the cases cited above, it may appear that court-annexed mediation is on the rise in the UK and that parties are under a lot of pressure to pursue ADR. It is clear, however, that it is very dependent on the individual judge or the particular culture in a court, whether there will be referrals to mediation or other forms of ADR.[49] So, already within a few years after the introduction of the CPR and an initial rise in mediated cases, mediation was on the decline again. While settlement rates traditionally have been, and are, very high, in general ADR has not become popular in or around English litigation: the courts have developed teeth but often they are reluctant to use them.

2.2.6. No Court Proceedings before Mediation Attempt

In several cases mediation has been made mandatory in the most drastic sense. First we will look at Norway. According to the Marriage Act 1991, which came into force

45 Quote from the website <http://www.cedr.co.uk/index.php?location=/news/archive/20041101.htm> (last consulted 5 September 2006); about contract clauses, see the case of *Cable & Wireless* v *IBM* [2002] EWHC 2059 (Comm Ct).

46 *Halsey* v *Milton Keynes General NHS Trust* (2004) EWCA Civ 576. In this case, the mediation offers by the claimant were recognized as 'somewhat tactical' and they were not rewarded by a favourable cost decision.

47 Case of *Burchell* v *Bullard & Ors* [2005] EWCA Civ 358 (08 April 2005); more recently, see the case of *Burne* v *A* [2006] EWCA Civ 24.

48 Civil procedure rules, 41st update, April 6, 2006.

49 Pel & Spliet 2003, p. 1897; Gatenby 2002, see paragraph 'ADR orders'.

on 1 January 1993, mediation is compulsory for spouses who separate, if the marriage has resulted in offspring and one or more children are under 16 years of age.[50] There is an exception for specific cases, such as cases of domestic violence.[51] The purpose of mediation is not to bring the spouses back together. Secondly the 2005 Law on Disputes (*Tvisteloven*) introduced *rettsmekling*, i.e. mandatory mediation, initiated by the judge, in some courts.

Both in Italy and in Norway it has been felt that it should not be possible to sabotage mediation. Therefore the mediator must keep track of the parties' behaviour, so that, in case the mediation fails, the judge may impose a costs sanction. The Italian law[52] also prescribes that if parties in a mediation do not reach a solution, the mediator has to present a settlement proposal.

In England mediation in family cases is a prerequisite to obtain legal aid. Finally in Germany, the States (*Länder*) have the possibility to make mediation compulsory under Article 15a EGZPO, mainly for neighbour disputes, disputes related to persons' reputations and for small claims (max. € 750,-).

A special field is that of collective or individual labour conflicts, where mediation is often compulsory. An example is France with the procedure at the *bureau de conciliation*, of the *Conseil de Prud'hommes*, in individual labour cases and Spain where parties in a labour conflict may not put their case before the *Magistratura de Trabajo* before they have attempted mediation or conciliation conducted by an employee of the *Servicio de Mediación, Arbitraje y Conciliación*. If no agreement is reached, the court will again attempt to reach a friendly settlement by way of mediation.

The Scandinavian countries also discourage participants who want to litigate or strike in labour conflicts. Norway knows the procedure before the *Riksmeklingsmannen* (state mediators) in collective labour disputes and when the Swedish National Mediation Office decides that a risk of industrial action exists, or if such action has already been initiated, the National Mediation Office may appoint a mediator without the agreement of the parties concerned. In Denmark the peace obligation forms the basis for solutions when it comes to disputes over rights in labour cases. These conflicts should - contrary to disputes over interest - in no circumstances be solved by use of industrial action. Disputes over rights have to be solved according to the procedural rules on mandatory conciliation and binding judicial decisions. The conciliator is empowered to promote a solution for the conflict in the form of a 'conciliation proposal' (*mæglingsforslag*).

3. The Problems with Mandatory Mediation

In section 2, I have introduced some examples of compulsory mediation in Europe. We have seen how pressure may be exerted on parties to comply with mediation. Is

50 Cf. Section 26 Marriage Act of Norway.
51 Cf. Section 23 Marriage Act.
52 Law No. 5 of 17 January 2003.

it all for the best? Is mediation always the better solution, and even if it were, is mandatory mediation the better solution?

In my answer to this question I will make a distinction between more 'empirical' aspects and more 'fundamental' aspects. Most fundamental aspects are developed in relation to mediation in general. It goes without saying that objections to mediation in general count even more heavily in case mediation is not completely voluntarily.[53]

3.1. *Empirical Aspects of Mandatory Mediation*

The first empirical question is whether mediation will still lead to positive results, if the parties' participation is not based on their free will. Perhaps they will simply refuse to cooperate and frustrate settlement because they feel forced to comply with the mediation process. That assumption supports the main argument behind the reasoning of Dutch courts, when they abstain from enforcing mediation clauses. Because parties are allowed to end mediation at any time, it does not make sense to force a party into what may be no more than a mere formality. 'You can lead a horse to the water but you can not make it drink'. They may be right, especially considering the fact that in such cases one party has already explicitly refused ADR. But it is not the only possible way to look at it: the England and Wales High Court (Commercial Court) has taken the opposite stance[54] as have German courts.[55]

Anyway it is different when the law or the court obliges parties to enter into mediation. Advocates of mediation sometimes claim that mediation should be made mandatory because people that initiate litigation instead of mediation have not necessarily refused mediation: either they do not know enough about mediation or they are afraid to propose mediation because it would make their case seem weak in the eyes of their opponent.[56] Mandatory mediation deals with this last objection. No one is the weaker party if mediation is not a choice.

Furthermore it cannot be said that mandatory mediation does not work. The success rates - meaning that a settlement has been achieved - are often not nearly as high as in voluntary mediation.[57] Actually sometimes they are significantly lower. But in absolute terms the results are worth the trouble. When 10% of the potential litigants choose mediation and the settlement rate would be as high as 80%, the settlement rate is 16. Compare this to a participation of 100% (in a mandatory

53 Rhode 2004, p. 477.

54 In *Cable & Wireless* v *IBM* [2002] EWHC 2059 (Comm Ct): 'For the courts now to decline to enforce contractual references to ADR on the grounds of intrinsic uncertainty would be to fly in the face of public policy as expressed in the CPR and as reflected in the judgement of the Court of Appeal in *Dunnett* v *Railtrack* (..)' and 'The reference to ADR is analogous to an agreement to arbitrate. As such, it represents a free-standing agreement ancillary to the main contract and capable of being enforced by a stay of the proceedings or by injunction absent any pending proceedings'.

55 Van den Bosch 2002, p. 52.

56 In the author's practice as a lawyer clients have often expressed that fear. It is also recognized e.g. by Partington 2004, p. 105.

57 Genn 2005, p. 14.

scheme) and a much lower settlement rate of only 25%. The total settlement rate is still over 3 times higher when compared to the situation where mediation is strictly voluntary (50 over 16).

Voluntary	10% of 200 = 20 choose mediation →	80% of 20 settle, is 16
Mandatory	100% of 200 = 200 in mediation →	25% of 200 settle, is 50

In fact, the lower success rate (in my example 25%) is used as an argument pro mandatory mediation. It shows that the mediators or the courts do not pressure parties into a settlement.[58] If they did, the settlement rates would be higher. This is obviously not a completely convincing argument: perhaps the settlement rate would be only 5% if it were not for the pressure of the mediator. Also, in some case studies the reported results of compulsory mediation were actually as good as in voluntary mediation. Can it be concluded that in these cases the mediator exerted undue pressure?

Another factor is perhaps more troubling. Several authors have described what happened in court-annexed mediation with a compulsory character.[59] Especially when mediation is used as a case-management device and there are many participants, the work load of the mediators, or the mediating officials, is high. Besides, the process becomes a routine, aimed at settlement. This is precisely the message that is conveyed to the parties, i.e. that the purpose of the conference is to achieve a settlement. Also, it is emphasized how undesirable the alternative is: the unpredictability, the risks and the emotional stress of the court's decision: horror stories. What also may happen when mediation becomes a routine, is that the mediation is not just facilitative and interest-based, but instead the mediator tends to evaluate the legal aspects of the case and even suggests what may be a likely outcome. For these reasons, and more, an observer has named the 'settlement officials' *quasi-adjudicative* – just like judges. As a result, the process is not only non-voluntary to enter into, but the parties live under the impression that they should settle; they feel coerced.[60] And it is not only the parties that believe so, as is illustrated by the lists of strategies and techniques mediators may utilize to pressure parties into settlement.[61]

These are coercive aspects, all aimed at achieving a settlement. This is troubling for at least two reasons. In the first place, generally everybody agrees that no-one should be forced to settle his case if he is entitled to bring it to court. Yet when the amount of pressure on parties is high enough, settlements become compulsory.[62] Secondly, as Mendel-Meadow puts it, we may see the corruption of

58 Wissler 1997, p. 593 & p. 600. She does find lower satisfaction rates when mediation is mandatory as compared to when it is voluntary.

59 Ingleby 1993; Nolan-Haley 1996; Menkel-Meadow 1991.

60 Abel 1982, p. 271-272; see also the (other) literature mentioned by Wissler 1997, p. 572, fn. 39.

61 Abel 1982, p. 271-272; Nolan-Haley 1996, references in fn. 64.

62 This is why Nolan-Haley 1996, 61, pleads for legal representation for parties in mediation. In my opinion this is putting the cart before the horse.

both processes, by which she refers to both the settlement process and the process of adjudication.[63]

3.2. *Normative Objections against Mandatory Mediation*

What are normative, or fundamental, considerations? I refer to certain characteristics in ADR or informal justice that differ from important elements of *formal* justice, or litigation. Although the criticism is often more theoretical than empirical, the idea is of course that normative aspects have an impact on what actually happens.

It is not daring to say that formal justice - used here as a synonym for litigation - is about guarantees,[64] guarantees regarding due process, leading to a fair treatment of both parties and a fair decision that is based on reality. This is for example expressed by:[65]

- the independence and the professionalism of the judge;
- the formal equality of the parties (the parties have the same rights to be heard and to speak out, to obtain legal assistance etc.);
- the structure of litigation procedures;
- the physical distance that remains between the parties, the formalized exchange of information;
- the formalities of a court trial: court building, black robes etc.,[66] that remind us of higher, public values.

A very important observation is that the formal institutions assume that parties are in fact *not* equal.[67] That is why all these features are so important. They compensate for the inequality and aim at guaranteeing that despite the inequality of the parties, they are treated on an equal footing, giving them the same opportunities, the same *arms*.[68] Hence the rhetoric of Abel: 'Given a choice unconstrained by resources, how many of those seeking vindication of a right would choose a paralegal over a lawyer or a legally-untrained mediator over a judge?'[69]

63 Menkel-Meadow 1991, p. 33.

64 Cf. Article 6 *ECHR*. Van Boneval Faure 1893, p. 195 writes: 'De gelijkheid der partijen, in tegenstelling van hunne ongelijkheid bij eigenrichting, wordt door de regeling der procedure beoogd'. ('The equality of parties, as opposed to their unequality when they take justice in their own hands, is the intended purpose of civil procedure'). Also Delgado *et al.* 1985, p. 1368.

65 Delgado *et al.* 1985, p. 1387 *et seq.*

66 In Dutch courtrooms a picture of the queen over the head of the judge reminds the litigants that justice is done in the name of the queen.

67 Fiss 1984, p. 1076; Delgado *et al.* 1985, p. 1394, fn. 267; Roberts 1993, p. 455.

68 Delgado *et al.* 1985, p. 1374.

69 Abel 1998, p. 1026; his rhetoric may well be based on empirical grounds, according to the results of the experiment by Thibaut, Walker and others, quoted by Delgado *et al.* 1985, fn. 223-225 and text.

In mediation it is assumed that parties equal each other in political power, wealth and social status.[70] This is a misapprehension, and it disadvantages weaker parties. If there is a dispute between parties of unequal power, it is unlikely that mediation will lead to just results, unless there are legal means as a last resort. 'One cannot have equity and informality at the same time'. Or, again, as Abel puts it: 'In the absence of state norms and coercive power, the outcome is more likely to reflect and reproduce existing power inequalities'.[71]

Much of this criticism can already be found in the classic article of Owen Fiss[72] who claimed that differences in power and wealth may lead to unjust settlements:

- the poorer party has more difficulty to estimate the results of regular trial (being a one shotter and not a repeat player) and is likely to make the wrong choices when negotiating;
- the poorer party needs the money as soon as possible and, because of this, will settle;
- also, the poorer party has to settle because he cannot afford the costs of legal and other expertise.

Even more basic is the criticism expressed two centuries earlier by Jeremy Bentham, who wrote: 'Another mode of termination [of a lawsuit, RV] is by what is called *compromise*; which, being interpreted, is *denial of justice*'.[73] As Twining explains, '[c]ompromise, even in situations of equality of bargaining power when parties freely consent, involves the sacrifice of rights (...)'.[74] Chronologically between Bentham and Fiss, on the continent, Von Jhering shared these ideas:

> 'das Preisgeben eines verletzten Rechts ist ein Akt der Feigheit, der der Person zur Unehre und dem Gemeinwesen zum gröβten Schaden gereicht; der Kampf um das Recht ist ein Akt der ethischen Selbsterhaltung, eine Pflicht gegen sich selbst und die Gemeinschaft'.[75]

So, while negotiating and settling is to an important extent based on differences in power and the assessment of these differences, adjudication is aimed at avoiding unjustified advantages by applying the rule of law.

70 Fiss 1984, p. 1076; Delgado *et al.* 1985, p. 1394 and fn. 267, quoting Abel.
71 Which does not necessarily express his own view, Abel 1998, p. 1026.
72 Fiss 1984, p. 1076; see also Luban 1995, p. 2619.
73 Twining 1993, p. 384.
74 Twining 1993, p. 385, adds that Bentham anticipated modern commentators in doubting whether bargaining is ever really equal or consent truly free.
75 Von Jhering 1872; nevertheless, he distinguishes between an opponent who for example claims the ownership of a certain good in good faith, and 'a thief'. In the first case the best way out, depending on his evaluation of the outcome of the case, can be settlement, p. 30.

These are all objections on the micro level of individual disputants.[76] It is possible to extend this line of argument to a macro political field, which can be (if perhaps inadequately) summarized in two points:

1. Informal justice stands in the way of social reform, because it neutralizes and channels conflict.[77] Conflict is redefined as mere miscommunication. Rebels, those who are dissatisfied with social inequality or unfair situations in society, are persuaded to give up their grievances and exchange conflict for 'peace and harmony'.[78] Of course, in this vision, social harmony equals support for the existing capitalist structures.

2. Mediation is about private interests and not about public values. Mediation lacks public accountability and may undervalue public interests.[79] It does not require appointed or elected officials - like judges - to enforce norms that are subject to democratic or judicial oversight. Like Deborah Rhode states: 'Informal procedures aimed at private settlements may provide (1) insufficient development of legal precedents, (2) inadequate deterrence of unlawful conduct, or (3) ineffective safeguards for third party interests'.[80]

Finally some feminist criticism should at least briefly be mentioned. It focuses mainly on the situation where women are opposed by men; we find this situation often in family mediation, like divorce mediation (which is an important field where mandatory mediation can be found).[81] One of the most important aspects of this criticism is that women valuate relational aspects higher than men and will more easily give up some material interests in order to save the relationship. This tendency may be induced by the setting of the mediation process with its high emphasis on the relationship, emotions and settlement. Besides, it is obvious that women are often in a worse position in society than their soon-to-be-ex-husbands, financially or otherwise. As said before, mediation does not repair these differences but denies them.[82] Also, the mediation process 'often imposes a rigid orthodoxy as to how [the parties] should speak, make decisions, and be. This orthodoxy is

76 It is worth mentioning the pragmatical yet somewhat biased opinion of the Oberlandesgericht Hamm (quoted by Althammer 2006, p. 72): 'dass im Verhältnis zwischen freiwilliger Schlichtung und Staatlichem Rechtsweg in der Regel ein Vorrang für die Beschreitung des Rechtsweges besteht, weil hierdurch ein zur Vollstreckung geeigneter Titel erlangt wird'.

77 Cf. J. Auerbach: 'Without legal power the imbalance between aggrieved individuals and corporations, or government agencies cannot be redressed', quoted by Delgado *et al.* 1985, p. 1395. See Abel 1982, p. 286 *et seq.*

78 Delgado *et al.* 1985, p. 1391 *et seq.*

79 Delgado *et al.* 1985, p. 1398; Luban 1995, p. 2622.

80 Rhode 1998, p. 1011.

81 Grillo 1991, p. 1547.

82 Wissler 1997 refers to several studies that deny that as a rule women are worse of than men in mediation, p. 574; Grillo 1991 acknowledges that 'the existence of substantial client satisfaction [in divorce cases, RV] with some models of mediation cannot be completely discounted', Grillo 1991, p. 1549.

imposed through subtle and not-so-subtle messages about appropriate conduct and about what may be said in mediation', which is detrimental to many women and some men.[83] The criticism is - of course - much more extensive than can be set forth here.

In the light of this criticism it is interesting to know that Californian courts have developed a 'presumption of undue influence': 'when an interspousal transaction advantages one spouse, the law presumes such transactions to have been induced by undue influence'.[84] However, this presumption of undue influence cannot be applied to marital settlement agreements reached through mediation, because '[i]n this regard, the presumption of undue influence in marital transactions must yield to the policies favouring mediation and finality of judgments' (*sic*) and 'voluntary participation and self-determination are fundamental principles of mediation'; applying this presumption would jeopardize the institution of mediation.[85] So the presumption of undue influence, very adequate to protect women who have agreed to a settlement under undue spousal pressure, is swept aside because the agreement was reached in mediation, on the basis of the ideals of voluntariness and self-determination. This can hardly be viewed as something else than hypocrisy, considering the fact that as early as 25 years ago mediation has been made mandatory by Californian laws in many instances.[86]

4. Conclusion

A basic presumption of mediation is that it should be a voluntary process. But in many instances, mediation has become mandatory to some extent; not only in the US, but also in Europe. This is a development that has to be considered critically: both for empirical reasons, and because of normative objections to mediation in general. To illustrate the normative objections to mediation, the mediation process is compared with some theoretical aspects of formal (court) proceedings. The drawbacks of mediation are felt even more heavily when people cannot choose for or against mediation but are forced to comply.

The mixture of empirical and normative considerations as presented above leaves questions unanswered, like how we should valuate empirical results and how the formal guarantees of court proceedings materialise in practice. But nevertheless it supports the main thesis of this article, which is that mediation, however valuable it often can be, is not a panacea and that there are many dangers in mediation, especially in mandatory mediation, which should be taken into account when instituting court-annexed mediation projects.

83 Grillo 1991, p. 1550.

84 *In re Marriage of Haines* (1995) 33 Cal. Ap4th 277, 293.

85 See *In re Kieturakis*, 2006 WL 78602 (Cal. Ap1 Dist. 2006), 29 March 2006. The ex-wife showed her financial dependence and need by filing an income and expense declaration on that date listing no income and monthly expenses of $ 9,326; now that may seem a lot, but it is still only half that of the ex-husband.

86 Although not in the case at hand.

Bibliography

Abel 1982
Abel, R.L., 'The Contradictions of Informal Justice', in: Abel, R.L. (ed.), *1. The Politics of Informal Justice*, New York: Academic Press, 1982, p. 267-320.

Abel 1998
Abel, R.L., 'Big Lies and Small Steps: A Critique of Deborah Rhode's Too Much Law, Too Little Justice: Too Much Rhetoric, Too Little Reform', *Georgetown Journal of Legal Ethics*, 1998, p. 1019-1027.

Althammer 2006
Althammer, C., 'Mediation als prozessuale Last', *JuristenZeitung*, 2006, p. 69-76.

Andrews 2003
Andrews, N., *English Civil Procedure. Fundamentals of the New Civil Justice System*, Oxford: Oxford University Press, 2003.

Boettger 2004
Boettger, U., 'Efficiency Versus Party Empowerment - Against a Good Faith Requirement in Mandatory Mediation', *The Review of Litigation*, 2004, p. 1-46.

Van Boneval Faure 1893
Van Boneval Faure, R., *Het Nederlandsche Burgerlijk Procesrecht, I*, Leiden: E.J. Brill, 1893.

Van den Bosch 2002
Van den Bosch, T., 'Tot mediation verplichtende bepalingen in overeenkomsten: een vergelijking tussen Nederland en Duitsland', *Tijdschrift voor Mediation*, 2002, p. 52-53.

Brenninkmeijer *et al.* 2003
Brenninkmeijer, A.F.M. *et al.*, *Handboek Mediation*, Den Haag: Sdu uitgevers, 2003.

Brown & Marriott 1999
Brown, H.J., Marriott, A.L., *ADR Principles and Practice*, London [etc.]: Sweet and Maxwell, 1999.

Combrink-Kuiters, Niemeijer & Ter Voert 2003
Combrink-Kuiters, L., Niemeijer, E. & Ter Voert, M., *Ruimte voor Mediation. Evaluatie van projecten bij de rechterlijke macht en gefinancierde rechtsbijstand*, Den Haag: Boom Juridische Uitgevers, 2003.

Delgado *et al.* 1985
Delgado, R. *et al.*, 'Fairness and Formality: Minimizing the Risk of Prejudice in Alternative Dispute Resolution', *Wisconsin Law Review*, 1985, p. 1359-1404.

Editor's note 1990
Editor's note, 'Mandatory Mediation and Summary Jury Trial: Guidelines for Ensuring Fair and Effective Processes', *Harvard Law Review,* 1990, p. 1086-1104.

Fiss 1984
Fiss, O., 'Against Settlement', *Yale Law Journal,* 1984, p. 1073-1090.

Gatenby 2002
Gatenby, J., *ADR & The English Courts: Current Issues & Future Trends,* Addleshaw Booth & Co, 2002, <http://www.sccinstitute.com/_upload/shared_files/artikelarkiv/gatenby.pdf> (last consulted 20 March 2007).

Genn 1998
Genn, H, *Central London County Court Mediation Pilot: Evaluation Report,* LCD Research Series, No. 5/98, 1998.

Genn 2005
Genn, H., *Solving Civil Justice Problems: What might be best?,* Paper for the Scottish Consumer Council Seminar on Civil Justice, 2005.

Grillo 1991
Grillo, T., 'The Mediation Alternative: Process Dangers for Women', *Yale Law Journal,* 1991, p. 1545-1610.

Ingleby 1993
Ingleby, R., 'Court Sponsored Mediation: The Case Against Mandatory Mediation', *The Modern Law Review,* 1993, p. 441-470.

Von Jhering 1872
Von Jhering, R., *Der Kampf um's Recht,* Vienna: Verlag der G.J. Manz'schen Buchhandlung, 1872.

Kuhn 1984
Kuhn, S.C., 'Mandatory Mediation: California Civil Code Section 4607', *Emory Law Journal,* 1984, p. 733-778.

Luban 1995
Luban, D., 'Settlements and the Erosion of the Public Realm', *Georgetown Law Journal,* 1995, p. 2619-2662.

Mackie *et al.* 2004
Mackie, K. *et al.* (eds.), *The EU Mediation Atlas: Practice and Regulations,* London: Butterworths Law, 2004.

Menkel-Meadow 1991
Menkel-Meadow, C., 'Pursuing Settlement in an Adversary Culture: A Tale Of Innovation Co-Opted or "The Law Of ADR"', *Florida State University Law Review*, 1991, p. 1-46.

Nolan-Haley 1996
Nolan-Haley, J.M., 'Court Mediation and the Search for Justice Through Law', *Washington University Law Quarterly*, 1996, p. 47-102.

Partington 2004
Partington, M., 'Alternative Dispute Resolution: Recent Developments, Future Challenges', *Civil Justice Quarterly*, 2004, p. 99-106.

Pel & Spliet 2003
Pel, M. & Spliet, M.M.A., 'Implementatie van mediation naast rechtspraak: Court-annexed mediation in Engeland... een lichtend voorbeeld?', *Nederlands Juristenblad*, 2003, p. 1897-1902.

Rhode 1998
Rhode, D.L., 'Too Much Law, Too Little Justice: Too Much Rhetoric, Too Little Reform', *Georgetown Journal of Legal Ethics*, 1998, p. 989-1018.

Rhode 2004
Rhode, D.L., 'Essay: Frivolous Litigation and Civil Justice Reform: Miscasting the Problem, Recasting the Solution', *Duke Law Journal*, 2004, p. 447-483.

Roberts 1993
Roberts, S., 'Alternative Dispute Resolution and Civil Justice: An Unresolved Relationship', *Modern Law Review*, 1993, p. 452-470.

De Roo & Jagtenberg 2003
De Roo, A. & Jagtenberg, R., *De praktijk van mediation in ons omringende landen*, Rotterdam/Den Haag: Erasmus Universiteit/WODC, 2003.

Twining 1993
Twining, W., 'Alternative to What? Theories of Litigation, Procedure and Dispute Settlement in Anglo-American Jurisprudence: Some Neglected Classics', *Modern Law Review*, 1993, p. 380-392.

Verkijk 2005
Verkijk, R., 'Conciliation in the Netherlands', in: Van Rhee, C.H. (ed.), *European Traditions in Civil Procedure* (Ius Commune Europaeum, 54), Antwerpen/Oxford: Intersentia, 2005, p. 207-212.

Verkijk 2005a
Verkijk, R., 'Conciliation in England and Wales', in: Van Rhee, C.H. (ed.), *European Traditions in Civil Procedure* (Ius Commune Europaeum, 54), Antwerpen/Oxford: Intersentia, 2005, p. 223-231.

Verkijk 2005b
Verkijk, R., 'Mediation in wetgeving in Nederland?', *Tijdschrift voor Civiel Procesrecht*, 2005, p. 34-40.

Winston 1996
Winston, D.S., 'Participation Standards in Mandatory Mediation Statutes: "You Can Lead A Horse to Water ..."', *Ohio State Journal on Dispute Resolution*, 1996, p. 187-206.

Wissler 1997
Wissler, R.L., 'The Effects of Mandatory Mediation: Empirical Research on the Experience of Small Claims and Common Pleas Courts', *Willamette Law Review*, 1997, p. 565-604.

N. Betetto

COURT-BASED MEDIATION AND ITS PLACE IN SLOVENIA

1. Introduction

Mediation is a voluntary and confidential conflict-resolution method. It is generally understood[1] to be a short-term, structured, task-oriented, participatory intervention process. Disputing parties work with a neutral third party, the mediator, to reach a mutually acceptable agreement. It is viewed as more expeditious, inexpensive, and congenial for parties than adjudication, more responsive to the needs of litigants and procedurally simpler than adversarial problem solving. Because it is a compromise rather than a combat, it can preserve business relationships and deliver creative settlements. Usually there are fewer enforcement problems.

The litigation fuels the parties' anger and suspicions, making it hard for them to think realistically about the dispute or talk constructively with each other about the settlement. A mediator, by contrast, is able to do the following:

- call a cease-fire and separate the combatants;
- convene all the stakeholders, as well as their lawyers, and allow them to state demands and make arguments directly to each other, getting potential emotional grievances off their chests;
- talk privately with each side's principal actors about the strengths and weaknesses of their legal case, asking questions that force them to re-examine their optimistic assumptions, the consequences of defeat and the impact of the litigation on them and their businesses;
- question everyone off-the-record about the non-legal issues in the case and their real goals;
- develop packages of options, conducting shuttle diplomacy if necessary;
- assist the parties' drafting of a durable settlement agreement.

Take for example the case where the tenants in an urban apartment complex suffer serious interruptions of services caused by the breakdown of the heating system.

1 Nolan Haley 1992, p. 56.

After conditions become intolerable they start a rent strike, but the landlord insists that they pay their rent and brings the case to court.

This simple case example and other practical cases illustrate the truth about litigation, which is the following: the legal system often operates like a procrustean bed, forcing litigants to make arguments and seek remedies that may have little to do with what they most care about. The parties in the dispute often litigate over inflammatory and largely irrelevant issues.

2. Court-based Mediation Schemes

Court-based (court-attached, court-annexed) alternative dispute resolution procedures are (1) administered by the court, and (2) different from the traditional litigation process.[2] The judge-hosted settlement conferences should not be treated as a form of alternative dispute resolution. In administering a court-based programme, a court generally provides a roster of neutral persons who conduct the sessions, establishes criteria for inclusion on the roster and adopts rules regarding such matters as case selection, methods for assigning neutrals to the case, confidentiality guarantees and guidelines for conducting the ADR sessions. Court-based alternatives in the United States[3] involve a limited number of ADR methods: arbitration, mediation, early neutral evaluation and summary jury trial.

Some court-based programmes automatically refer certain types of cases to the ADR process.[4] In other programmes cases enter the ADR process after referral by a judge or through voluntary participation by the parties. The outcome is not binding unless the parties agree to be bound.

The incorporation of ADR, mediation in particular, into the dispute resolution process, both inside and outside the courts, presents the court system with the basic question: Should ADR, mediation in particular, have a role at all in courts?

3. Should Mediation have a Role in Courts?

A core function of the courts as public institutions is, beyond any doubt, to serve the needs of individual litigants and thereby to maintain public confidence in society's capacity for peaceful dispute resolution.

3.1. *The Arguments against In-court Mediation*

The arguments against providing in-court mediation are that courts should not divert resources from their public mission – to declare and apply the law – to secondary, alternative programmes designed solely to aid parties in settling their disputes. The opponents of in-court mediation believe when a court resolves a dispute publicly, it not only serves litigants' private interests, but also serves the

2 Stienstra & Willging 1995, p. 3.

3 Stienstra & Willging 1995, p. 4.

4 Parties can request that their case be removed from the programme.

public interest by passing visible judgements. When a court or its representatives in an alternative proceeding evaluates a case privately and facilitates a settlement, it primarily serves individual, short-term interests of the litigants. The methods courts use in declaring the law give the public confidence in the law. Such procedural traditions enhance public acceptance of case outcomes and legal rulings. Reasoned decisions give meaning and context to abstract rules of law, enabling individuals to understand their legal positions, and to avoid disputes or settle them privately. By ruling publicly in concrete cases, courts serve as public guides that others can use to predict how courts will apply the law in the future. In contrast, alternative processes thwart the formal dispute resolution and law-making processes by siphoning disputes away from them, even though not all cases filed lead to trials and not all trials lead to judicial rulings. In most cases, parties settle their claims with little or no formality. Referring such cases to ADR, however, removes them from the processes that allow the parties and the court to assess their importance for the development of the law. The eligibility requirements of the typical court-based mediation programme sweep into such programmes cases involving legal principles along with cases involving pecuniary interests.

3.2. *Arguments in Support of In-court Mediation*

The proponents of in-court mediation argue that courts provide a forum for the peaceful resolution of disputes and thus serve the core responsibility of ensuring society's safety and stability. Courts also preserve the rule of law and develop and refine the legal norms through public adjudication, conducted according to written rules and resulting in recorded decisions that preserve individual rights, sustain public values and provide guidelines for future behaviour. Courts cannot, however, fulfil their dual function of peacemaker and law giver if they are not available to disputants nor have the confidence of the public. To be available, courts must be affordable and must provide the assistance of a neutral decision maker in a timely fashion. To generate public confidence, courts must provide both a process and an outcome that are seen as fair by litigants and the public. For many cases over many years, the traditional adjudicatory process has provided the means for peaceful and fair resolution of disputes. Procedural rules have afforded individual parties due process and the written decisions have established and reinforced public values. In adhering solely to traditional dispute resolution methods in all cases, however, courts impose a stringent process. For some parties, the traditional adversarial framework, although providing a resolution, does not provide the conciliation they seek. For others, the procedural rules make the process too costly to pursue. Even for those who intend to proceed to trial - to seek, for example, a new precedent or to resolve an important public policy issue - the traditional process may impede or prolong case resolution, rather than promote it. When courts cannot meet litigants' needs, they risk becoming an esoteric and distant institution in the citizens' lives. To retain the confidence of the public and to preserve their role as peacemaker and law giver, the courts must change as the needs of those they serve change.

For many litigants, alternative procedures provide benefits or opportunities not available to them through traditional adjudication. Instead of adjudication's exclusive focus on legal and factual contentions, mediation helps parties clarify and address issues driving (and sometimes stalling) the litigation. Instead of adjudication's 'winner takes all' approach, appropriate in some, but not all cases, mediation permits parties to fashion more creative and mutually satisfactory outcomes. Where adjudication is rigid, mediation is flexible. Where adjudication reserves control for the judicial decision maker, mediation provides parties with greater control over the dispute resolution process and outcome.

Common sense alone suggests that meeting the standards of the ideal system requires deploying a whole battery of dispute resolving mechanisms. Even if a court's most important role is to declare and preserve the law, this function can be carried out only through real cases and real litigants who bring disputes to court. It is the litigants' perceptions of their case's outcome and processing that form the basis for much of the public's faith in the courts.

Some litigants are best served by traditional adjudicatory processes. Others need a less elaborate, less costly, or less adversarial procedure. These needs have probably always been present, but are augmented today by a greater diversity of cases in courts compared with the past and a greater diversity of litigants. When substantial numbers of litigants in courts cannot satisfactorily resolve their disputes - or when the public believes this is true - the courts have failed in their most fundamental functions.

Some will argue that if courts shift their focus to meeting the needs of individual litigants, they will retard the development of the law by removing law-making cases from judicial decision-making. Even in the traditional adjudicatory system, as in alternative procedures, potentially law-making cases settle because the parties choose to do so. No judge would force the parties in such cases to go to trial because a new legal principle might be set.

Moreover, legal rules alone do not ensure societal well-being. Unwritten norms, too, are powerful guides for behaviour, and courts, like other institutions, help establish and maintain important norms. In doing their work, for example, courts present to citizens a model for how to resolve disputes. The adjudication model, while teaching much that is good, emphasizes conflict rather than cooperation, secrecy rather than openness, and dependence on authorities rather than oneself for the resolution of problems.

It is possible to conceive a different court in which mediation would be required in most civil cases, one in which those in disagreement would be directly involved in the resolution of their cases. The central purpose of such a court would be to promote self-determination and consideration for others. Mediation would serve not only the needs of the individual litigant, but critical public values as well, and adversarial interactions and judge-imposed outcomes would be displaced by cooperative problem solving and party-generated solutions.

4. Designing a Court-based Mediation Programme

Courts should address the following questions when considering whether and how to implement a court-based mediation programme:[5]

- what problems is the court trying to solve by providing a court-based mediation programme?
- what are the court's goals in having a mediation programme?
- does the court want a facilitative or evaluative mediation process?
- when in the litigation should mediation occur?
- will the court itself provide mediation, or will the cases be assigned to private institutions?
- will the programme provide for compulsory participation of parties, or will it be based on the principle of voluntariness?
- what kinds of cases should be referred to mediation?
- how will the programme be financed?
- will parties have to pay the mediation service?
- who will be mediators?
- what level of confidentiality will be guaranteed?
- what kinds of rules and forms should there be?
- how shall the programme be managed?
- how shall the programme be integrated into the case-management process?
- how shall the programme be evaluated?

4.1. *Court-based Mediation – Assignment of Cases to Private Institutions?*

In a country where mediation has practically no tradition and therefore no ADR private institutions exist, such as Slovenia, courts must address the question whether they themselves should provide mediation or whether the cases should be assigned to private institutions. The balance of reasons favours the court providing mediation itself.

Courts should establish alternatives that are located in and monitored by the courts themselves. They should do so for three reasons: equal access, fair process and the maintenance of a broad-based public-sector justice system.

First, the courts' public function is, in significant part, to help citizens resolve disputes. In doing so, the courts should provide all citizens with access to whatever process is appropriate to the case. Whatever the appropriate method, citizen-litigants would rightfully be shocked if a public institution told them to turn to the private market for assistance, particularly if private organisations hardly exist. Even if alternative procedures offered by the private market existed, a lot of citizens could not afford them. The courts owe these litigants in particular the opportunity of a court-based alternative procedure.

5 See Stienstra 2002, conference material.

Second, the courts have a responsibility to guarantee a fair process and a just outcome to litigants. Once a case is filed, it ceases to be a mere private business. It also becomes the public's business. When a court's dispute resolution methods include referral to alternatives, such as mediation, the court must guarantee the quality of those methods and can best do so by establishing them as a part of its own system of case resolution. It can specify how cases are to be selected for mediation and whether certain types of cases are to be exempt because they are inappropriate for ADR. It can spell out the procedures for assigning neutrals to cases and establish training and certification requirements for these neutrals. It can specify as well how the mediation sessions are to be conducted and can protect the confidentiality of information exchanged at these sessions. In establishing these procedures and safeguards, the courts protect litigants. Their purpose is to ensure that both the stronger and the weaker party in a case have equal access to information and equal power to negotiate a resolution. The courts can protect parties from pressure to settle and protect one party from another who is not negotiating in good faith. The courts' involvement, in turn, is likely to enhance the parties' faith in the process, motivate the neutral to provide superior service, and allow ongoing evaluation of the system.

Some will object that administration of ADR is a too intrusive role for courts since it attempts to regulate the interactions between attorneys and clients. Once parties have chosen to file a case in court, however, and once the court has determined that mediation is appropriate, the court has an obligation to provide parties with the same protection as afforded by traditional procedures. This protection does not necessarily exist in the private market, which may be one of the reasons litigants choose to come to court.

The third reason why courts should provide mediation is to fulfil their role as public institutions established to resolve citizens' disputes and to declare and apply the law. To suggest that citizens should take their disputes elsewhere, or that they can come to court but that they are unlikely to have a chance to present their case to neutrals, can only prompt public doubt in the justice system. Confining mediation and other ADR methods to the private sector would result in the creation of a private justice system, whose effect would be to undermine the courts' peace-keeping and law-making functions far more drastically than court-based ADR possibly could.

4.2. *Selection of Cases and Timing of Referral*

When courts choose between cases or categories of cases for which mediation is offered, such choices should be made on the basis of clearly articulated criteria. Such criteria might include the following:

- there is high probability that mediation will be successful in the particular cases or category of cases, in terms of both the number and quality of settlements;
- even if there is not a high probability that mediation will be successful in the particular case or category of cases, continuing litigation would harm non-parties;

- the dispute involves important continuing relationships;
- the case, if not mediated, is likely to require lasting involvement by the court.

The following considerations may militate against the suitability of referring cases to mediation:

- there is a need for public sanctioning of conduct;
- repetitive violations of statutes or regulations need to be dealt with collectively and uniformly;
- a party or parties are not able to negotiate effectively themselves or with the assistance of counsel.

Although the timing of a referral to mediation may vary depending upon the type of case involved and the needs of the particular case, referral should be made at the earliest possible time that parties are able to make an informed choice about participation in mediation. Courts should provide opportunities on a continuing basis for both the parties and the court to determine the timing of a referral to mediation. They should also establish presumptive deadlines for the mediation process, which may be extended by the court upon a showing by the parties that continuation of the process will assist in reaching a solution.

5. The Court-based Mediation Programme of the District Court of Ljubljana

Since 2002 the District Court of Ljubljana has been offering litigants in civil, family and commercial cases the opportunity to resolve their disputes through mediation. Mediation is presented to parties as a voluntary, confidential, fast, free-of-charge dispute resolution procedure, in which a neutral third party (the mediator) helps the litigants find a consensual resolution of the dispute. This procedure is non-binding until the parties agree to be bound by it and does not affect an eventual litigation in any way. The only condition for mediation is that both parties agree to solve their dispute with the help of a mediator. Sessions are informal; mediators talk to parties in joint and separate sessions (caucus). The mediation procedure is as long as parties and the mediator think it is appropriate. If the parties reach a solution they may agree to be bound by the agreement signed in front of a judge in a form of a court-settlement, which becomes a final (and enforceable) judicial decision. All communication regarding mediation procedures is confidential. If the mediator is a judge the case cannot be assigned to him or her after the mediation process.

5.1. *Court-based Mediation Planning*

Court-based mediation planning of the Ljubljana District Court focused on three key areas:

- setting up a coalition;
- conducting analysis;
- adopting a formal programme.

Four key persons formed a coalition: the president of the District Court of Ljubljana, the Head of the Civil Department and his deputy and the former Head of the Civil Department (at the moment of establishing the coalition a court of appeal judge). The participation of the former Head of the Civil Department was particularly important as it provided management continuity and thus programme efficiency during a longer period of time. At the same time it provided direct communication and programme promotion at the court of appeal.

The selection of judges for the team, which aimed at initiating changes and improvements, was very important. The team had to include individuals who were experienced yet who would not utilize their experience to apply yesterday's solutions to today's problems. The leading team had to be open-minded, it had to share the vision of how to draft a programme. This was important in order to legitimate the process of change.

The second stage was to establish an internal alliance. Within the civil sector of the court a discussion was initiated between judges and specialised staff members about possible approaches to encourage consensual dispute resolution within civil procedure. Different strategies of promoting participation in drafting and implementing the mediation programme were used: communication to 'sell the idea', and presentations on how the new approach could help clients, the courts and judges; training with the goal to allow the employees to adapt to the new programme; and negotiations and flexibility in the short-term planning of the programme. The inclusion of stakeholders in the negotiations to legitimize the process to implement mediation services in the courts was advantageous, as at the end the judges' interest in participating in the programme was greater than expected. It is estimated that the main reason for the support of mediation was the transparency of the process in adopting decisions and engaging in permanent dialogue with all stakeholders.

The third step of establishing a coalition was to establish an external alliance. Unlike the programmes of court-based mediation in the USA, the UK and the Netherlands, where implementation of these programmes followed the top-down policy, in Slovenia the policy was implemented bottom-up. Due to initial ignorance about the advantages of mediation, the District Court of Ljubljana programme was not supported by the key players of judicial policy – the Supreme Court, the Judicial Council and the Ministry of Justice. A statement was made to the effect that this kind of dispute resolution was unsuitable and therefore not recommended. Such statements made by the key players of the judicial policy in the field of alternative dispute resolution have an important impact as the courts must rely on them when designing new programmes, obtaining budget appropriations, and defining requirements for mediators.

A statement of support by the key players should make the following points in order to garner support and create momentum for mediation programmes in the courts:[6]

- alternative dispute resolution and adjudication in traditional judicial proceedings should be treated equally;
- alternative dispute resolution should be seen as a logical component of time standards for dispute resolution, by which particularly advocates' support is needed;
- a policy should make options available for the parties to the dispute and thus wider access to justice; as clients go where the service is the best and the costs are the lowest, promotion of the fact that alternative procedures are free of charge or of modest costs in comparison with judicial proceedings is needed;
- financing support for the programme will be offered by the Ministry of Justice. The Ministry should further help to create plans to reduce the transaction costs of the court and create targets for cases to be solved in shorter times;
- a declaration of intent that the courts should be authorized to provide alternative dispute resolution, in order to ensure that the courts are able to redefine if necessary the quality standards, and monitor, evaluate and re-adapt the programme to the needs and expectations of the customers.

As the key players of the judicial policy made no such statement of support for the role of alternative dispute resolution in the Slovenian courts, the procedure of setting up the external alliance was more difficult and risky. More clarification was needed to explain why alternative dispute resolution is necessary than to explain how to offer and use these services. The court was setting up external alliances by obtaining the support of the Law Faculty in Ljubljana regarding the legal admissibility of the mediation programme despite there being no explicit regulatory framework. There was no support of the bar association, the Attorney General and insurance companies (the most common players in judicial proceedings).

The court planned its programme on the basis of its needs, as well as the needs of the disputants and the advocates. The methods applied included collecting statistical data; conducting a functional analysis; and conducting a comparative legal analysis.

The statistics regarding the court backlogs showed that before 2001 the court needed 21 months on average to settle a civil case. Functional analysis showed that in the period from 1995 to 1999, 80% of cases were settled by the end of the first hearing. This date confirmed the hypothesis that the earlier the mediation is offered the bigger are the chances for success. At the Law Faculty in Ljubljana, two comparative legal analyses of court-based mediation were ordered by the court. They confirmed the standpoint of the court that from the procedural point of view, the existing provisions of the Civil Procedure Act, laying down the obligation of the

6 See Zalar 2002.

court to help parties to settle throughout the whole procedure, provided a sufficient legal framework to start the programme.

The Courts Act (statutory) and the Court Rules (secondary law) provided a substantive legal framework for the introduction of court-based mediation. Both lay down the obligation of the court to adopt a programme for solving court backlogs when the number of cases the court receives annually is higher than the number of pending cases. The District Court in Ljubljana used the framework for alternative dispute resolution in two ways. In the programme of reducing backlogs, mediation was defined as an experimental pilot programme, which would last two years. This allowed the programme to be modified based on the analysis of its strengths and weaknesses. The experimental nature of the programme when it was launched also allowed for great flexibility. The second advantage of the legal framework for alternative dispute resolution was that the court itself was able to define and prescribe the principles and rules of mediation, as well as the standards for the selection, appointment, dismissal, training and assessment of mediators.

One year after the implementation of the programme, the Civil Procedure Act was amended. It authorizes the court to stay the procedure if parties demand an order to attempt alternative dispute resolution. It was easy for the legislature to subscribe to such an amendment due to the support from existing data on the performance of the experimental programme.

The legal framework for alternative dispute resolution, however, implies certain risks. The principle of confidentiality as the fundamental mediation principle is particularly relevant in relation to the judicial proceedings. Parties would be reluctant to participate in mediation if in case of unsuccessful mediation their openness would return like a boomerang in litigation. Everything that is said or submitted in writing during mediation should stay confidential in relation to the judicial proceedings. Unsuccessful mediation should not affect the position that the parties held prior to the mediation. This standard is so important that it should be protected by procedural law. The District Court in Ljubljana enforced this protection by offering the parties who were willing to participate in mediation the chance to sign a statement of confidentiality and evidence prohibition. A question could be raised, however, how the confidentiality principle would be protected by the court in case a violation of the statement occurred.

5.2. *Referral of Cases to Mediation*

The court offers mediation automatically in all family cases, all pain and suffering damage cases and other damage cases, all commercial cases, all cases about a division of property (except when one party has given notice that it is not interested in mediation). Judges can offer mediation in all cases at any stage of the procedure.

The court sends parties and their lawyers a mediation offer in writing. This includes a description in detail of the rules of the procedure, the potential outcome of the procedure, the mediators' qualifications and how the parties can enforce the exclusion of a mediator in a case of conflict of interests. Practical information such as the whereabouts of the mediation and the time and costs aspects of the procedure are also included. The letter proposing mediation is a general one and it is not tailored to the specific subject of the case.

The average rate of acceptance of the mediation offer from both parties is 30%. Although it is believed Slovenian people are real fighters, the acceptance rate compared with international experience (where it ranks from 5 to 25%) is rather high. This means that the parties in Slovenia are willing to resolve their conflicts using mediation when this idea is presented to them in a proper way and when they are provided with an experienced mediator. The court guarantees that mediation will start within three months (in family cases in 14 days) after the parties have accepted the mediation offer. This saves a lot of time compared to lengthy judicial procedures. An additional incentive for the parties is that mediation is free and that the agreement is enforceable as a court-settlement.

5.3. *The Mediators*

The first mediators were judges who provided their service as »pro bono« mediators in addition to their regular judicial tasks. The reason for this choice was that judges enjoy a good reputation and have a certain authority, both of which might raise the public trust in mediation. Now the list of more than sixty mediators includes judges, retired judges, lawyers and psychologists. The role of mediators with no legal background is confined to co-mediator. While the judges serve 'pro bono', other mediators are paid on a contractual basis.

The court sees the offering and maintaining of good-quality court-based mediation as one of its responsibilities. It provides basic (forty hours) and advanced mediation training organized by the ADR office. Special attention is paid to the continuous education of mediators.

A mediator is selected at random from the list of mediators. There is no attempt to match the mediator's background and the case assigned. In case parties have doubts about the impartiality of the mediator, they can request another mediator on the same grounds that they can request a judge to be excluded from hearing a case. Once the mediator has been selected, he suggests the date of the mediation session. When the parties express their consent to mediate in litigation, the ADR office immediately sets a date for the first mediation session.

5.4. *Organizing Mediations*

The District court of Ljubljana has a special office for alternative dispute resolution which is responsible for information and clarifications, management, monitoring and adaptations of the mediation programme, as well as for all communication with the public concerning court-based mediation. It sends out letters offering mediation, registers all cases, organizes mediation sessions, and handles communication concerning mediation with judges, lawyers, mediators and clients. It sends out the invitations to, and cancellations of mediation sessions, keeps statistical data and takes care of the promotion, monitoring and evaluation of the programme.

Furthermore, it organizes meetings and intervision meetings for mediators and initiates the mediators' training programmes.

5.5. *Monitoring*

Statistical data have been recorded since the beginning of the project. The data that are kept are the following:

- rate of expressed consents;
- number of cases in which mediation was successful;
- number of cases referred to mediation;
- party satisfaction, which is measured by anonymous questionnaires the parties fill out on a voluntary basis;
- number of mediation sessions required to reach a settlement.

5.6. *The Mediation Procedure*

The parties and their lawyers are invited to the ADR office. The mediation sessions (joint and separate) take place in the court building. During the sessions no written record is made. When an agreement is reached between the parties, a district court judge has to take part in completing the process of mediation. All judges of the Civil Department of the District Court of Ljubljana are in a twice a week 'call on duty' schedule. Even if the mediator is a judge. The final agreement, in order to have the force of a court-settlement, has to be signed in front of a judge who was not mediating the case. This judge checks the draft agreement on its admissibility and proper formulation. He can improve the text of the agreement and make some remarks.

The mediation procedure is as long as the parties and mediator wish. In approximately 58% of civil cases, 39% of family cases and 54% of commercial disputes, mediation finishes successfully during the first session. In the District Court of Ljubljana, there are 15 to 25 sessions a week.

6. The Future

Clear and achievable goals and targets of case management are the most important pillars for growing support and acceptance of the court-based programme in the District Court in Ljubljana.[7] A long-term and lasting goal of the programme should be the implementation of an effective system of timely and tailor-made dispute resolution, which can be compared with recent standards within the EU. It is essential to recognize that the objectives and goals of different players in the field are not necessarily the same. Those involved in mediation and case management should choose their approaches accordingly.

7 For details see Pel 2005.

The Ministry of Justice, the Judicial Council and the Supreme Court are responsible for maintaining a broad public justice system and reducing the existing backlogs. It is therefore very important to gain the support of those institutions through showing them good results and the need for support and sufficient funding. Furthermore, the support of 'repeat-players' like governmental bodies, insurance companies and lawyers is indispensable. Mediation is still a relatively unknown and thus unpopular option to almost all players in this field in Slovenia. Good information and communication (rather than arguments) are essential for encouraging everyone to co-operate.

Bibliography

Nolan Haley 1992
Nolan Haley, J.M., *Alternative Dispute Resolution*, St. Paul: West Publishing Co., 1992.

Pel 2005
Pel, M., *Slovenia Court-annexed Mediation Project*, 2005, unpublished.

Stienstra 2002
Stienstra, D., *Core Issues to Address in Designing a Mediation Programme*, Southeast European Regional Conference on Alternative Dispute Resolution, Ljubljana 2002, (conference material).

Stienstra & Willging 1995
Stienstra, D. & Willging, T.E., *Alternatives to Litigation: Do They Have a Place in the Federal Courts?*, Federal Judicial Center, Long-Range Planning Series, 4/95, 1995.

Zalar 2002
Zalar, A., *Policy Issues of Court-annexed mediation in Slovenia*, Southeast European Regional Conference on Alternative Dispute Resolution, Ljublana, 2002 (conference material).

M. Vukelić

ALTERNATIVE DISPUTE RESOLUTION AND MEDIATION IN CROATIA

1. Legal Basis

The development of an alternative dispute resolution system is of particular interest for the Republic of Croatia and one of the priorities of the reform of the justice system.[1]

By the adoption of the Arbitration Act (2001) and the Mediation Act (2003), an adequate legal framework was created.

The Mediation Act

When the Mediation Act (*Official Gazette* No. 163/03) was adopted, its purpose was to alleviate some of the burden on the courts by introducing alternative dispute resolution and establishing a legal framework for such dispute resolution. For the purpose of the implementation of the Act, a number of new measures have been planned in order to encourage parties to resolve disputes peacefully. These measures include continuous training and the introduction of criteria for the selection of persons who can act as mediators, for informing the public and all entities on the advantages of peaceful dispute resolution, media coverage and promotion of mediation, and the establishment of a network of centres for mediation.

According to the Mediation Act, mediation is a procedure whereby parties make an attempt to resolve their dispute amicably with assistance provided by one or more mediators who help the parties reach a settlement, without imposing on them a binding solution (Article 2 of the Conciliation Act).

Mediation is limited to disputes concerning patrimonial issues, and especially to civil, commercial and labour disputes. Disputes that do not concern patrimonial issues (such as marital disputes, family disputes, and disputes strictly concerning strictly personal rights) are not covered by this Act (Article 1 of the Conciliation Act).

1 The data used is from the working material of the Croatian Ministry of Justice (Development of Alternative Dispute Resolution).

The Labour Act regulates the possibility of voluntary and compulsory conciliation in collective labour disputes. Mediation is compulsory in the case of disputes concerning the conclusion, amendment or renewal of collective agreements or similar disputes (Article 214 of the Labour Act). The Act also foresees the possibility of mediation in individual labour disputes.

The Civil Obligations Act provides that the contracting parties may agree on a third party to interpret the contract in the case of disagreements. The parties may not initiate a dispute until they obtain an interpretation of the contract. The participants in a relationship governed by the law of civil obligations have a duty to make an attempt to resolve disputes by coordination, mediation or in some other amicable way (Article 321 of the Civil Obligations Act).

The Civil Procedure Act allows for the possibility of concluding court settlements (Article 321(3)). The person who intends to file a suit may try to reach a settlement through the court. The person who intends to file a suit against the Republic of Croatia has the duty to address the State Attorney's Office to make an attempt at amicable dispute resolution (Article 186(a) of the Civil Procedure Act).

The Family Act provides that in certain cases it is compulsory to have a conciliation procedure if the procedure for dissolution of a marriage was initiated by a complaint or by a joint petition, and the spouses have children (Article 44 of the Family Act).

The Criminal Procedure Act, according to the principle of purposefulness, prescribes that the State Attorney may reject criminal charges in cases of less serious criminal acts provided that there is an agreement between the injured party and the suspect, and after the suspect fulfils one of the obligations laid down by law (Article 175 of the Criminal Procedure Act). The same Act states that judges in criminal procedures for criminal acts subject to private prosecution may summon the parties to make an attempt at conciliation before scheduling the main hearing (Article 443 of the Criminal Procedure Act).

The Act on Juvenile Courts (Article 63) provides that with the aim of extra-judicial settlement of problems concerning juvenile delinquency, and under the conditions provided by law, the State Attorney for minors may decide not to initiate a criminal procedure. These conditions correspond to the view that initiating criminal procedure would not be purposeful, given the nature of the criminal act and the circumstances under which it was committed, the previous living conditions of the minor in question and his personal characteristics.

The Trades and Crafts Act (Article 78) provides that a Court of Honour is to be established and work within the Croatian Chamber of Trades and Crafts, and that it is to decide on violations of good customs in the performance of trades and crafts, the non-performance of obligations of its members, and violations of the statute and other deeds of the Croatian Chamber of Trades and Crafts.

The Act on the Croatian Chamber of Economy (Article 12) provides that there is a Court of Honour within the Croatian Chamber of Economy that decides on violations of good business practice in the performance of commercial activities and trade in goods and services, the non-performance of obligations of members of the Chamber and violations of the statute and other deeds of the Chamber. The Court of Honour may issue measures against members of the Chamber in the event of infringements of social discipline.

The Arbitration Act regulates domestic arbitration, the recognition and enforcement of arbitration awards, and the competence and activities of courts in arbitration cases. Parties may agree on domestic arbitration for the settlement of disputes concerning rights of which they may freely dispose (Article 3).

The Insurance Act (Article 273) provides that insurance companies are under a duty to establish a procedure for extra-judicial resolution of disputes between insured parties, that is, contractors of insurance (i.e. clients and insurance companies). Under the conditions of insurance, the insurance company is under an obligation to make information on the procedure for extra-judicial dispute resolution available to the public.

2. Organisations for ADR and Mediation

In Croatia, where the first institutional arbitration was established in 1853, there are a number of bodies outside the judicial system that are available to parties for alternative dispute resolution.

The Permanent Arbitration Court at the Croatian Chamber of Economy is the leading arbitration institution in the Republic of Croatia.

The Centre for Mediation at the Croatian Chamber of Commerce was established in 2002 to resolve disputes between companies.

The Centre for Mediation at the Croatian Association of Employers was established in 2004. The Chamber represents entrepreneurs and employers and is based on voluntary membership.

The Centre for Mediation at the Croatian Chamber of Trades and Crafts was established in 2004. The Chamber represents traders/craftsmen. Membership is compulsory.

The Croatian Mediation Association was established in 2003 with the aim of promoting, developing and improving the institute of mediation in the Republic of Croatia.

The Office for Social Partnership was established within the framework of the Economic and Social Council. Twenty-nine educated mediators have been appointed. The mediation procedure in collective labour disputes began to be used systematically in 2003.

Social welfare centres conduct mediation procedures in divorce proceedings.

The professional services for extra-judicial settlement (a non-governmental organization) provides mediation services in cases where criminal acts are committed by minors/young adults.

Proposal for the organisation of alternative dispute resolution in Croatia:

1. ADR in Courts
   a. in offices for mediation in civil cases;
   b. in services for out-of-court settlement in criminal cases;
2. ADR in organisations for mediation and arbitration institutions;
3. ADR in the Office for Social Partnership;
4. ADR in centres of the Office for Social Partnership;
5. ADR in centres for ex-trial proceedings in consumer disputes.

Mediation in Courts

The basic planned features of mediation in courts:

1. mediation proceedings are conducted in relation to disputes for which a court procedure has already been instituted;
2. mediation proceedings are free of charge for parties;
3. mediation is performed by judges certified as mediators after a training programme at the Judicial Academy;
4. mediation is conducted at court premises;
5. a case solved by mediation is included in the judicial quota;
6. each court must have a mediation commissioner/office for mediation which are in charge of administrative tasks related to mediation, of informing citizens and of qualitative and quantitative analysis of conducted mediation proceedings;
7. the court must provide a judge on call who will, even outside working hours, decide on a court settlement on the basis of the agreement between the parties to the mediation proceedings.

From April to October 2006, the Commercial Court in Zagreb received 226 mediation cases. Of that number, 65 procedures have been concluded, 32 of which successfully.

Mediation has also begun in 8 municipal courts.

3. Education and Informing the Citizens

To date, around 150 persons have successfully completed different mediation training programmes in Croatia. Another 160 persons will be trained within the framework of the project 'Strengthening of mediation as a type of alternative dispute resolution'. Trainers for training programmes will be educated separately.

Cooperation with law faculties is planned in order to introduce mediation as an elective subject.

The Ministry of Justice is planning to undertake a series of measures in order to increase the level of awareness of citizens about alternative dispute resolution: creating a web-page on ADR, issuing special information materials, and organising media campaigns for the promotion of mediation proceedings. In conjunction with mediation associations, a monthly newsletter on ADR will be published.

4. The Development of ADR

Courts, public prosecution services, mediation organisations and arbitration institutions, ADR associations, faculties of law, and the ministries responsible for social welfare, labour and consumer protection shall all participate in the development of ADR.

The following activities are planned in order to stimulate ADR:

1. regulation of attorney and court fees in order to positively influence mediation proceedings;
2. establishment of a refund of court fees to parties in cases of successful mediation proceedings;
3. inclusion of successfully completed mediation proceedings in judicial quotas;
4. permission and encouragement of judges, when adjudicating court expenses, to take into account the behaviour of the parties in relation to the call for mediation and their behaviour during the mediation proceedings;
5. legally binding financial institutions and other business subjects to ensure mechanisms for out-of-court proceedings;
6. introduction of obligatory mediation in individual labour disputes;
7. prescription of obligatory mediation in cases concerning the compensation of damage;
8. securing of funds and more authority for the Public Prosecution Services for settlements in mediation proceedings;
9. organisation of expert discussions on the introduction of a settlement conference before a judge, a settlement week or obligatory arbitration in small claims disputes.

On 30 May 2006 the Ministry of Justice concluded with the Croatian Employer's Association, the Croatian Chamber of Commerce, the Croatian Chamber of Trades and Crafts an agreement on joint participation in the PHARE 2005 project 'Strengthening of Mediation as an Alternative Dispute Resolution Method' – the main purpose of which is to develop mediation as an alternative dispute resolution method.

5. Online Mediation

The possibilities for online mediation need to be explored as it has specific advantages: savings in relation to the costs, the possibility of dispute resolution from one's own home, and the avoidance of potentially uncomfortable encounters with the opposite side. Sophisticated software, assisting parties to make settlements, has already been developed and can be applied.